CHILD ABUSE TORT CLAIMS AGAINST PUBLIC BODIES

Child Abuse Tort Claims Against Public Bodies

A Comparative Law View

Edited by

DUNCAN FAIRGRIEVE and SARAH GREEN
British Institute of International and Comparative Law

Routledge
Taylor & Francis Group
LONDON AND NEW YORK

First published 2004 by Ashgate Publishing

Reissued 2018 by Routledge
2 Park Square, Milton Park, Abingdon, Oxon OX14 4RN
711 Third Avenue, New York, NY 10017, USA

Routledge is an imprint of the Taylor & Francis Group, an informa business

First issued in paperback 2018

Typeset by Tradespools, Frome, Somerset

A Library of Congress record exists under LC control number: 2004046334

ISBN 13: 978-0-815-38799-2 (hbk)
ISBN 13: 978-1-138-61905-0 (pbk)
ISBN 13: 978-1-351-16188-6 (ebk)

Contents

Foreword

*Allan Levy QC**

In this excellent book leading practitioners and academics investigate how the factual circumstances contained in the landmark House of Lords cases of *X v Bedfordshire CC*[1] (local authority's alleged failure to deal with abused children in the community) and *Barrett v Enfield LBC*[2] (local authority's alleged negligence regarding a child in their care) in England would be dealt with in various different common law and European jurisdictions, including the United States, Canada, Australia and New Zealand, South Africa, France and Italy.

In a revealing overall exercise in comparative law the authors consider, for instance, the characteristics of government liability in their own legal system; whether there have been similar cases to the English ones and, if so, the result and the reasoning; what public policy aspects or other control mechanisms were relied upon; if no cases, the reasons for this absence; the availability of alternative sources of compensation; what damages are available and how they are calculated; and particular procedural aspects. Where appropriate, suggestions for reforms in these areas are put forward.

In reality the various jurisdictions are concerned to a large extent with the same concepts and similar discussions are triggered. It becomes a question of degree and detail. A central common dilemma that emerges is: in what circumstances will, and should the law convert a general duty to abstain from inflicting harm on another to a positive duty to act to protect another from foreseeable harm. Public policy looms large in the scheme of things. How public policy should be formulated, and by whom, are aspects that could fill a book on their own. What emerges on the present topic is the suggestion that there is a significant divide between the common law jurisdictions and at least some of the continental European countries such as Italy and Germany and perhaps the Netherlands.

It appears that the latter countries give immunity to the family unit which is not easily disturbed, if at all. However, in England and Wales, for example, the issues around immunity or protection from litigation has centred on the liability of public bodies: in other words whilst there is a public policy behind the Children Act 1989 that in the normal way a child is brought up by his or her natural family, there is also a clear recognition that child abuse occurs and

* 17 Bedford Row.

that the state in certain clearly defined circumstances must intervene and then may possibly be liable in tort for its actions.

This distinction arising from the degree to which the family unit remains sacrosanct or is only regulated in narrow and exceptional circumstances, also has something to say about the existence or otherwise of children's rights in the various jurisdictions. In some jurisdictions the existence of the rights is questionable. Even in the United Kingdom, despite the Human Rights Act 1998 and the United Nations Convention on the Rights of the Child (ratified by all the countries covered in the book except the United States), children's rights are still in their infancy legally.

Public policy has some of the characteristics of the British climate: it is changeable and often unpredictable. It needs to be noted that since the successful conference, under the auspices of the British Institute of International and Comparative Law, which inspired this book, the decision in *X v Bedfordshire CC* has been successfully attacked on behalf of children in the case of *JD and others v East Berkshire Community NHS Trust.*[3] The Court of Appeal decided that subsequent decisions had significantly restricted the effect of the Bedfordshire case and therefore:

> it follows that it will no longer be legitimate to rule that, as a matter of law, no common law duty of care is owed to a child in relation to the investigation of child abuse and the initiation and pursuit of care proceedings. It is possible that there will be factual situations where it is not fair, just or reasonable to impose a duty of care, but each case will fall to be determined on its individual facts (Paragraph 84).

The Court of Appeal also reached the firm conclusion that *X v Bedfordshire* could not survive the Human Rights Act 1998. The position of parents, however, was held to be different. As the child's interests were said to be in 'potential conflict with the interests of the parent' there were 'cogent reasons of public policy for concluding that, where child care decisions are being taken, no common duty of care should be owed to the parents' (paragraph 86). For this aspect the Court of Appeal relied on the support of the Privy Council decision in the New Zealand case of *B v Attorney-General.*[4] The decision in respect of children will remain good law as the local authority are not trying to appeal to the House of Lords. The parents, however, in the three cases that were heard together are seeking leave to challenge the Court of Appeal's findings.

This book provides an intriguing and thought-provoking survey of the internal workings of eleven different jurisdictions across the legal globe. The material also provides the means by which a fascinating exercise in comparative law can be carried out. Law reformers in particular can extract the best and most practical aspects to re-enforce their own systems. For the academic, ideas proliferate. For the more general reader the wealth of information provided is exceptional.

Notes

1 [1995] 2 AC 633.
2 [2001] 2 AC 550.
3 [2003] EWCA 1151.
4 16 July 2003, unreported.

Chapter 1

Suing Health Authorities in Ireland: Recent Legal Developments

*Ann Power**

Introduction

Judicial and legislative developments in recent years have made the functions, powers and duties of health boards a subject of legal analysis and debate in Ireland. One of the most important developments has been in the area involving the protection of children. Clearly, the functions and duties of health boards extend beyond the remit of child-care. Health boards have been parties to litigation spanning a wide variety of areas including adoption, unfair dismissal, mental treatment, hospital services and consent to medical treatment. Often in cases alleging medical malpractice, such as in the recent series of cerebral palsy cases, a health board may be joined as co-defendant against whom vicarious and/or direct liability for negligence is alleged. However, this paper focuses, primarily, upon the legal issues arising in litigation involving health boards and their responsibilities towards children since most of the recent legislative and judicial developments have arisen in that context. Having addressed, briefly, the historical evolution of such responsibilities, this paper will consider:

1 the role of health boards in child abuse litigation;
2 the duties of health boards to parents;
3 the duties of health boards to children at risk;
4 the duties of health boards and children in care;
5 health boards and children with special needs;
6 the role of health boards and consent to medical treatment of children.

Historical Background

The *Ministers and Secretaries Act, 1924* established the Department of Local Government and Public Health for 'the administration and business of public services in connection with local government and public health'. Section 2 of the *Ministers and Secretaries (Amendment) Act, 1946* established a

* Barrister-at-Law, Dublin.

Department of State to be styled and known as An Roinn Sláinte. The functions of the Department of Health have been defined as including:

> the administration and business relating to the preparation, effective carrying out and co-ordination of measures conducive to the health of the people, including in particular measures for the treatment and care of persons suffering from physical defects or mental illness.[1]

Pursuant to section 7(1) of the *Health Authorities Act, 1960* a 'health authority'[2] was obliged to perform all the functions which, immediately before its establishment, were performed by the relevant local authorities under the *Health Acts, 1947* to *1958*.[3] Under those Acts a health authority was obliged, specifically, 'to safeguard and improve the health and physical condition of children in its functional area'.[4] Health authorities also inherited functions of local authorities under Part I of the *Children Act, 1908*, and section 2 of the *Children (Amendment) Act, 1957*.[5]

The Health Act, 1970

The *Health Authorities Act, 1960* was repealed almost in its entirety[6] by the *Health Act, 1970*. In accordance with the general policy of devolved executive responsibility, new health boards were established under the provisions of Part II of the *Health Act, 1970*. Under the 1970 Act, a health board is a body corporate with perpetual succession. It may sue and be sued in its corporate name. Health boards were legally established on 1 October 1970.[7] However, the process of appointing members was not completed until November 1970 and health boards did not become responsible for the operation of health services until 1 April 1971.[8]

No express responsibility for child protection Section 6 of the *Health Act, 1970* provides that

> a health board shall perform the functions conferred on it under this Act and any other functions which, immediately before its establishment, *were performed by a local authority* in the functional area of the health board in relation to the operation of services as identified in subsection (2).

In relation to children, health boards, therefore, inherited the responsibilities of local authorities which had been imposed by the authorities pursuant to Part 1 of the *Children Act, 1908*. The duties in question were very limited. Local authorities had no statutory responsibility in relation to safeguarding children at risk (which is covered by Part II of the 1908 Act) and thus no such responsibilities passed to the newly established health boards. Thus, there is no provision in the 1970 Act authorising a health board to enter the home of a child who may be at risk and to remove such a child from there. Nor does the Act specify the procedure to be followed in cases of suspected child abuse. Under the 1970 Act, a health board's duties in relation to child health services were limited to the provision of health examinations and treatment services to children attending national schools.[9]

Assumed Responsibilities under the Children Act, 1908

Notwithstanding the foregoing, health boards, once established, had, in fact, become involved in making applications in appropriate cases for children to be placed in care, with the boards themselves being appointed as 'fit persons'. This practice was based on the provisions of the *Children Act, 1908*, particularly sections 20, 24 and 34. Section 20(1) provides that a constable

> *or any person authorised by a justice*, may take to a place of safety any child or young person in respect of whom an offence under this Part of this Act, has been, or there is reason to believe has been, committed.

The main statutory provisions dealing with the prevention of cruelty to children are contained in the *Children Act, 1908*. Section 21 of that Act provides that where a person having the custody, charge or care of a child or young person has been convicted of committing an offence under the Act, or committed for trial for such offence the Court may order that:

> the child be taken out of the custody, charge or care of the person so convicted... and be committed to the care of a relative of the child or *some other fit person*, named by the Court.

Section 24 of the 1908 Act deals with the question of suspected abuse of children and provides for the issuing of a warrant authorising any *constable* named therein to search for such a child and to remove the said child to a place of safety until he can be brought before the Court. It further provides that '*the Court... may commit the child to the care of a relative or other fit person*' in like manner as if the person in whose care the child was *had* been committed for trial. The expression 'fit person' includes any society or body corporate established for the reception or protection of poor children or the prevention of cruelty to children.[10]

The problem of the legal status of health boards in cases involving child abuse was addressed in *The State (D & D) v G and Others.*[11] In that case, a child was ordered to be committed to the care of the Midland Health Board as a 'fit person' under the *Children Act, 1908* by a District Justice. The Supreme Court found that health boards could not be designated 'fit persons' for the purpose of the *Children Act, 1908*. In analysing the issue Finlay CJ noted that the 1970 Act transferred certain powers previously exercised by the local authorities to health boards, specifically, powers exercised under Part 1, but not Part II, of the 1908 Act. He rejected the contention that the duties imposed on health boards pursuant to section 66(2) of the 1970 Act extended to the universal nature of the provisions contained in Part II of the 1908 Act, provisions which deal, *inter alia*, with the search for and removal of children at risk, the detention of children in places of safety and the maintenance of children when committed to care. He continued:

> Having regard to the universal nature of the provisions contained in Part II of the Act of 1908 in respect of the protection and welfare of children, and, in particular, in respect of the making of care orders and the designation of fit persons, it would appear to me extraordinary if the Health Board by virtue of an obligation to make available to children over the age of six years a health service, provided only that they are attending a national school..., could be construed as making a health board a fit person, presumably in respect of such children under the Act of 1908, but having no function of a like kind in regard to other children, even of the same age who did not happen to be attending such schools. It would, in my view, be an unwarranted extension of the obligations imposed on a health board by that subsection to consider that they are a fit person.

Finlay CJ concluded, however, by stating that

> it is appropriate that a health board, its servants or agents, should become involved *as interested persons*, in making applications to the Court under sections 24 or 21 of the 1908 Act where the welfare of a child at risk has been brought to their notice.

The Children Act, 1989

In the aftermath of *The State(D) v G*, and to ensure the validity of the numerous 'fit person' orders that had been made prior to that case, the Oireachtas acted quickly to enact legislation[12] ensuring that the term 'fit person' included and was deemed always to have included, a health board established under the 1970 Act. The *Children Act, 1989* further provided that the functions of a health board shall include and be deemed always to have included the functions conferred on a fit person by the 1908 Act.

Guidelines on Non-Accidental Injury and Child Abuse

Awareness of the problem of child abuse has exploded as a social, political and legal phenomenon in the past ten years. Protecting children at risk is complex, uncertain and unpredictable and often requires a difficult and delicate balancing of conflicting interests. The publication in 1980 of the Department of Health's *Guidelines on Non-Accidental Injury to Children*[13] contributed towards promoting awareness of the problem of child abuse though not child sexual abuse. Since that time, various legislative and administrative reforms have tried to keep pace with growing awareness of the problem, culminating, to date, with the most recent publication in September 1999 of the National Guidelines for the Protection and Welfare of Children: *Children First.*[14] It is important to note that as Guidelines, *Children First* should be regarded as representing the *minimum standards* that ought to prevail in the area of child protection.

The Role of Health Boards in Child Abuse Litigation

Concomitant with increased awareness of the problem that child abuse posed in this jurisdiction, there came, slowly, at first, but with increasing rapidity, an upsurge in the number of civil actions taken against those organisations and institutions charged, statutorily or otherwise, with the care of children. Although the *Children Act, 1908* did not impose upon health boards any specific statutory duties in relation to the care of children, the reality was that since their establishment, health boards had, in fact, been assuming a role in the care of children in need of protection. Thus, when survivors of abuse sought legal redress for the wrongs suffered, health boards, frequently, found themselves as defendants in many civil actions. The other Defendants in many of the civil actions involving childhood abuse that are currently pending before the Courts, tend to be the State and the religious congregations responsible for the operation and management of residential institutions.

Residential Institutional Abuse

In some cases, however, that are currently before the Courts, particularly those involving institutional abuse, health boards have been joined as defendants in circumstances where the alleged abuse occurred at a time which pre-dated the existence of the boards. In view of the very limited responsibilities for children that health boards inherited from their predecessors, there is a strong argument for contending that there is no legal basis for joining health boards in actions where the abuse pre-dates the establishment of the boards. One might, reasonably, expect that the vast majority of those residential abuse cases will be taken out of the Court system and will be transferred, instead, to the recently established Residential Institutions Redress Board. With the enactment of the *Residential Institutions Redress Act 2002*, the Redress Board is empowered to make significant awards and claimants are required to pass a significantly lower threshold of proof than would otherwise be required by a Court. A claimant is required to prove his or her identity, the fact of residence in an institution, the fact of abuse and the injury suffered. Claimants are relieved of the onus of proving negligence which would obviously be imposed upon them if they were to proceed with civil actions.

Child Abuse – An Ongoing Phenomenon

One cannot assume that increased awareness of the problem of child abuse equates with a diminution in the incidence thereof. If child abuse in this jurisdiction was as vast a social problem as the plethora of civil actions and criminal trials would suggest, there is no valid reason for assuming that the phenomenon itself has diminished or disappeared. There are few, if any, grounds for believing that the problem has resolved and that litigation will cease as soon as 'past' cases have been heard. In the absence of conclusive evidence of the fact that the incidence of child abuse has diminished dramatically, health authorities might, reasonably, proceed on the assumption that children are as vulnerable and are as likely to be abused today as they were in the past. The exploitation and abuse of children is likely to continue unless the legislative and administrative measures designed to protect them are working effectively, evaluated consistently and revised accordingly.

The Child Care Act, 1991

The *Child Care Act, 1991* is the main legislative device established by the State for the welfare and protection of children. Section 3(1) of the *Child Care Act, 1991* imposes upon a health board a positive statutory function to promote the welfare of children residing within its functional area. The Act authorises the interference with familial relations whereby a child can be removed from the care, custody and authority of his parents and delivered into the care of a State agency, namely, a health board.

Section 3 of the *Child Care Act, 1991* provides:

1 It shall be a function of every health board to promote the welfare of children in its area who are not receiving adequate care and protection.
2 In the performance of this function, a health board shall:
   a take such steps as it considers requisite to identify children who are not receiving adequate care and protection and co-ordinate information from all relevant sources relating to children in its area;
   b having regard to the rights and duties of parents, whether under the Constitution or otherwise, regard the welfare of the child as the first and paramount consideration, and in so far as is practicable, give due consideration, having regard to his age and understanding, to the wishes of the child; and
   c have regard to the principle that it is generally in the best interests of a child to be brought up in his own family.
3 A health board shall, in addition to any other function assigned to it under this Act or any other enactment, provide childcare and family support services, and may provide and maintain premises and make such other provision as it considers necessary or desirable for such purposes, subject to any general directions given by the Minister under section 69.

A health board that fails to have regard for the various duties attaching to its statutory functions pursuant to Section 3 is likely to attract potential litigants from two sources:

1 parents whose rights are not adequately regarded; and
2 children whom a health board fails, initially, to identify and, subsequently, to protect.

The Duties of Health Boards to Parents

The main purpose of section 3(2) is to strike a fair balance between the competing interests of children, parents and health boards, whilst regarding the welfare of the child as paramount. Whilst most of the litigation, to date, has tended to come from adult survivors whose childhood welfare had allegedly been neglected, health boards are also exposed to the risk of being sued by parents whose rights have been denied or disregarded. Unless specific structures are in place which demonstrate, objectively, that due regard has been had for the rights of parents as required by section 3(2)(b), health boards throughout the country are at risk of being sued.

Section 3(2)(b) *obliges* health boards to have regard to the constitutional and other rights and duties of parents. Boards are also required to have regard to the principle that it is generally in a child's best interests that he be reared within his own family. In making decisions about children's welfare, health boards should be able to demonstrate, in practical terms, how adequate regard is had for parental rights. One of the consequences of the emerging litigation culture is that some professionals, fearful of being sued, may resort to a more cautious and defensive approach to their work. At times, such defensive practices may result in a child being removed, unlawfully, from the care of his/her parents. The irony is, of course, that such defensive actions may, in fact, precipitate further litigation – the plaintiffs, this time, being parents alleging breach of constitutional and other rights.

The question as to whether a parent in such circumstances could bring an action in negligence and breach of statutory duty against a local authority was considered by the English Courts. In *M (A Minor) and Another v Newham London Borough Council,*[15] a mother and her child sued the local authority for its alleged failure to carry out its statutory duties with care. In *M*, the child, who had been sexually abused, was unnecessarily taken into care on the advice of a social worker and a psychiatrist who failed to take an accurate case history. The local authority obtained a Court order removing M from her mother and restricting access to her. When it became apparent that the psychiatrist had erroneously identified the abuser as the mother's co-habitee, the local authority recommended the rehabilitation of the Plaintiff with her mother. By that time, however, the child had been separated from her mother for almost a year and both mother and child claimed to have suffered a positive psychiatric disorder as a result thereof.

When the matter came before the House of Lords, the Court acknowledged that very difficult decisions were involved in striking the balance between protecting the child from immediate feared harm and disrupting the relationship between the child and its parents. However, it decided, on public policy grounds, that it was just and reasonable for local authorities to enjoy immunity from suit in the discharge of their statutory duties. Thus, they held that no private cause of action in negligence and breach of duty arose. There can be little doubt but that *M* and the similar and related matters of *X (Minors) v Bedfordshire County Council*[16] were products of 'policy-guided' considerations in Britain. In view of the constitutional rights of the family it is unlikely, in my view, that the Courts in this jurisdiction would follow the reasoning of the English Courts in such matters.

The decision of the House of Lords in *M v Newham County Council* was appealed to the European Court of Human Rights (ECtHR). The applicants complained of an unjustified interference with their family life under Article 8 of the European Convention for the Protection of Human Rights and Fundamental Freedoms (1950) and further complained that they had no access to a fair trial under Article 6. On 10 May 2001, the ECtHR delivered its decision and found that the conduct of the local authority had, in fact, constituted an unjustified interference with family life and thus the United Kingdom had been in breach of Article 8 of the Convention. It also reiterated the principle established in its earlier decision of *McMichael v United Kingdom*[17] namely, that failure to disclose relevant documents to parents during procedures to place a child in care did not afford requisite protection of the parents' interests under Article 8 of the Convention.

The European Convention will be incorporated, presently, into domestic law in this jurisdiction. Health boards that fail to have regard for parental rights in the discharge of their duties pursuant to section 3 of the *Child Care Act, 1991* would face difficulties in defending such disregard in view of the provisions of both the Convention and the Constitution. Health boards have a duty to adopt procedures that ensure that due regard is given to parental rights and duties in matters involving State intervention in families.

The Duties of Health Boards to Children at Risk

Section 3 of the *Child Care Act, 1991* imposes upon health boards statutory obligations towards children, whose welfare it is the duty of health boards to promote. A close reading of the *Child Care Act, 1991* confirms, however, that the wording of section 3(2)(a) does not limit a health board's duty to those children whose cases actually come to the attention of the board. Its duty is to children in its area who are not [*in fact*] receiving adequate care and attention.[18] In discharging that general duty a health board is obliged to *take steps to identify* children at risk.[19]

Exercising Discretionary Powers

Section 16 of the of the *Child Care Act, 1991* imposes upon a health board a statutory duty to instigate care proceedings in respect of a child in its area who requires care and protection. The section provides:

> Where it appears to a health board with respect to a child who resides or is found in its area that he requires care or protection which he is unlikely to receive unless a Court makes a care order or a supervision order in respect of him, it shall be the duty of the health board to make application for a care order or a supervision order, as it thinks fit.

The *Child Care Act, 1991* provides for various types of orders being made by the Court in respect of a child brought to its attention including an emergency care order,[20] an interim care order,[21] a care order committing the child to the care of the health board for so long as he remains a child or for such shorter period as the Court may determine,[22] and a supervision order.[23]

Section 16 envisages a health board exercising a discretion prior to discharging its duty to apply for a Court order. However, the cases currently being processed before the Courts today establish that *it is, precisely, in the exercise of its discretion that a health board is most vulnerable to litigation.* Consideration, therefore, must be given as to how discretionary powers ought to be exercised by health boards so that the risk of incurring liability in negligence, breach of duty and/or breach of constitutional rights may be reduced.

The Standard of Care

In December 1997 the High Court commenced its hearing of the first civil action relating to child sexual abuse – *McColgan v The Northwestern Health Board and Desmond Moran.* Lawyers had hoped that the Court, in that case, would enunciate clear, legal principles that would guide health boards in this developing and complex area of public law. However, the eventual settlement of the case postponed, until another day, the clarification of Irish law in this area. Until legal principles in this area of law have been enunciated by the Irish Courts, health boards should proceed on the basis that they must be able to demonstrate that *reasonable care* was taken in decisions pertaining to children at risk of abuse.

Clearly, every decision is contextual but the standard principles of reasonableness in negligence should be applied consistently and without exception. The greater the likelihood of harm to a child, the more probable it is that a Court will regard it as unreasonable (and thus, negligent) for a health board to fail to take steps to protect that child. Where the potential injury to a child is great then a Court may find that even a slight risk (such as delaying the taking of action for several hours) may constitute negligence. The gravity of a threatened injury is a relative matter and whilst the calculated risk of abuse occurring may be the same for two children, the results may be far more serious for one than the other. In assessing alleged negligence the Court will, undoubtedly, have regard to the difficult and complex nature of the work of health boards in this area and to the inevitable 'inter-agency' approach that must be adopted when dealing with such cases. (This factor weighed so heavily in the deliberations of the House of Lords in the *Bedfordshire* cases that their Lordships found that no personal cause of action would lie against a health authority for alleged negligence or breach of duty in this area.) It is, however, doubtful whether regard for the difficult work of health boards would be sufficient to convince a Court in this jurisdiction to follow the House of Lords' policy-guided reasoning in this instance.

Doubtful Cases

There may arise circumstances where the conditions pertaining to a particular child are not unequivocally indicative of child abuse. Suspicions regarding the welfare of a child may arise where little concrete evidence may be available to confirm or substantiate such concerns. A child may make an allegation of abuse and then, subsequently, retract it. Investigations, following a report of suspected abuse, may yield little by way of corroborative evidence. Sometimes, health board personnel may have no more than a recurrent and persistent doubt in relation to the welfare of a particular child. How ought a health board respond in such situations so as to reduce the risk of subsequent litigation?

Such uncertainties prevailed in the matter of *Re H (Minors) (Wardship: Sexual Abuse)*,[24] the facts of which may be summarised, briefly, as follows. The case concerned four children, E, C, R and N. The mother of the first three was the sister of the fourth child's mother. Both families lived together in one household and the living arrangements were highly undesirable. R's mother noticed that R had blood on her pants and she contacted her local General Practitioner who referred the child to a Consultant Paediatrician. The consultant's findings were 'highly suggestive' of child sexual abuse and the local authority was notified.

The authority obtained a place of safety order and commenced wardship proceedings, which had the effect of making all four children wards of court. Medical examinations and video-taped interviews of the other three children were described as 'negative' and there was no physical evidence of sexual abuse of E, C or N. Notwithstanding these findings the local authority sought interim care orders in respect of all four children in view of the presumed risk which, it stated, must attach, given the history of R. The parents opposed the application and the Court at first instance dismissed the local authority's application. In making his determination Heald J stated:

> I take the view that I am here left with a case where there is a real possibility that R has been sexually interfered with. It is no higher than that, and on the scale of remote possibility, real possibility, distinct possibility and probable, it is fairly low on the scale.[25]

He made an order continuing the wardship proceedings but returned the children into the care of their parents with a supervision order in favour of the authority. The local authority appealed.

The Court of Appeal held that in cases involving allegations of sexual abuse of children, two stages were involved in the Court's decision-making process. The first stage required an evaluation of the evidence of fact and expert opinion. The second stage required a judicial exercise of discretion, with the test of the welfare of the child being paramount. It was held that the Court should have regard to the danger that in seeking to protect children from sexual abuse (by placement with foster-parents, however loving and skilled), society might cause other, and possibly greater harm to children by taking them away from the only home they might have known and from parents, however inadequate, to whom they were attached. Against the risk of possible further abuse of R, there had to be balanced all the risks of removing her and her siblings from their parents, siblings and extended family.

In dismissing the appeal, the Court of Appeal held that Heald J had correctly balanced those risks. However, the Court noted that frequently local authorities are faced with situations that give rise to doubt. It concluded that refusals of their applications for care orders should not discourage them from acting in cases of uncertainty. Balcombe LJ stated:

> We wish to make it clear that in no way do we seek to criticise the council for making the application before Judge Heald, nor for appealing his order to this Court. Society has entrusted local authorities with this difficult and demanding task of protecting children from abuse. In the exercise of this task they, and the social workers who have to do the work on the ground, will always be exposed to criticism. If they do not seek to remove a child who is at risk of abuse (whether sexual or otherwise) from its home, and that child is subsequently abused, or even, in the worst cases, killed, they are criticised. If, on the other hand, they do seek to remove a child whom they believe to be at risk, they are criticised as being authoritarian and for disregarding parental rights. They must always be entitled to bring a case before the Court, upon which the burden of decision then rests.[26]

Whilst nothing can immunise a health board from the risk of suit, there is, in my view, one standard rule that might, reasonably, apply in circumstances where doubts and uncertainties prevail in relation to the welfare of a child. Notwithstanding its duty to have regard to the rights of parents, in cases where doubts and uncertainties about the safety and welfare of a child obtain, a health board should bring the matters before the Court and make an appropriate application pursuant to section 16 of the 1991 Act. If difficult decisions are to be made in such delicate and complex circumstances then, arguably, it is preferable that those determinations are made by the Court 'upon which the burden of decision rests'. The High Court, in this jurisdiction, has also confirmed recently, albeit in a slightly different context, that the ultimate responsibility for children in need of care rests with the Court.[27]

The Legal Basis of Actions

Whilst Irish law remains in a state of uncertainty with regard to the liability of a health board in the event of abuse suffered by a child within its area, one can, at this point, say that health boards *may* be liable in damages if the act complained of constitutes:

1 a breach of statutory duty;
2 the commission of a recognised tort, such as, trespass or negligence;
3 an infringement of a personal constitutional right.

Breach of Statutory Duty

The question arises as to whether a breach of statutory duty on the part of a health board will give rise to a private cause of action within this jurisdiction. Very occasionally a statute will state explicitly that breach of the statute does[28] or does not[29] give rise to a cause of action. Generally, however, the statute will be silent on the matter and the Courts will engage in the fictitious exercise of imputing legislative intention in order to determine whether a cause of action follows on foot of a breach of statutory duty.

In considering alleged breaches of statutory duty, this 'fictitious' exercise was conducted in the United Kingdom in the decision of *X v Bedfordshire*. Lord Browne-Wilkinson held that where difficult and sensitive decisions have to be taken in a statutory framework, very clear language would be needed to establish a right to damages under statute where an erroneous decision was taken. Such a right, he concluded, was not to be found in the *Children's Act 1989*. He went on:

> Most statutes which impose a statutory duty on local authorities confer on the authority a discretion as to the extent to which, and the methods by which, such statutory duty is to be performed. It is clear both in principle and from the decided cases that the local authority cannot be liable in damages for doing that which Parliament has authorised. Therefore if the decisions complained of fall within the ambit of such statutory discretion they cannot be actionable in common law.[30]

The same question was considered by the High Court in this jurisdiction in *Stephens v The Eastern Health Board*[31] where Mr Justice Geoghegan examined the matter in the context of the *Child Care Act 1999* and stated:

> I take the view that no breach of any of the provisions of the Child Care Act 1999 gives rise to an action for damages for breach of statutory duty. Breaches of the Act can be remedied by Judicial review because that will ensure the actual performance of the duties as distinct from absolution for performance in return for money.

Health boards, however, should be slow to take solace from the judgments cited herein. Whilst those cases may suggest that they will not be held liable in damages for breaches of statutory duties, they do not, by any means, address all of the relevant legal considerations. *Stephens* may represent a statement of Irish law on the narrow question of damages for breach of a health board's statutory duty (and I am not convinced that this decision would be upheld today). That aside, however, a health board in breach of its duties to children in this jurisdiction could be found liable in damages if the act complained of constituted the commission of a recognised tort, such as negligence or trespass.

Breach of Common Law Duty

The House of Lords in *X v Bedfordshire* also refused to impose a common law duty of care on local authorities having regard to the difficult circumstances in which such authorities often exercise their discretionary powers. It recognised that the task of an authority and its servants in dealing with children at risk is extraordinarily delicate in that the work is inter-disciplinary, involving the participation of the police, educational bodies, doctors and others. Their Lordships cited from the *Report of the Inquiry into Child Abuse in Cleveland 1987* which stated:

> It is a delicate and difficult line to tread between taking action too soon and not taking it soon enough. Social services whilst putting the needs of the child first must respect the rights of the parents; they also must work if possible with the parents for the benefit of the children. These parents themselves are often in need of help. Inevitably, a degree of conflict develops between those objectives.[32]

In the *Bedfordshire* cases the Court concluded that it would not be just and reasonable in such circumstances to impose a common law duty of care on the local authority in relation to the exercise of its powers and duties. Accordingly, it held that a claim for damages in negligence also failed as being non-justifiable. The Court further held that a local authority was not vicariously liable for the actions of social workers and psychiatrists instructed by it to report on children who were suspected of being sexually abused. Once again, its rationale was that it would not be just and reasonable to impose such a duty of care on the local authority as it would be contrary to public policy so to do.

There is no doubt that the reasoning of their Lordships in the *Bedfordshire* cases is incontrovertibly based on policy considerations and such cases are unlikely to be of persuasive authority in this jurisdiction. One could not, reasonably, envisage a Court in this jurisdiction denying the existence of a common law duty of care on the part of a health board such as would amount to a 'blanket immunity' from suit for the negligent exercise of discretionary powers.

Breach of Constitutional Right

A plaintiff in this jurisdiction may also succeed against a health board on the grounds that failure to provide the requisite care and protection amounted to an infringement of a personal constitutional right. The willingness of the Courts to countenance a re-shaping of remedies in the light of the Constitution is nowhere more evident than in the context of the law of torts.

> Where an existing tort is ineffective to protect constitutional rights, the Courts may either modify the definition of the tort or permit the Plaintiff to sue directly for infringement of constitutional rights.[33]

The *Statute of Limitations (Amendment) Act, 2000* changed the law on the limitation period applicable to cases involving childhood sexual abuse insofar as it expanded the meaning of the term 'disability' as defined in the earlier Statutes of Limitations. Until that time and indeed even now, many actions were and are being framed in terms of a breach of constitutional rights, presumably, because the criteria for determining liability for infringement of constitutional rights are not, necessarily, identical with those appropriate to tort law. Thus, whilst a plaintiff in this jurisdiction *may* fail in a claim for breach of statutory duty, he or she may, nevertheless, succeed if the breach in question can be characterised either as negligence *simpliciter* or as a negligent breach of his or her constitutional right.

The Duties of Health Boards and Children in Care

Some of the litigation currently before the Courts in this jurisdiction involves allegations of abuse, negligence and want of care against health boards in failing, subsequent to having taken children into care, to provide adequate care and protection. Where a child is in the care of a health board, that board has a statutory duty pursuant to section 36 of the Act of 1991 to provide care for the child, subject to its control and supervision. Such care may be provided by placing the child with foster parents or in a residential facility or, in some cases, by arranging for its adoption. The *Child Care (Placement of Children in Foster Care) Regulations, 1995* and the *Child Care (Placement of Children in Residential Care) Regulations, 1995* came into effect on 31 October 1995. These Regulations impose duties upon health boards in relation to, *inter alia*, the selection and screening of carers and the management and monitoring of care placements.

In *W v Essex County Council*[34] the Court of Appeal upheld a claim brought by foster parents against the local authority. The foster parents and their four minor children brought actions against Essex County Council and a social worker employed by Essex. The local authority, according to the foster parent, had not disclosed that the child had been abused and had been suspected of abusing others. The claim arose out of the fostering of G, then aged 15, on the grounds that the local authority and the social worker were aware that G was an active sexual abuser, it being accepted that G had received a caution three years earlier for indecent assault on his sister. During the month that G spent with the foster family he had sexually abused the children then aged 7 and 12 years. The Court of Appeal held that the local authority in that case owed a duty of care to the foster family not to place it at risk from a known sexual abuser and that the claims in negligence should not have been struck out.

However, in 1997 the Court of Appeal in England held that a *child* placed with foster-carers by a local authority in a negligent manner cannot sue the local authority for damages which such negligent placement might have caused. In *H v Norfolk County Council*[35] the applicant was a 22-year-old man who had been taken into care at the age of 4 and placed with foster parents until he was 14. He alleged that he had been physically and sexually abused by his foster-father and that the council had been negligent in failing to supervise his placement, to investigate reports of abuse and to remove him from foster care. Relying upon the *Bedfordshire* principles, the judge struck out the applicant's claim on the ground that it disclosed no reasonable cause of action. The plaintiff applied for leave to appeal against the order and contended that the trial judge had failed to distinguish between the instant fostering case and the position vis-à-vis natural parents in the *Bedfordshire* cases. The Court of Appeal, however, held that the same public policy reasons that precluded allowing damage claims against local authorities by children outside the care system must also serve to preclude damages by children *in* foster care. The interlocking roles of the various agencies, the Court held, could not be disentangled.

The Court of Appeal made a similar ruling in another case involving allegations of negligent placement in foster care. In *Barrett (A.P.) v London Borough of Enfield*,[36] the plaintiff was taken into the care of the defendant authority when he was ten months old and remained in care until he was 17. In the Statement of Claim he alleged that the defendant negligently made two placements with foster parents, moved him six times to different residential homes, failed to provide him with proper social workers and failed to make proper arrangements to re-unite him with his mother. He further alleged that such negligent treatment caused him to leave the care of the local authority when he attained the age of majority without family or attachments and suffering from a psychiatric illness leading to his having an alcohol problem and a propensity to harm himself.

Counsel for the plaintiff in *Barrett* argued that where a health authority has been granted a wide degree of discretion in relation to decisions about children, and acts *in loco parentis*, then its duty includes a duty to provide the child with the standard of care which could be expected of a reasonable parent. This duty, it was submitted, included a duty to provide a home and education, to take reasonable steps to protect him from physical, emotional, psychiatric or psychological injury and to promote his development. Moreover, the plaintiff argued that it was the defendant's duty at all times to provide competent social workers whose responsibility it was to monitor the various aspects of the plaintiff's welfare. The negligence alleged against the defendant consisted of the way in which the plaintiff was placed with the various foster parents and homes.

The Court of Appeal *per* Lord Woolf MR stated that whilst the policy considerations in fostering cases are not identical to those in the *Bedfordshire* cases (where the child was not actually *in* care), nevertheless they were strictly comparable and, taken cumulatively, had sufficient potency to override the competing consideration that 'wrongs should be remedied'. He added that, in relation to decisions of the local authority of which complaint was made,

> ... it would be contrary to the public interest and therefore not just or reasonable to impose a duty of care.

As in the *Norfolk* case, the Court of Appeal, relying on *Bedfordshire*, upheld a decision to strike out his claim for failure to disclose a cause of action. Lord Woolf MR stated that the very fact that the defendant was stated to have been in the position of a parent to the plaintiff at the material time brings home the public policy aspects of the situation. He held that although a parent could be liable to a child for negligently driving a car he should not, nor should the local authority, be liable in making decisions 'with regard to their children's future'. The decision was appealed to the House of Lords.

Surprisingly, the House of Lords in *Barrett* reversed the Court of Appeal. Its judgment, delivered in June 1999, suggests something of a shift in thinking in the jurisdiction in this area of public law. It is interesting to note that whilst the House of Lords, in Britain, has, heretofore, refused to impose a duty of care on local authorities in the exercise of their statutory discretion, some of their Lordships have now expressed the view that once the discretion has been exercised and the decision to take a child into care has been made, different legal considerations apply.[37] Clearly, there is no *logical* reason why a 'blanket immunity' from suit that applies to local authorities in respect of statutory discretion exercised prior to taking a child into care should not also apply in respect of those exercised post-admission into care.

Barrett would suggest that the 'blanket immunity' provided to local authorities in Britain is now under review. What caused such a change? In the intervening period between *Bedfordshire* and *Barrett*, the European Court of Human Rights in *Osman v Ferguson*,[38] upheld a claim by the Osmans that their rights under Article 6 (the right to a fair and public hearing) of the European Convention on Human Rights had been infringed.[39] The Osmans had sought to bring proceedings in the United Kingdom against the police alleging negligence in the prevention of crime. On the basis of the same type of policy considerations that applied in *Bedfordshire*, the proceedings in *Osman* had been struck out by the Court of Appeal. The decision of the Strasbourg Court, however, has clearly influenced the House of Lords insofar as it can no longer apply a 'blanket immunity' to local authorities who fail in performance of their duties. In allowing the appeal in *Barrett* Lord Browne-Wilkinson stated:

> In view of the decision in the Osman case it is now difficult to foretell what would be the result in the present case if we were to uphold the striking out order. It seems to me that it is at least probable that the matter would then be taken to Strasbourg. That Court, applying its decision in the Osman case..., would say that we had deprived the plaintiff of his right to have the balance struck between the hardship suffered by him and the damage to be done to the public interest in the present case if an order were to be made against the defendant council.[40]

Lord Slynn in *Barrett*, however, had held that the Court must have jurisdiction to consider whether there is a duty of care owed and whether it has been broken. He concluded:

> I do not see how the interests of the child can be sufficiently protected otherwise.

Whilst the Courts in this jurisdiction have not ruled on the specific question of liability for negligent placement of children in care, I am of the view that they would be more likely to follow the reasoning of Lord Slynn in *Barrett* than that of the Court of Appeal in *Norfolk*. If a Court were to find that a child had been injured as a result of a negligent placement by a health board, it would, in my opinion, have little difficulty in allowing such a plaintiff to recover damages against such a board for negligence and breach of duty.

Health Boards and Children with Special Needs

In recent years, numerous cases involving children with particular behavioural difficulties have appeared in the non-jury list, usually before the Court of Mr Justice Kelly. The problems encountered by such children range from homelessness, substance abuse and neglect to emotional deprivation and psychological disorders. Frequently, these children sometimes described as 'out of control', manifest serious conduct disorders and need to be cared for and treated in secure units. For many years, however, they have been unable to find placements due to the lack of such secure facilities designed to meet their particular needs. Invariably, health boards have been involved in cases wherein the jurisdiction of the High Court has been invoked in an effort to ensure that the constitutional rights of such children are protected by the State. These cases include *DB (A Minor) v The Minister for Justice and Others*;[41] *TD (A Minor) v The Minister for Education and Others*;[42] *TD (A Minor) v The Minister for Education and Others*;[43] and *DH (A Minor) v Ireland and the Attorney General.*[44]

In 1995 Mr Justice Geoghegan, in *FM v The Minister for Education and Others*,[45] recognised the duty of the State to provide adequate and suitable accommodation for such disturbed children. The applicant in that case was a twelve-year-old child whose father was unknown and whose mother – dead at the time of the application – had lost contact with him since an early age. He was ultimately diagnosed as suffering from what was described as a 'hyperkinetic conduct disorder' by a consultant psychiatrist who recommended that he should spend a period of time in a secure unit which could contain him safely while addressing his behavioural difficulties.

It was submitted on behalf of the Ministers and the other respondents that there was no constitutional obligation on the State to provide services beyond what was then available so as to cater for the particular needs of a person in the position of the applicant. The trial judge rejected that contention, saying that he was satisfied that, in the case of children with 'very special needs' which could not be provided by their parents or guardians, there was a constitutional obligation on the State to cater for those needs in order to vindicate the constitutional rights of the child. The Court in *FN* held that a child has a constitutional right to be fed and to live, to be reared and educated and to have the opportunity of working and realising his or her full potential and dignity as a human being and that those rights must be protected and vindicated by the State. Geoghegan J stated:

> In summary I take the view that the State is under a constitutional obligation towards the applicant to establish as soon as reasonably practical, either by use of section 58(4) of the Act of 1908 or otherwise, suitable arrangements of containment with treatment for the applicant.

Notwithstanding the considerable lapse of time since Mr Justice Geoghegan's decision, the High Court heard that the State had failed to make the appropriate arrangements for such children. Mr Justice Kelly was highly critical of the manner in which the executive had dealt with the problem of facilities for children with special problems, describing the delays and reversals in departmental policy as 'a scandal'. He had rejected arguments based on lack of resources, financial or otherwise, and held that the State and statutory bodies had clear constitutional duties to provide for the accommodation needs of children with special needs. It should be noted that in no case had any conviction been recorded against any of the disturbed children. However, due to the lack of available places in sufficiently secure units with appropriate facilities for minors with behavioural problems, they were being held in detention centres intended for the reception of children convicted of criminal charges, a situation which had given rise to considerable concern on the part of the Court.

On 25 February 2000, Kelly J made mandatory orders against the Ministers for Education and Science and Health and Children directing them '*to take all steps necessary to facilitate the building and opening of secure and high support units*' in different parts of the State and he specified dates by which such special care units were to be opened. Such facilities were necessary, he held, if the State was to ensure that its statutory obligations were fulfilled and the constitutional rights of minors upheld. He expressly stated that he was not dictating policy as such policy had already been decided. The order which Kelly J made was, in his view, one that would ensure that the Minister would 'live up to his word' and carry his policy into effect.

The Respondents appealed to the Supreme Court which delivered its judgment on 17 December 2001.[46] The Court, by a majority of four to one, reversed Kelly J's judgment and discharged the mandatory orders made against the State. The Chief Justice acknowledged that it was understandable that the High Court should have found it necessary to take the step of granting a declaration that the executive had been in breach of its constitutional duty to the applicants in specific cases. The issue, however, was whether the Court was also entitled to make an order specifying in detail the manner in which it was to carry out its functions so as to remedy the breach. Keane CJ stated:

> I am satisfied that the granting of an order of this nature is inconsistent with the distribution of powers between the legislative, executive and judicial arms of Government mandated by the Constitution. It follows that, as a matter of principle, it should not have been granted by the trial judge, however much one may sympathise with his obvious concern and exasperation at the manner in which this problem had been addressed at the legislative and executive level. It is of fundamental importance that each of the organs of Government should not only carry out the duties imposed on it by the Constitution but should recognise, . . . that the Constitution also defines the boundaries within which they are confined in carrying out their functions.
>
> The difficulty created by the order of the High Court in this case is not simply that it offends in principle against the doctrine of the separation of powers, though I have no doubt that it does. It also involves the High Court in effectively determining the

> policy, which the executives are to follow in dealing with a particular social problem.
> There is no reason in principle why the executive should not adopt a flexible and open-minded approach to the problems of children with special needs while at the same time ensuring that their constitutional right to have those needs met is respected.

Mr Justice Murphy agreed with the Chief Justice that Kelly J was not entitled to make the mandatory order in question as a means of vindicating the constitutional rights of the applicants. He went further and questioned the existence of the constitutional right in respect of which the order was made. He held that with the exception of the State's obligations in relation to the education of citizens, there was no provision in the Constitution which imposes an obligation of the State to provide accommodation, medical treatment, welfare or any other form of socio-economic benefit for any of its citizens, however needy or deserving.

Mr Justice Hardiman's analysis centred on whether it was constitutionally possible or desirable to increase the power of judges so as to enable them to dictate social policy. In his judgment in *Jamie Sinnott v The Minister for Education and Others*,[47] he earlier indicated:

> that Court intervention would be justified if, almost impossible to imagine, the political branches of government were to cease to make any provision for primary education.

But he stressed that a power available to deal with an absolutely extreme situation must not be applied to another less acute. In the present case, he was satisfied that enormous efforts had been made at considerable expense to address the needs of the applicant.

Denham J dissented and held that in the exceptional circumstances of the cases in question it was within the Court's jurisdiction to make the mandatory order. She was of the view that the order was a proportionate response, in exceptional circumstances, to protect the rights of the applicants.

Whilst the doctrine of the separation of powers is, undoubtedly, a central pillar upon which constitutional government rests, the Supreme Court in *TD* could be regarded as a disappointing resolution of a serious problem. It did not give any indication as to how the executive, with its 'flexible and open-minded approach', was to ensure that the constitutional rights of vulnerable minors were to be respected in practical terms. In view of the delays and failures on the part of the executive to discharge its obligations to such minors, it is hardly surprising that they should seek relief from the Courts. If, despite available resources and stated policy, the executive will not vindicate their constitutional rights and the Supreme Court will not compel the executive so to do, one wonders about the value, in practical terms, of the State's acknowledgement of these children's constitutional rights.

The Role of Health Boards and Consent to Medical Treatment of Children

In *The North Western Health Board v W and W*[48] the question which the Court had to consider was whether the parents of a 14-month-old child could be required by an Order of the Court to permit the health board to conduct a medical test – known as the PKU test – on their child. The facts can be stated as follows. A test exists, known as the PKU test, which enables it to be ascertained whether a child, who may look healthy and well, is suffering from certain biochemical or metabolic disorders which can be extremely serious but are also treatable if identified at an early stage. The test is generally carried out on a newborn infant between 72 hours of age and 120 hours of age to be most effective. Blood is dropped on to a card – known as a Guthrie card – which is then sent to the Children's Hospital, Temple Street, Dublin, where it is tested for four metabolic conditions and one endocrine condition. The four metabolic conditions are phenylketonuria, galactosaemia, homocystinuria and maple syrup urine disease. The endocrine condition is hypothyroidism. All the conditions in question cause either mental handicap or life-threatening illness unless they are detected early.

The risk to a child of having the heel test done is minimal. Even where the test is carried out badly and incorrectly, the worst that could occur is that the little lancet which is used might introduce infection in the skin or at worst in the bone. There is no indication that this has ever happened since the test was first adopted in Ireland in 1966.

In January 1998, a working group appointed by the Minister for Health furnished a report on metabolic disorders to the Minister. In their recommendations, the working group said that 'screening for metabolic disorders must be considered an integral part of the management of newborn infants'. They then went on to consider the responsibility of health boards, hospitals, health board community care services, general practitioners and midwives and parents for ensuring that every infant is so screened. They were of the view that the ultimate responsibility to ensure that the highest possible number of infants are screened should be placed on the health boards.

The parents in *W* refused to allow their child, 'Paul', to be subjected to the test as it would involve the puncturing of a blood vessel. It was their strong religious belief that nobody should be allowed to injure any person. Conscious of its obligations under the *Child Care Act, 1991*, the health board sought a declaration that it was in the best interests of Paul that the PKU test be carried out on him, and that the refusal of his parents to consent to the carrying out of the test was a failure to vindicate his personal rights. The board also sought a mandatory injunction requiring the defendants to furnish their consent to the test.

The health board argued that in circumstances where a parental decision exposed the minor to the risk of such significant disability, the Court could and should override the parents' decision and uphold the child's rights to bodily integrity and to life. The parents argued that the general rule in this jurisdiction was that parents should be left to do their best, even if individual decisions appear wrong, except in exceptional circumstances where there was a direct and serious threat to the health or life of the child. They rejected the notion that the Court in this case should make a decision of general application on matters of social policy.

In the High Court, McCracken J was concerned with what he saw as a rapid progression towards '*the brave new world in which the State always knows best*'. He considered the provisions of the *Child Care Act, 1991* and noted that section 3 undoubtedly imposes an obligation on health boards to promote the welfare of children in its area 'who were not receiving adequate care and protection'. He accepted that, in this regard, the welfare of the child must be the first and paramount consideration. He noted that the Act is primarily concerned with situations where, for a child's welfare, it is necessary that the child be taken under the care of some institution other than the family. He also noted, however, that the welfare of the child was not the only matter to be considered under section 3 of the Act and that the rights of the parents and the position of the family unit is clearly both recognised and emphasised therein. In considering Article 41.1 of the Constitution, he stated:

> Parents constantly make decisions of this nature, and subject their children to risks which objectively may not be justified, and which may have disastrous results. Examples outside the medical field may be decisions to allow a child to cycle to school on a busy road, or decisions to allow a teenager to find his or her own way home from a disco. Of course, in extreme cases the putting of children into a situation of risk may justify State intervention, but such cases would be extreme and therefore exceptional cases. In the medical field, the State provides many facilities for the protection of children, such as inoculations and vaccinations, but it does not compel the parents to have their children inoculated or vaccinated. There is in fact a far stronger case to be made that some vaccinations should be compulsory in the common good where the vaccination is against an infectious disease such as diphtheria or meningitis, but the State has chosen to leave it to the decision of the parents to have these vaccinations.

The High Court refused to grant the relief sought and the health board appealed its refusal.

On appeal, the Supreme Court, by a majority of four to one, upheld the finding of the High Court and refused to grant the declaration and injunction sought by the board. The Chief Justice, delivering his dissent, relied on a number of authorities in support of his decision. He referred to the case of *In Re C (a child) HIV Test*[49] which involved the issue as to whether the Court could order a baby to be subjected to a test for HIV where the mother was herself infected with HIV. In that case, a General Practitioner to whom the baby was taken for a developmental examination, expressed grave concern that the baby might already have been infected with HIV and that, if not, continued breast-feeding might make her so. She said that the baby should be tested for the infection. Since the parents disagreed, the doctor said that she felt obliged to speak to officers of the local authority and experts at Great Ormond Street Hospital. A Consultant Paediatrician at that hospital was also of the view that the baby should be tested for infection. The parents having refused to agree to the test, the local authority applied for a direction that a sample of blood be taken from the baby. The baby was not a ward of court and the application was made under the *Children Act, 1989*. The parents withheld their consent on the ground that the application for an order was 'an affront to their parental autonomy'. They also relied on what they claimed was medical evidence that the test was unnecessary and of no value.

In his judgment, Wilson J said that, on the evidence before him, 20% of babies infected with HIV would develop a serious AIDS-related illness within the first year of life unless they were treated with a prophylactic. The concerns of the parents in that case arose, not simply because of what they regarded as a wrongful medical and legal intrusion into their lives, but because of their objection to the treatment which might be indicated and, as the parents saw it, forced upon them, if the test were to be carried out. Having said that he had tried to be 'appropriately imaginative' about the position of the parents, Wilson J pointed out that the baby had rights of her own, reflected in both national and international law. He summed up his conclusion as follows:

> In order that her rights should be properly articulated, the baby in this case has been represented by the Official Solicitor. A Court will always look critically at the submission of the child's representative and in my experience in a significant minority of cases disagree with it. In this instance, however, I agree with the Official Solicitor that the case for testing the baby is overwhelming. I order it to take place.

The Chief Justice also relied upon *In Re W (a minor)*[50] in which the Court of Appeal considered the situation in which a minor, suffering from anorexia nervosa, refused medical treatment. The condition was such that she would suffer permanent physical damage without such treatment. In the Court of Appeal, Nolan LJ, with whom Lord Donaldson MR and Balcombe LJ agreed, said:

> If the child's welfare is threatened by a serious and imminent risk that the child will suffer grave and irreversible mental or physical harm the Court when called upon has a duty to intervene. It makes no difference whether the risk arises from the action or inaction of others or from the action or inaction of the child. Due weight must be given to the child's wishes, but the Court is not bound by them.

In that case, the order of the judge that the minor should be removed to and treated at a specialist hospital was upheld.

Keane CJ also considered the case of *In Re E (a minor)*, in which a 15-year-old boy who had leukaemia urgently required a blood transfusion as a lifesaving measure. As devout Jehovah's Witnesses, the boy and his parents had refused to consent to this procedure which was contrary to the tenets of their faith. The boy having been made a ward of court, the hospital authority sought the leave of the Court to treat him as they considered necessary, including giving transfusions of blood and blood products. Counsel for the parents opposed the application on the grounds that it was an abuse of the process of the Court, as it would be wrong for a judge in wardship proceedings to interfere in these circumstances and exercise that jurisdiction so close to the ward's sixteenth birthday. After that date, it was agreed that the boy would be capable of making his own decisions for all purposes as to all kinds of medical treatment.

Ward J, who described the case as 'one of life and death', said that he found that the influence of the teaching of the Jehovah's Witnesses was 'strong and powerful'. The very fact that the family could contemplate the death of one of its members was, he said, 'the most eloquent testimony of the power of that faith'. He summed up his views finally as follows:

> A has by the stand he has taken thus far already been and become a martyr for his faith. One has to admire – indeed one is almost baffled by – the courage of the conviction that he expresses. He is, he says, prepared to die for his faith. That makes him a martyr by itself. But I regret that I find it essential for his well being to protect him from himself and his parents and so I override his and his parents' decision.

Adopting the principles enunciated in the above cases, the Chief Justice was satisfied that the test should be carried out on Paul. The health board, he noted, was charged with promoting the welfare of children in their area and that this was not a case in which the State, through the health board, was claiming that 'it knows best'. Rather, this was a case in which it was beyond doubt that, if this test was not administered, Paul could suffer death or serious brain damage. If that were to occur, the responsibility would not be that of the parents alone. The Chief Justice held that the defendants had refused to protect and vindicate, so far as practicable, the constitutional right of Paul to be guarded against unnecessary and avoidable dangers to his health and welfare. The Courts, in his view, can and should.

The rest of the Supreme Court did not agree. Denham J believed that what was at issue was the balancing of responsibility between parental rights, the health board and the rights of the child as a member of a family and as a person. She accepted that the health board had statutory functions in this regard but that these had to be considered in the context of the constitutional rights of the family and the child. Applying the test of 'weighing and balancing constitutional principles', she concluded that the Court should not interfere with parental decision.

Mr Justice Murphy confessed that he would be impatient with the attitude of the parents in this case. He stated:

> I am alarmed by the real possibility (happily not a probability) that the young boy may be a victim of one of the metabolic conditions which the PKU test could so easily detect and that, because of the absence of detection and treatment, he could suffer appalling consequences. In that event at least the North Western Health Board will have the comfort of knowing that they took every possible step to secure the welfare of the infant.

Notwithstanding his alarm, however, he refused to interfere with the parents' decision, taking solace in the Supreme Court having interpreted the Constitution and the law to the best of its fallible ability.[51]

Murray J and Hardiman J also refused to interfere with parental autonomy in this area. Their decisions were based, *inter alia*, on the fact that the family as a moral institution enjoyed certain liberties under the Constitution which protect it from undue influence by the State. In addition, Mr Justice Hardiman expressed more general concerns about the notion of compulsion in the context of medical treatment. He cited the well-known American case of *Buck v Bell*[52] as 'a chilling example of logic, rationality and utilitarianism taken to an extreme'.

Buck v Bell was the attempt of Carrie Buck, an inmate of a State institution for the 'feeble minded', to avoid compulsory sterilisation on the basis, alternatively, of the equal protection clause and the due process clause of the 14th amendment to the United States Constitution. Hardiman J noted that 'to our contemporary sensibilities it seems outrageous that she found no protection'. He cited the opinion of Justice Oliver Wendell Holmes who spoke for the Court (save for one dissenting judge) in the following terms:

> We have seen more than once that the public welfare may call upon the best citizens for their lives. It would be strange if it could not call upon those who already sap the strength of the State for these lesser sacrifices, often not felt to be such by those concerned, in order to prevent our being swamped with incompetence. It is better for all the world, if instead of waiting to execute degenerate offspring for crime, or to let them starve for their imbecility, society can prevent those who are manifestly unfit from continuing their kind. The principle that sustains compulsory vaccination is broad enough to cover cutting the fallopian tubes. Three generations of imbeciles are enough.

Although Hardiman J accepted that there was no comparison between the types of treatment at issue, he was satisfied that the lesson of *Buck v Bell* was that:

> It is better to hesitate at the threshold of compulsion, even in its most benevolent form, than to adopt an easy but reductionist utilitarianism whose consequences may be unpredictable. Ample scope must be given to the fundamental values of human dignity, as well as those of positive logic.

Whilst one may readily agree with Hardiman J's hesitation at the threshold of compulsion, is it the case that insistence upon such a beneficial and simple test as the PKU test would constitute or even tend towards 'a reductionist utilitarianism'? Hardiman J's wariness of 'a purely utilitarian rationale' in favour of a principled approach must be welcomed. However, there remain unresolved questions in relation to how the child's personal rights enshrined in the Constitution are vindicated in a principled manner.

Conclusion

Health boards have been playing a central role in developing the law as it relates to children in this jurisdiction. The full implications of the powers and duties imposed upon health boards under the *Child Care Act, 1991* continue to be explored by the Courts.[53] As yet, many important questions relating to the liability of health boards, particularly, in the area of child sexual abuse, have yet to be addressed and we must wait until the Courts deliver further guiding principles in this evolving and important area of public law.

Notes

1 White Paper: Outline of Proposals for the Improvement of the Health Services, 1947 (P. No. 8400).
2 Defined in section 2 of the *Health Act, 1947* as 'a council of a county or a corporation of a county borough'.
3 The *Health Acts, 1947–1958* contain various provisions relating to wide-ranging areas of public health, such as, the control of infectious diseases, the regulation of health institutions and the provision of mother and child services.
4 See section 22 and section 23 of the *Health Act, 1947*.
5 Part I of the 1908 Act provides for infant life protection and section 2 of the 1957 Act makes provision for the notification to a health authority by persons receiving children for reward.
6 Save for section 15(8), 15(9) and section 24 and the Fourth Schedule.
7 Health Boards Regulations 1970 [S.I. 170 of 1970].
8 Health Authorities (Dissolution) Order, 1971 [S.I. 117 of 1971]. See also Brendan Hensey, *The Health Services of Ireland* (Dublin: Institute of Public Administration, 1988), p.60.
9 Section 66(2).
10 Section 38, *Children Act, 1908*.
11 1990 ILRM 130.
12 *The Children Act, 1989*.
13 *Guidelines on the Identification and Management of Non-Accidental Injury to Children* (Department of Health, 1980).
14 *Children First: National Guidelines for the Protection and Welfare of Children* (Dublin: Stationary Office, 1999).
15 [1995] 3 AER 353–401.
16 Ibid., 353.
17 *McMichael v United Kingdom* (1995) 20 EHRR 205, [1995] 2 FCR 718.
18 Section 3(1).
19 Section 3(2)(a).
20 Section 13.
21 Section 17.
22 Section 18.
23 Section 19.
24 [1991] 2 FLR 416.
25 Ibid. at 419.
26 Ibid. at 424.
27 *Eastern Health Board v McDonnell* [1999] 1 IR 174.
28 See, for example, *Competition Act 1991*, section 6; *Electoral Act 1992* section 159.
29 See, for example, *Post and Telecommunication Services Act 1983*, section 15(2); *Litter Pollution Act 1997* section 14 (no action for damages by reason of failure of local authority to exercise their statutory functions).

30 [1995] 3 AER 353 at 736.
31 High Court, 17 July 1994.
32 *Report of the Inquiry into Child Abuse in Cleveland* (1987) at 244.
33 Kelly, J. *The Irish Constitution* (3rd ed.) at 708.
34 [1998] 2 FLR at 278.
35 [1997] 1 FLR 384.
36 Brandt J delivered judgment in the first instance. The House of Lords, thereafter, delivered judgment of 17 June 1999: *Barrett v Enfield LBC* [1999] 3 ALL ER 193; [1999] 2 FLR 426.
37 See, for example, the judgment of Lord Slynn.
38 [1993] 4 AER 344.
39 *Osman v United Kingdom (The Times* 5 November 1998).
40 Ibid. at page 2.
41 High Court 29 July 1998.
42 High Court 4 December 1998.
43 High Court 25 February 2000.
44 High Court, 12 May 2000.
45 [1995] 1 IR 409.
46 *TD [A Minor] & Others v The Minister for Education and Others*, Supreme Court, 17 December 2001.
47 Supreme Court, 12 July 2001.
48 Supreme Court, 8 November 2001.
49 [1999] 3 FCR 289.
50 [1992] 4 AER 648.
51 At page 5 of his Judgment.
52 274 US 200.
53 See, for example, *The Western Health Board v KM*, Supreme Court, 21 December 2001.

Chapter 2

Child Abuse Claims against Public Authorities under the Human Rights Act 1998

*Jane Wright**

Introduction

In *Z v United Kingdom*, the United Kingdom government confidently asserted that after October 2000 a victim of a violation of a convention right would have a right to take proceedings against the public authority under the Human Rights Act 1998 ('HRA') and the courts would be empowered to award damages.[1] In *Z*, the European Court of Human Rights made the then largest awards ever in respect of personal injury after it had been conceded by the government that Bedfordshire County Council had failed to prevent four siblings from suffering appalling neglect and ill-treatment by their parents, contrary to Article 3 of the European Convention on Human Rights ('ECHR'). In principle, where children are grievously let down by the public authority with responsibility for them they may in future, on analogous facts, have a remedy under the HRA.[2] While the European Court of Human Rights may have retreated from *Osman v United Kingdom*[3] in relation to the Article 6 right to a fair trial in *Z*, it nevertheless found that there had been a violation of Articles 3 (inhuman and degrading treatment) and 13 (right to an effective remedy). The aim of this paper is to evaluate the potential of the HRA to afford a remedy to victims of abuse on facts analogous to those that arose in *Z*, and to identify the limitations inherent in the HRA, particularly in relation to time limits, that will provide a serious obstacle to securing justice for some victims. It is necessary also to consider the capacity of the HRA to influence the development of the common law through the court's role as a public authority under section 6 HRA.

It is inevitable that some of the discussion that follows is speculative. The HRA is in its infancy and it remains to be seen how English courts will shape case law in response to the demands of the Strasbourg jurisprudence.

* University of Essex.

The Obligation on Public Authorities under Section 6 HRA

Section 6(1) HRA makes it 'unlawful for a public authority to act in a way which is incompatible with a Convention right' and by virtue of section 2(1) HRA, English courts are required in determining questions that arise under the Act to take account of Strasbourg jurisprudence. This means that in addition to their statutory duties prescribed by English legislation such as the Children Act 1989, public authorities are now bound by the duties that inhere in the ECHR. The corollary of the rights set out in the ECHR is the imposition of duties on public authorities by virtue of section 6(1) HRA. There is a large body of ECHR jurisprudence developed by the European Court (and former Commission) of Human Rights ('ECtHR') that has fleshed out the bare bones of the Convention text and to which English courts must turn in order to 'bring home'[4] the Convention rights. Section 6(2) provides that subsection (1) of section 6 will not apply if the authority could not have acted differently by reason of one or more provisions of primary legislation. In order to discover the nature of the obligation under section 6(1) it is therefore necessary to ascertain exactly what the ECHR requires of states. The following discussion will therefore identify the rights that are most likely to be of relevance in child abuse litigation, as well as outlining the scope of those rights.

The Convention rights that bind public authorities are set out in Schedule 1 HRA and include two rights that are likely to be of particular significance in relation to child abuse claims: Article 3 which prohibits torture and inhuman or degrading treatment or punishment and the Article 8 right to respect for private and family life. While human rights may be viewed traditionally as obligations of non-interference in citizens' lives by the state, recent years have witnessed an extensive development of ECHR case law, the thrust of which is that the state may have a positive duty to act to secure the rights set out in the ECHR: it was the positive obligation under Article 3 that was significant in *Z v United Kingdom*. The effect of these positive obligations is that a public authority may be required to act when the ill-treatment is meted out by private individuals, such as parents and other carers. The positive obligation derives from reading Article 1 ECHR according to which states are obliged to 'secure [the Convention rights and freedoms] to everyone within the jurisdiction' together with the relevant article.

Thus, in *A v United Kingdom*,[5] the ECtHR found that the United Kingdom had violated Article 3 when a young boy was beaten by his stepfather. In *A*, it was held that children in particular require effective protection, in the form of effective deterrence against breaches of their personal integrity. On the issue of positive obligations, in *Z* the Commission held that the

> protection of children who by reason of their age and vulnerability are not capable of protecting themselves requires not merely that the criminal law provides protection against Article 3 treatment but that, additionally, this provision will in appropriate circumstances imply a positive obligation on the authorities to take preventive measures to protect a child who is at risk from another individual.[6]

In *Z*, before the ECtHR, the government did not contest the Commission's finding that the treatment suffered by the four applicants reached the level of severity prohibited by Article 3 and that the United Kingdom had failed in its positive obligation to protect the children from inhuman and degrading treatment contrary to Article 3.

It might be argued that since Article 1 has not been incorporated into English law by the HRA there is no room to read Article 3 as importing a positive obligation. However, as Clayton and Tomlinson have observed, the omission of Article 1 is consistent with the fact that the HRA is a domestic instrument.[7] It would have made no sense to incorporate Article 1 as the HRA is the vehicle through which the Article 1 obligation is implemented at domestic level. In any event, Strasbourg jurisprudence relating to Article 1 and the development of positive obligations is to be taken into account by English courts under section 2 and as Lord Slynn has indicated it is appropriate to give a purposive construction to the Act,[8] namely to bring home the ECHR rights.

Article 3 violations are reserved for the most egregious forms of ill-treatment. Torture is a term that is applied to especially cruel treatment. In *Ireland v United Kingdom*,[9] the ECtHR defined torture as 'deliberate inhuman treatment causing very serious and cruel suffering', a view that was confirmed recently in *Aksoy v Turkey*.[10] In order for treatment to be 'inhuman' it must reach a minimum level of severity and any assessment will be relative and take into account such things as the duration of the treatment, its physical and mental effects and, the sex, age and state of health of the victim.[11] In *Z*, the Commission had no doubt that the level of severity contemplated by Article 3 had been reached, taking account of the following: the children were under-nourished and frequently locked in their rooms in a soiled and unhygienic state and they disclosed signs of emotional abuse and neglect: the Criminal Injuries Compensation Board had found that they had suffered appalling neglect and had made awards of compensation based on physical and psychological injury. In addition two of the children were undergoing therapeutic treatment and it was likely that another would be in need of psychological treatment. In a more recent decision, *E v United Kingdom*,[12] the EctHR held that sexual and physical abuse of children over a long period of time by their mother's cohabitee constituted inhuman and degrading treatment.

The next question that arises is about when exactly states/public authorities do have a positive obligation to act. According to the case law on positive obligations under Article 3, the test is the same that was applied by the ECtHR in *Osman v United Kingdom*[13] regarding Article 2 (the right to life). A state comes under a positive obligation to act when there is a real and immediate risk of ill-treatment contrary to Article 3 of which they know or ought to have knowledge.[14] It will be no answer to a claim under Article 3 that the public authority was not aware of ill-treatment where the circumstances were such to suggest that an investigation should be made or that the facts required a situation to be monitored.[15]

As to the measures that should be taken by the public authority, Strasbourg jurisprudence indicates that the measures should provide effective protection and include reasonable steps to prevent ill treatment.[16] It is implicit in *Z v*

United Kingdom that Bedfordshire County Council, the relevant public authority, should have invoked the powers available to it to remove the children from their home at a much earlier stage. At the time of writing it remains to be seen how the Strasbourg criteria regarding the establishment of a duty to act and the scope of action required which have been laid down in *Z*, and indeed in *Osman v United Kingdom*, will be transposed into English law. As we have seen, for the positive duty to act to arise, there must be 'a real and immediate risk of harm to an identified individual'. Put another way, this would seem to require a very high degree of forcibility, in the words of Lord Morris of Borth-Y-Gest in *Home Office v Dorset Yacht*,[17] the risk must be glaringly obvious. When this test is satisfied, the local authority is required to provide effective protection and to take 'reasonable steps'[18] to prevent ill-treatment. According to the Commission in *Z*, the local authority had failed 'despite the means reasonably available to them' to take any positive steps to bring the ill-treatment to an end.[19] One question that arises is whether resource considerations may be taken into account in determining whether such a positive obligation to act has been discharged.

According to *Osman v United Kingdom*, resources may be taken into account in determining the scope of a positive duty to act under Article 2 ECHR. The ECtHR held that

> bearing in mind the difficulties involved in policing modern societies, the unpredictability of human conduct and the operational choices which must be made in terms of priorities and resources, [the positive obligation under Article 2] must be interpreted in a way which does not impose an impossible or disproportionate burden on the authorities.[20]

The Commission in *Osman* noted that the obligation will vary:

> having regard to the source and degree of danger and the means available to combat it. Whether the risk to life derives from disease, environmental factors or from the activities of those acting outside the law, there will be a range of policy decisions relating, *inter alia*, to the use of state resources, which it will be for the contracting states to assess on the basis of their aims and priorities subject to these being compatible with the values of democratic societies and the fundamental rights guaranteed in the Convention.[21]

There is no discussion in *Z*, of the role that resources might play in assessing whether a positive duty under Article 3 has been discharged. It is perhaps important to remember that the discussion in *Osman* centred around the concept of operational measures, which would seem to relate to measures of personal protection. Clearly, where an individual(s) is in danger there may well be very difficult resource allocations to be made in terms of manpower. In contrast, the issue in *Z* was the failure to institute care proceedings (the means reasonably available to the local authority). Varying views have been expressed by commentators. Mole has argued that resource arguments cannot be used to justify a failure to discharge the positive obligation under Article 3, because the obligation is absolute.[22] Miles, on the other hand, differentiates the negative and positive obligations inherent in Article 3 (and Article 2) and suggests that it is less clear that the positive obligation excludes consideration of resources.[23] There is little support for the Miles view. As she points out, in *Olsson v Sweden*,[24] the state argued that the placement of children in foster-homes a long way from each other and from their parents was caused partly by the limited number of foster-homes. In finding a violation of Article 8, the court held that administrative difficulties could only play a secondary role. The ECtHR has not discussed the relevance of resources in any of the recent cases concerning positive obligations under Article 3 (see *A v United Kingdom*, *Z v United Kingdom* and *E v United Kingdom*) in contrast with the caselaw under Article 2 (see for example *Osman v United Kingdom* and *Kilic v Turkey*).[25] Indeed, in *D v United Kingdom*,[26] where it was found that deportation of a convicted drug smuggler in the terminal stages of AIDS to St. Kitts where the level of medical care and family support would be grievously inadequate would be a violation, the ECtHR stressed the absolute nature of the Article 3 obligation. Although, the reasoning is not in terms of positive/negative obligations, the crux of the case is that the state had a positive obligation to continue to provide medical care for a person for whom it had assumed responsibility: deportation would violate that obligation. The Court held that:

> in exercising their right to expel such aliens, contracting states must have regard to Art. 3 of the convention, which enshrines one of the fundamental values of democratic societies. It is precisely for this reason that the court has repeatedly stressed in its line of authorities involving extradition, expulsion or deportation of individuals to third countries that Art. 3 prohibits in absolute terms torture or inhuman or degrading treatment or punishment and that its guarantees apply irrespective of the reprehensible nature of the conduct of the person in question (see, most recently *Ahmed v Austria* (1997) 24 EHRR 278 and *Chahal v UK* (1997) 23 EHRR 413, [1996] 1 CLY 3130).

However, there is arguably some support for Miles where the Court has indicated that the state/public authority is expected to take 'reasonable' steps and to take measures 'reasonably available to them'. It is noteworthy though that in none of the cases concerning positive obligations under Article 3 has the ECtHR alluded to its well known dictum that in determining whether a positive obligation exists:

> regard must be had to the fair balance that has to be struck between the general interest of the community and the interests of the individual, the search for which is inherent in the whole of the Convention [*emphasis added*].[27]

As Miles has observed, an obvious difference between the domestic context and the Strasbourg arena is that liability under the HRA is imposed on individual public authorities under section 6, rather than on the state. A local authority might argue that a failure to act was a result of lack of resources attributable to decisions taken by central government.[28] It is suggested that English courts should resist the type of argument that attempts to shift responsibility from the public authority, to which statutory or other responsibilities have been devolved, to central government. Were they to accept such argument there is a possibility that a victim would become remediless as the means available to protect children are cast upon the responsible public authorities under the Children Act, not the Secretary of State.

Article 8 ECHR, which requires the state to respect the right to private and family life is also likely to be of relevance in child abuse claims. The concept of private life is not limited to matters of 'privacy' as English lawyers might understand but encompasses a person's physical and psychological integrity.[29] While the argument in *Z v United Kingdom* was that the local authority had procrastinated for too long before removing the children, conversely in *TP and KM v United Kingdom*,[30] the claimants argued that the removal of the child into care was an interference with the Article 8 right that could not be justified under Article 8(2). Any interference with the right to respect for private and family life must be in accordance with the law and must pursue a legitimate aim and be 'necessary in a democratic society'. In *TP and KM*, the place of safety order was issued under section 28 of the Children and Young Persons Act 1969 and was aimed at protecting the 'health or morals' and 'the rights and freedoms of the child'. The English court had been satisfied that there was strong evidence that the child had been sexually abused and removal to the care of the local authority was to protect her from that risk.

The ECtHR has held that the state will enjoy a wide margin of appreciation when taking a decision to take a child into care, but stricter scrutiny is called for in respect of further limitations. Although Article 8 contains no explicit procedural requirements, Strasbourg jurisprudence has a well-developed body of jurisprudence the thrust of which is that the decision-making process must be fair and safeguard Article 8 interests. Thus in *TP and KM*, the ECtHR recalled its dictum in *W v United Kingdom*:

> What has to be determined is whether, having regard to the particular circumstances of the case and notably the serious nature of the decisions to be taken, the parents have been involved in the decision-making process, seen as a whole, to a degree sufficient to provide them with the requisite protection of their interests. If they have not, there will have been a failure to respect their family life and the interference resulting from the decision will not be capable of being regarded as 'necessary' within the context of Article 8.[31]

On the facts in *TP and KM*, the failure to submit to the court promptly the question of whether a videotaped interview of the child should be made available deprived the parent of adequate involvement in the decision-making process concerning the daughter and consequently Article 8 was violated. If the video had been disclosed there would have been an opportunity for the mother to deal with allegations that her daughter could not safely be returned to her care.

Where a victim alleges that a public authority has acted incompatibly with an ECHR right, and therefore unlawfully under section 6(1) HRA, proceedings may be brought against that public authority under section 7. The following discussion will outline the action under section 7.

The Action against a Public Authority under Section 7 HRA and Time Limits

Where a person claims that a public authority has acted unlawfully under section 6(1) HRA he/she may bring proceedings against the authority (section 7(1)(a)) or rely on the Convention right or rights in any legal proceedings (section 7(1)(b)), provided that he/she is a victim of the unlawful act. According to section 7(7) a person will be a victim of an unlawful act only if he/she would be a victim for the purposes of Article 34 of the Convention if proceedings were brought in the ECtHR in respect of that act. This means that a person must be

> actually affected by the violation he alleges . . . [there is] no kind of *actio popularis* for the interpretation of the Convention; it does not permit individuals to complain against a law *in abstracto* . . .[32]

Thus, the effect of section 7 is that in a case where Convention rights are engaged a child abuse victim may seek a remedy at common law, such as negligence, as well as taking proceedings under section 7 HRA.

Under section 8(1) HRA, where a court finds that any act of a public authority is (or would be) unlawful, 'it may grant such relief or remedy, or make such order, within its powers as it considers just and appropriate'. Damages may only be awarded by a court with power to award damages in civil proceedings[33] and no award of damages is to be made unless the court is satisfied that the award is necessary to afford just satisfaction to the person in whose favour it is made.[34] The general view of commentators[35] is that the effect of section 8(3)(a) is that the damages remedy under section 8 is residual so that an award under the HRA will only be made where, for example, no common law remedy lies and this view is supported by what little authority there is.[36]

In many ways the action under the HRA may be perceived as an attractive remedy: there is no need to establish a duty of care at common law so that where facts engage ECHR rights and concern the child who is not yet cared for by the local authority the restrictive decision of *X v Bedfordshire County Council*[37] ('*Bedfordshire*') is of no application. In addition, English courts are required when determining whether to award damages and the amount of an award to take into account the principles applied by the ECtHR in relation to the award of (just satisfaction) compensation.[38] Strasbourg jurisprudence demonstrates that far wider heads of damage may be compensated under the ECHR than under English tort law: just satisfaction has been awarded for 'trauma, anxiety and feeling of injustice',[39] 'feeling of helplessness and frustration',[40] and 'distress, anxiety and humiliation'.[41] However, there are significant limitations to the availability of the section 7 action to child abuse victims as a result of the time limits prescribed by the HRA and as Mole has pointed out that there may be many claimants whose cases pre-date the HRA.[42]

Time Limits

Proceedings against a public authority under section 7 must be brought within one year of the date on which the act complained of took place, unless the court finds it equitable having regard to all the circumstances to extend the period.[43] The problem section for some claimants is section 22(4) HRA according to which section 7 (the action against a public authority) does not apply to an act taking place before the coming into force of that section, namely, 2 October 2000. Thus, in a case with facts analogous to *Bedfordshire* no claim would lie against the relevant authority under the HRA, even assuming that the court was prepared to extend the limitation period under section 7(5).

It might be thought that one way of circumventing the limitation of section 22(4) would be to rely on the court's role as public authority: by virtue of section 6(3) HRA 'public authority' includes a court and a number of authorities have been decided on the basis that in developing the principles of the common law, the court must ensure that it takes account of ECHR obligations.[44] Indeed, the development of a right of privacy that is arguably taking place[45] has occurred in response to this perceived obligation on the court. However, there are a number of authorities decided at the highest level that suggest that the scheme of remedies (if it can be called that, given that there is no 'right' to damages under the Act) for unlawful action by public authorities cannot be circumvented through reliance on the court in its role as public authority under section 6(1).

The effect of a number of decisions is that the HRA would appear not to have retrospective effect, where the defendant is a public authority.[46] In *R v Lambert*[47] and *R v Kansal*,[48] which both concerned criminal appeals, the House of Lords examined the meaning of section 22(4)HRA and decided that a defendant whose trial took place before the coming into force of sections 6(1) and 7(b) cannot rely on an alleged breach of his Convention rights by a court or prosecutor that occurred before 2 October 2000. The only exception is that stated in section 22(4): Convention rights may be relied upon whenever the act in question took place where 'proceedings are brought by or at the instigation of a public authority'. Section 22(4) does not apply to appeals against criminal conviction as they are not proceedings brought by or at the instigation of a public authority. In *Lambert*, the appellant had been convicted of possession and intent to supply a controlled drug contrary to the Misuse of Drugs Act 1971. He argued that the trial judge had violated Article 6(2) ECHR (presumption of innocence) by directing the jury that the burden of proof was on the defendant to prove that he did not know that he possessed a controlled drug. The majority view of the House of Lords on the interpretation of section 22(4) was expressed by Lord Slynn as follows:

> It is to be noted that section 7(6)[49] distinguishes between proceedings brought by a public authority and 'an appeal against the decision of a court' whereas section 22(4) extends the application of section 7(1)(b) only where proceedings are brought by a public authority. This appears to indicate that an appeal by an unsuccessful defendant is not to be treated as a proceeding brought by or at the instigation of a public authority albeit in other contexts an appeal may be considered as part of the proceedings initiated by a particular party.[50]

There were clearly strong policy considerations at work in these cases. As Lord Hutton observed, he did not consider that 'in enacting section 22(4) Parliament intended that a conviction which was validly and lawfully imposed should be quashed on an appeal perhaps many years later'.[51] The House of Lords in *Lambert* and *Kansal* were concerned that many convictions could be reopened. As Lord Hope observed the majority view has yet to be tested in a civil case and he indicated that a narrow view of the ratio should be taken:

> It would be unsatisfactory if the majority view were to be regarded as having pre-empted the question whether section 22(4) applies to civil appeals, to which the concern about past convictions does not apply.[52]

It should be pointed out that *Lambert* was followed in *Kansal*, notwithstanding that three members of the House of Lords considered that *Lambert* was wrongly decided but held that in the interests of certainty the decision should be followed. Subsequently, in *Clingham v Royal Borough of Kensington and Chelsea*,[53] notwithstanding that by virtue of *Kansal*, the HRA was not directly applicable, the House of Lords agreed at the invitation of all counsel to deal with appeals concerning section 1 Crime and Disorder Act 1998 as if the HRA was applicable.

In *Wainwright v Home Office*,[54] Laws LJ, relying on *Lambert*, took the view that section 22(4) HRA demonstrated that when 'Parliament wanted the [HRA] to act retrospectively it says so',[55] and that the HRA could not be relied upon to introduce a 'retrospective right to privacy which did not exist at common law'.[56] The claimants sought damages following a strip search on a prison visit that had been carried out in a distressing and humiliating manner. Buxton LJ described the treatment of Mrs Wainwright and her son as 'deplorable'.[57] There was no question that the strip search itself was not permitted, the complaint went to the manner in which it was carried out. Counsel for the claimants argued that section 3 HRA (which requires that so far as it is possible to do so, primary and subordinate legislation must be read and given effect in a way which is compatible with Convention rights) should be applied to Prison Rule 86 so that it complies with Article 8 ECHR (the right to respect for private life). Lord Woolf MR (with whom Mummery and Buxton LJJ agreed) held that the decisions in *Lambert* and *Kansal* were 'consistent with the general presumption that legislation should not be treated as changing the substantive law in relation to events taking place prior to legislation coming into force'.[58] The HRA could not 'be relied on to change substantive law by introducing a retrospective right to privacy which did not exist at common law'.[59] Although, the Court of Appeal did not consider the scope of the court's obligation under section 6(3) explicitly, the implication of the judgments is clearly that the non-retrospective nature of the HRA generally cannot be circumvented through reliance on the court's role as a public authority under section 6.[60]

The question whether the court should develop the tort of negligence where pre-HRA facts engage ECHR rights was considered, *obiter*, by the Court of Appeal in *K v Secretary of State for the Home Department*.[61] In *K*, the claimant had been raped by a convicted sex offender who had been recommended for deportation. The offender was released by the Home Secretary under powers conferred by para 2(3) of Schedule 3 to the Immigration Act 1971. In a unanimous decision the Court of Appeal held that the Secretary of State owed no duty of care to the claimant as the facts disclosed no nexus between the claimant and the defendant: the only nexus that existed was between the defendant and the rapist.[62] In other words, a special relationship of proximity was not established on the facts. However, counsel for the claimant argued that the common law should be interpreted to safeguard the claimant's rights under the ECHR. On the facts this was a weak argument since the victim was unknown to the defendant and Laws LJ recalled the nature of the positive obligation laid upon the state under Article 2 ECHR (right to life) which speaks of a duty to take steps to prevent an offence where the authorities know of a 'real and immediate risk to the life of an identified individual or individuals'.[63] The reference to Article 2 is somewhat puzzling because in fact counsel had argued that the rape of the claimant amounted to inhuman and degrading treatment contrary to Article 3 ECHR. However, the test to determine when a positive duty to act arises is the same under Articles 2 and 3. Laws LJ expressed himself satisfied that the English common law on 'third agency cases'[64] conformed with the ECHR (he clearly did not have in mind *Bedfordshire* where as we have seen the European Court of Human Rights found a violation of Articles 3 and 13 (the right to an effective remedy). Laws LJ cited *Bromiley v UK*[65] where the European Court of Human Rights held that striking out a claim for want of proximity was consistent with Article 6 ECHR (the right to a fair trial[66]) and he did not speculate on what the outcome would have been had the facts engaged Article 3. Arden LJ[67] took a different tack and sounded a very clear warning note that no assumption that the common law will be developed to accommodate ECHR rights should be made. In her view it was quite unnecessary to examine the facts to see whether they engaged ECHR rights because they took place prior to the HRA coming into force. She stated that:

> ... the common law is very porous and susceptible to development in accordance with many influences, including Convention values. I assume for this purpose that a finding of a breach of Art. 3 would follow if the pleaded allegations were proved. However, as a matter of Strasbourg jurisprudence, it is established that Art. 6 does not guarantee the content of civil rights under national law (see for example *Z v United Kingdom* (2002) 34 EHRR 97). ... Art. 13 of the Convention confers the right to an effective remedy if a Convention right has been violated, and in any case

> occurring after the commencement of the Human Rights Act 1998, s.7 of that act is available. In those circumstances, I do not consider that there is a need for the common law to develop in the very significant way that would be necessary to accommodate this case (assuming for this purpose that such a course is open to the court). ... Since the material events occurred before the commencement of the Human Rights Act 1998, we need not decide the question whether the matters alleged mount to a breach of a positive obligation imposed on the state by virtue of Art. 3 of the Convention.[68]

Thus, according to Arden LJ the ECHR will be irrelevant in cases where the facts arose prior to 2 October 2000. The House of Lords has yet to rule on this issue but the gist of these judgments suggests that in those tort cases that do engage ECHR rights and that fall outside the time limits prescribed by the HRA, English courts may well leave claimants to pursue their remedy in Strasbourg. This attitude runs counter to the lofty expectations expressed in the White Paper, *Rights Brought Home*, which spoke of British people being able to argue for their rights in the British courts without the inordinate delay and cost of going to Strasbourg.[69]

More recently, a differently constituted Court of Appeal has signalled a new approach. In *MAK and RK v Dewsbury Health Care NHS Trust and Kirklees Metropolitan Council* (appeal consolidated with *JD v East Berkshire Community* and *RK and Another v Oldham NHS Trust and Dr. Blumenthal*[70]), which related to pre-HRA facts, a father and daughter claimed damages for psychiatric injury and financial loss after the father was wrongly accused of sexual abuse and denied access to his daughter for a short period of time. At first instance, it was held that the principles of *X (Minors)* were fatal to both claims. The Court of Appeal, however, held that in relation to the child's claim (but *not* that of the father) *Bedfordshire*[71] could not withstand the advent of the HRA. The Court of Appeal's reasoning proceeded in two stages. First, the Court responded to counsel's argument that *Bedfordshire* should be reconsidered because subsequent decisions of the House of Lords have varied the principles and 'the law has moved on'. Counsel relied particularly upon *Barrett v London Borough of Enfield*[72] and *Phelps v Hillingdon London Borough Council.*[73] In both these cases, various members of the House of Lords have questioned the merits of a number of the policy arguments that were put forward by Lord Browne-Wilkinson in *Bedfordshire* as self-evident justifications for denying a duty of care on the part of the local authority. Giving judgment for the Court of Appeal, Lord Phillips MR acknowledged that in neither *Barrett* nor *Phelps* had the House of Lords sought to depart from its previous authority, but he added the important qualification that: 'it is always possible for the House of Lords to reduce the impact of a previous decision by distinguishing it or confining it narrowly to its particular facts'.[74] He stated that in *Barrett*, 'much of the reasoning advanced by Lord Browne-Wilkinson had been called into question'.[75] Thus, Lord Slynn had endorsed the dictum of Evans LJ in the Court of Appeal in *Barrett* where he stated that:

> what is said to be a policy consideration, namely, that imposing a duty of care might lead to defensive conduct on the part of the person concerned and might require him to spend time or resources on keeping full records should normally be a factor of little, if any, weight. If the conduct in question is of a kind which can be measured against the standards of the reasonable man, placed as the defendant was, then I do not see why the law in the public interest should not require those standards to be observed.[76]

Lord Slynn had also doubted that alternative remedies (for example, the local government ombudsman) would be as effective as the recognition by the court that a duty of care is owed at common law. In *Phelps*, Lord Clyde doubted that the multi-disciplinary aspects to a claim could constitute a bar to action:

> It should be possible to disentangle the relevant parts played by particular individuals and identify where the alleged negligence occurred.[77]

Thus, in *Barrett* and *Phelps*, much of the reasoning that underpinned Lord Browne-Wilkinson's speech in *Bedfordshire* had been called into question and, according to the Court of Appeal in *MAK* and *RK*, the effect of these cases is to restrict *Bedfordshire* to the core proposition that decisions by local authorities whether or not to take a child into care are not reviewable by way of a negligence claim.

The Court of Appeal then proceeded to consider the combined impact of ECHR jurisprudence such as *Z v United Kingdom*[78] and *E v United Kingdom*[79] and the action under the HRA on that core proposition. The effect of the HRA is that where a claim is made under section 7 there will now be litigation against public authorities involving factual inquiries into the conduct of professionals involved. This fact led Lord Phillips to declare that:

> In these circumstances the reasons of policy that led the House of Lords to hold that no duty of care towards a child arises, in so far as those reasons have not already been discredited by the subsequent decisions of the House of Lords, will largely cease to apply. Substantial damages will be available on proof of individual shortcomings, which will be relevant alike to a claim based on breach of section 6 of the [HRA] and a claim based on a breach of a common law duty of care... the decision in [*Bedfordshire*] cannot survive the [HRA]... the absence of an alternative remedy for children who were victims of abuse before October 2000 militates in favour of the recognition of a common law duty of care once the public policy reasons have lost their force.

The effect of *MAK and RK* is that there is no longer any denial of a duty of care as a matter of law under the third head of *Caparo* but, as Lord Phillips observed, each case must be determined on its own facts and there may be cases where it would not be fair, just and reasonable to recognise a duty of care.[80]

The Court of Appeal did rely on public policy arguments to deny any common law claim to the father, on the basis that in such cases there is an inherent potential conflict between child and parent. As Lord Phillips observed the same view was taken by the Privy Council in *B v Attorney General*,[81] on appeal from the New Zealand Court of Appeal. It is relevant to note here that while the ECtHR has held that if balancing of interests between child and parent is necessary, the child's interests must prevail, it has on many occasions found that proceedings in relation to the care of children have violated a parent's rights.[82] The decision in *MAK and RK* means that in a case engaging pre-HRA facts, a claimant such as the parent in *TP and KM* will still have no remedy at common law. However, the lack of a common law remedy is arguably of less significance in the case of parents (for whom the limitation period in negligence is much shorter than that applicable to their children), who of course may have a claim under the HRA where the relevant facts occurred post 2 October 2000. The logic of the Court of Appeal decision is clearly flawed, given that the Court has taken the view that in the case of the child the common law must be consistent with the ECHR jurisprudence, but not in relation to parents.

The Court of Appeal's decision in *MAK and RK* appears to be an illegitimate overruling of a House of Lords' decision which it has recognised as being binding, at least in relation to the core proposition. It is clear that decisions of the House of Lords are absolutely binding on the Court of Appeal and that it is not open to the Court of Appeal to advise judges to ignore decisions of the House on the ground that they were decided *per incuriam* or are unworkable.[83] An otherwise binding precedent may either expressly or by necessary implication be repealed by statute,[84] but it is extremely doubtful that such a view could be taken of the impact of the HRA on the status of *Bedfordshire*, and the Court of Appeal has not attempted to elucidate exactly which provisions of the HRA justify its conclusion. The Court of Appeal has staked its claim to legitimacy on the fact that post-HRA victims will have a remedy under the HRA. This looks very like de facto retrospective effect, through the development of the common law and as we have seen the House of Lords has previously held that the HRA does not have retrospective effect.[85] Some support for the Court of Appeal's decision might arguably have been found in section 6(1) and 6(3) HRA, by invoking the court's own obligation to develop the common law in line with the ECHR. There is arguably some support for this view, albeit *obiter*, in the pre-HRA House of Lords' decision in *Reynolds v Times Newspapers*,[86] but *Lambert* and *Kansal* clearly present obstacles to this interpretation. However, both *Lambert* and *Kansal* could be distinguished because they related to criminal appeals where different considerations of public policy apply and, as discussed previously, Lord Hope expressed the view that they should not be determinative in civil claims. Nevertheless, it is plainly not acceptable for the Court of Appeal to state baldly that a binding decision of the House of Lords cannot withstand the enactment of a statute, but without justifying their decision by reference to specific statutory provisions. While it might be thought that the same result (non-applicability of *Bedfordshire*) could have been justifiably reached on the basis that subsequent House of Lords' jurisprudence in the shape of *Barrett* and *Phelps* have undermined the very premises on which Lord Wilkinson's leading speech was based, the House of Lords itself has not chosen to overrule its previous authority and has limited itself to restricting its application. It is understood that *MAK and RK* will be appealed and it remains to be seen what view the House of Lords will now take of the discredited authority that *Bedfordshire* appears to have become.

While *MAK and RK* evinces a clear intention to rectify the lacuna in the law created by the combined effect of *X (Minors)*, *Z v United Kingdom* and the limited availability of a remedy under the HRA due to the non-retrospectively principle, the Court of Appeal gives no indication as to *how* ECHR principles will be mediated into the English common law. It would seem logical to develop any test for establishing a duty of care in negligence on the basis of the criteria developed by the ECtHR in its jurisprudence under relevant articles. Thus, in the case of Article 3 for example, a duty of care involving a positive obligation to take reasonable steps to act would arise where a local authority is, or ought to be aware of abuse/risk of abuse. On this issue, though, Lord Phillips held that the Court was not suggesting that any duty of care should 'replicate' the duty not to violate Articles 3 and 8,[87] for liability might arise under the ECHR where the tort of negligence is not established. This question will now surely exercise the courts as they grapple with the means by which English law should accommodate the ECHR.

Notes

1 [2001] 2 FCR 246 at para. 107.
2 Assuming that the relevant facts occurred after 2 October 2000 – the claim against a public authority does not take effect retrospectively, see discussion *infra.*
3 [1999] FLR 193.
4 Adopting the wording of the White Paper which described the aim of the Human Rights Act 1998 as being to 'bring home' the Convention rights: *Rights Brought Home: The Human Rights Bill* (Cm 3782).
5 (1998) EHRLR 82.
6 (1999) 28 EHRR CD 65. The Commission also referred to Article 19 of the United Nations Convention on the Rights of the Child which requires states to take all appropriate measures 'to protect the child from all forms of physical and mental violence, injury or abuse'.
7 R. Clayton and H. Tomlinson, *The Law of Human Rights*, Oxford, Oxford University Press, 2000, at p. 147.
8 *R v Lambert* [2001] 3 WLR 206 at para. 29.
9 (1979–80) 2 EHRR 25.
10 (1997) 23 EHRR 553.
11 *Ireland v United Kingdom, supra* n.9 at para. 162.
12 [2002] 3 FCR 700.
13 *Supra* n.3.
14 *Z v United Kingdom, supra* n. 6 at para. 94, citing *Osman v United Kingdom, supra* n.3 at para. 116.
15 See *E v United Kingdom, supra* n.12.
16 *Z v United Kingdom*, ECtHR, *supra* n.1 at para. 73.
17 [1970] 2 All ER at 303.
18 *Z v United Kingdom, supra* n.1 at para. 73.
19 At para. 98.

20 *Osman*, *supra* n.3 at para. 116.
21 (1999) 29 EHRR 245.
22 N. Mole, 'Local Authorities and the European Court', [2001] Fam Law 667.
23 J. Miles, 'Case Commentary: Human rights and child protection', (2001) 13 CFLQ 431 at 438–40.
24 (1998) 11 EHRR 259.
25 [2000] ECHR 22492/93.
26 (1997) 24 EHRR 423.
27 *Rees v United Kingdom* (1986) 9 EHRR 56 at para. 57, where the EctHR was examining whether there was a positive obligation under Article 8 to recognise the post-operative status of a transsexual.
28 For discussion of this issue, see Miles, *supra* n.23 and R. Carnwath, 'Welfare Services – liabilities in tort after the Human Rights Act. Postscript' [2001] PL 475, in which he discusses *R v Gloucestershire C.C., ex parte Barry* [1997] AC 584, where the majority held that the Council was entitled to reduce its services on account of reduced resources.
29 *X and Y v The Netherlands* (1985) 8 EHRR 235, *Botta v Italy* (1998) 26 EHRR 241.
30 [2001] 2 FLR 549.
31 (1987) 10 EHRR 29.
32 *Klass v Germany* (1978) 2 EHRR 214.
33 Section 8(2).
34 Section 8(3)(a) HRA.
35 See D. Fairgrieve, 'The Human Rights Act 1998, Damages and English Tort Law', in D. Fairgrieve, M. Andenas, J. Bell (eds) *Tort Liability of Public Authorities in Comparative Perspective*, London: The British Institute of International and Comparative Law, 2002.
36 *Marcic v Thames Water Utilities* [2002] 2 All ER 55.
37 Cf *Barrett v London Borough of Enfield* [2001] 2 AC 550, the leading authority regarding children cared for by the local authority. With regard to *Bedfordshire*, see discussion below, text accompanying n.70.
38 Section 8(4) HRA.
39 *McMichael v United Kingdom* (1995) 20 EHRR 205.
40 *Papamichalopoulos v Greece* (1995) 21 EHRR 439.
41 *Campbell and Cosans v United Kingdom* (1982) 4 EHRR 293.
42 N. Mole, 'Local Authorities and Human Rights', [2001] Fam Law 487.
43 Section 7(5)(b).
44 See for example *Douglas v Hello! Limited* [2001] QB 967, *Venables v News Group Newspapers Ltd* [2001] 1 All ER 908.
45 *Campbell v Mirror Group Newspapers* [2003] 1 All ER 224 at para. 70.
46 The following discussion draws on the author's work in K. Stanton, M. Harris, P. Skidmore and J. Wright, *Stanton and Skidmore on Statutory Torts*, 2nd edn, London: Sweet & Maxwell, 2003.
47 [2001] 3 WLR 206.
48 [2001] 3 WLR 1562.
49 Section 7(6) HRA provides that: 'In subsection (1)(b) [of section 7 ie A person who has claimed that a public authority has acted or proposes to act in a way which is made unlawful by section 6(1) may … (b) rely on the Convention right or rights concerned in any legal proceedings] 'legal proceedings' includes [firstly] proceedings brought by or at the instigation of a public authority; and [secondly] an appeal against the decision of a court or tribunal'.
50 *Lambert*, *supra* n.140 at para. 99.

51 *Kansal*, *supra* n.141 at para. 104.
52 *Kansal*, ibid. at para. 54.
53 Judgment 17 October 2002, LEXIS.
54 [2002] 3 WLR 405.
55 *Wainwright*, ibid. at para. 29.
56 Ibid. at para. 40.
57 Ibid. at para. 62.
58 Ibid. at para. 27.
59 Ibid. at para. 40.
60 On appeal to the House of Lords ([2003] All ER (D) 279), counsel for the appellants accepted that the HRA did not have retrospective effect. Rather, it was argued that the House of Lords should declare that, in order for the United Kingdom to conform to her international obligations, there is a tort of invasion of privacy. The leading speech was given by Lord Hoffmann who took the view that there is nothing in Article 8 ECHR which suggests that 'some high level principle of privacy' is required to comply with Article 8. Instead, according to Lord Hoffmann, ECHR case-law embodies a range of violations that are instances of particular forms of privacy invasion and it is the state's responsibility to respond to the particularities of those individual findings. As with freedom of speech, privacy is a value underlying the rule of law rather than an independent principle of law capable of reduction to specific rules: LEXIS transcript.
61 [2002] EWCA 983, transcript: Smith Bernal.
62 Ibid. at para. 29.
63 *Osman v United Kingdom*, *supra* n.3 at para. 116.
64 Those factual scenarios where a claimant seeks to make the defendant legally responsible for harm arising from the criminal acts of a third party: *Home Office v Dorset Yacht Co. Ltd* [1970] AC 1004, *Osman v Ferguson* [1993] 4 All ER 344.
65 Application no. 33747/96.
66 Discussed, *infra*, text accompanying n.254.
67 Note that Arden LJ was *ad hoc* judge for the United Kingdom in *Z v United Kingdom* where she argued strongly against the finding of the European Court of Human Rights in *Osman v United Kingdom* that the Court of Appeal in its decision in *Osman v Ferguson* [1994] 4 All ER 344 had put the United Kingdom in violation of Article 6.
68 Ibid. at para. 45.
69 *Rights Brought Home: The Human Rights Bill*, *supra* n.1 at para. 1.14.
70 [2003] EWCA Civ 1151.
71 *Supra* n.37.
72 [2001] AC 550.
73 [2001] 2 AC 619.
74 *Supra* n.70 at para. 34.
75 *Supra* n.70 at para. 49.
76 [1998] QB 267, 380.
77 *MAK and RAK*, *supra* n.70 at para. 48.
78 *Supra* n.1.
79 *Supra* n.12.
80 *Supra* n.70 at para. 84.
81 Unreported 16 July 2003.
82 For example, *TP and KM v United Kingdom*, *supra* n.30.
83 *Cassell & Co Ltd v Broome* [1972] 1 All ER 801.
84 *Miliangos v George Frank (Textiles) Ltd* [1975] 3 All ER 801, per Lord Simon.

85 *R v Lambert*, *supra* n.47 and *R v Kansal*, *supra* n.48.
86 [1999] 3 WLR 1010.
87 *Supra* n.70 at para. 85.

Chapter 3

Child Abuse Compensation Claims: A Practitioner's Perspective

*Elizabeth-Anne Gumbel QC**

Introduction

Public authorities are responsible for providing a range of important services for children. These services include social services to protect children from neglect or abuse at home and educational services. Personal injury claims brought against a public authority or institution in which it is alleged that the Claimant suffered injury arising from sexual, physical or emotional abuse as a child are now an established area of litigation. In addition there are a number of claims arising out of the failure of education authorities to provide appropriate education for a child. Somewhat surprisingly this area of litigation has only developed since the mid-1990s. During the last eight years the House of Lords has set the parameters for such claims on four separate occasions.[1] Until the House of Lords confirmed that a claim brought against a public authority was arguable, such claims were regularly struck out. Before that the only means of obtaining compensation was through the criminal injuries compensation schemes. A scheme for compensating victims of crimes of violence was introduced in 1964. The scheme only provided compensation in limited circumstances and at a relatively restricted level. It did not include compensation for emotional damage or damage from a harsh regime in the absence of a crime of violence, nor did it include damages for failure to provide education. The scheme also frequently failed to provide compensation to the victims of sexual abuse or physical abuse on the ground that the victim had been involved in criminal offences.

Sexual and physical abuse by those in positions of trust with children has of course always occurred. Abusers and their employers have denied both the fact and the extent of the abuse. This has led to the present situation where abuse is being investigated by the police[2] for criminal prosecutions and by civil courts for compensation claims many years after the events. Paedophiles operating as far back as the 1950s are now being convicted of serious sexual offences and sentenced to long terms of imprisonment. The complainants, some now in their fifties, are having to relate the events of their childhood to police and in criminal courts. In the course of this process complainants have come to

* 199 Strand.

recognise that not only their abusers but also the public authorities and institutions employing the abusers should be held accountable for the damage done. Many victims of abuse in childhood have been unable to describe the events in their adult lives until forced to do so for a police enquiry. The psychiatric damage the abuse has caused is often not recognised by the victims and is left untreated for many years. The issue of limitation is therefore one that frequently arises in such claims and the Courts are still grappling with how to apply the limitation provisions in such cases. The statutory regime and the case law relating to limitation in personal injury claims does not provide any straightforward or fair solution to the issue and the approach to date has provided a range of imperfect solutions which makes it difficult for practitioners to advise clients.

The Early Development: *Stubbings v Webb*

Some of the earliest reported civil claims for compensation arising out of child abuse were claims brought by victims of abuse against their abusers. The best-known example is the case of *Stubbings v Webb* [1993] AC 498. In that case the Claimant was born in 1957 and at the age of two years placed by a local authority in the care of foster parents who later adopted her. In 1987 the Claimant brought proceedings against her adoptive father and stepbrother claiming damages arising out of the sexual abuse she suffered as a foster child and then an adopted child. The House of Lords held that such claims were properly categorised as trespass claims rather than negligence claims and should have a limitation period of six years. This period is fixed and not susceptible to any discretionary extension. The Claimant was not entitled to rely on any argument that she only had the requisite knowledge to bring proceedings after she had seen a psychiatrist in 1984 pursuant to sections 11 and 14 of the Limitation Act 1980. Further she could not rely on section 33 of the Limitation Act 1980 as these sections were held only to apply to cases of negligence, nuisance or breach of duty.

In considering the case of *Stubbings and Others v the United Kingdom* [1997] 1 FLR 105, the European Court did not follow the Commission who found violations of Article 14 (discrimination) in conjunction with Article 6 (lack of access to court). The European Court found that the restriction imposed by the Limitation Act 1980 was within the margin of appreciation allowed to the United Kingdom in circumscribing access to court. In the course of their judgment however the Court stated:

> There has been a developing awareness in recent years of the range of problems caused by child abuse and its psychological effects on victims, and it is possible that the rules on limitation of actions applying in Member States of the Council of Europe may have to be amended to make special provision for this group of claimants in the near future.[3]

The case of *Stubbings v Webb* gave rise to the anomalous position in the case of *S v W and Another* (Child abuse: damages) [1995] 1 FLR 862. In *S v W* a claim was brought by a Claimant against her father. The father had been convicted of five counts of incest involving the Claimant and had been sentenced to four years' imprisonment. The Claimant also brought proceedings against her mother who had known of the abuse and failed to protect her from it. The Court of Appeal confirmed the claim against the father was statute barred following *Stubbings v Webb*. However the Court of Appeal accepted that the claim could proceed against the mother, who was alleged to have negligently failed to prevent the father abusing the Claimant. In respect of the mother, the Claimant could rely on sections 11, 14 and 33 of the Limitation Act 1980. The Court of Appeal described how:

> It was a claim against the mother for an entirely independent tort involving acts of omission by her, such as constituted on her part a breach of her common law duty to take care of her child and not to expose that child to the unnecessary risk of injury or further injury.[4]

And

> As has been pointed out, the result of the judge's ruling was, as he rightly said, illogical and surprising. That fact is a good reason for inviting the attention of the Law Commission to the interrelation of these provisions and to the absence of any longstop limitation period of this and any other parts of the Act, for example section 28 of the Act which deals with persons under a disability.

By 1995 the position had been reached whereby claims arising out of the abuse of children could be brought against the abuser for assault and trespass provided they were brought within six years of the Claimant reaching majority or whilst the Claimant was a patient. In practical terms such claims would only provide compensation for victims of abuse if the abuser had means to satisfy a judgment. However, if a person could be identified who had failed to protect the child from abuse then, potentially, a claim could be brought outside the primary limitation period, provided the Claimant could show a later date of knowledge or persuade the court to exercise its discretion to allow the action to proceed. This has been an important principle in the development of claims against public authorities where identifying a claim in negligence has allowed claims to be brought with a discretion to extend limitation.

Further Development: *L v Hesley Hall Ltd*

The position then developed further with the decision in *L and Others v Hesley Hall Ltd* [2001] 2 WLR 1311 HL. In this case the House of Lords held that an employer will be vicariously liable for the acts of an employee who abuses children whilst in the course of purporting to carry out child care duties if the acts are carried out in the course of employment or are closely connected to it.

Although this claim was not against a public authority the principles apply to claims against local authority employees, including care workers, teachers and social workers.

In the case of *L v Hesley Hall Ltd* the Claimants were pupils at a privately owned residential school and alleged they were subjected to sexual abuse by a warden at the school. The warden was convicted of sexual abuse and sentenced to seven years' imprisonment. In a claim against the school for damages HH Judge Walker held the school could not be vicariously liable for the sexual abuse of an employee but could be liable for the employee's failure to report the abuse. The Court of Appeal allowed the Defendant's appeal and held that the failure to report was so closely connected to the sexual abuse itself that it was outside the course of the employee's employment and the Defendant could not be vicariously liable. The House of Lords reversed the decision of the Court of Appeal, overruled the case of *T v North Yorkshire County Council* [1999] IRLR 98 and found that the Defendant was vicariously liable for the warden's acts of abuse. The House of Lords found that the warden of the school had such close contact with pupils at the school that there was sufficient connection between the work he was employed to do and the acts of abuse he had committed for those acts to be committed within the scope of his employment. The Defendant could therefore be vicariously liable for those acts.

Lord Hobhouse described the position as follows (at paragraph 54 of the judgment):

> What these cases and Trotman's case in truth illustrate is a situation where the employer has assumed a relationship to the plaintiff which imposes specific duties in tort upon the employer and the role of the employee (or servant) is that he is the person to whom the employer has entrusted the performance of that duty. These cases are examples of that class where the employer, by reason of assuming a relationship to the plaintiff, owes to the plaintiff duties which are more extensive than those owed by the public at large and, accordingly, are to be contrasted with the situation where a defendant is simply in proximity to the plaintiff so that it is foreseeable that his acts may injure the plaintiff or his property and a reasonable person would have taken care to avoid causing such injury....
>
> The fact that sexual abuse was involved does not distinguish this case from any other involving the care of the young and vulnerable and the duty to protect them from the risk of harm.

This claim against the owners and managers of a private school had failed in negligence as the Judge found it could not be shown that the Defendants had been negligent in their care, selection and control of the warden. The claim succeeded on the basis the Defendant was held vicariously liable for the abuse perpetrated by the warden. The speeches of Lord Steyn (with whom Lord Hutton agreed), Lord Clyde and Lord Hobhouse describe the vicarious liability of the Defendant in terms of breach of duty. Lord Clyde describes how:

> It appears that the [Defendant] gave the warden a quite general authority in the supervision and running of the house as well as some particular responsibilities. His general duty was to look after and to care for, among others, the [Claimants]. That function was one which the [Defendants] had delegated to him. That he performed that function in a way that was an abuse of his position and an abnegation of his duty does not sever the connection with his employment. The particular acts that he carried out upon the boys have to be viewed not in isolation but in the context and the circumstances in which they occurred. Given that he had a general management of the house and in the care and supervision of the boys in it, the employers should be liable for the way in which he behaved towards them in his capacity as warden of the house. The [Defendants] should then be vicariously liable to the [Claimants] for the injury that they suffered at the hands of the warden.

Lord Millett however described the liability of the Defendants as vicarious liability 'for the warden's intentional assaults, not (as was suggested in argument) for his failure to perform his duty to take care of the boys'. This left open the important issue as to whether the vicarious liability of the Defendants in *L v Hesley Hall Ltd* gives rise to a cause of action for breach of duty with a three year limitation period (and the extension provisions of sections 11, 14 and 33 of the Limitation Act 1980) or whether it gives rise to a cause of action in trespass with a non-extendable six year limitation period.

Limitation

Following *Stubbings v Webb and L v Hesley Hall Ltd* there are particular limitation problems in abuse cases. In the case of *Various Claimants v. Bryn Alyn Community Homes Limited and Another* (Connell J, 26 June 2001) unreported, Connell J found that the claim for deliberate acts of abuse for which the Defendant was vicariously liable was subject to a non-extendable six year limitation period. The Court of Appeal confirmed this position in a decision given on 12 February 2003, *KR and Others v Bryn Alyn Community (Holdings) Limited and Royal and Sun Alliance PLC* [2003] EWCA *Civ 85*, and stated:

> In our view the correct approach is as Lord Millett has expressed it. Whether or not section 11 is in play, it is to identify the wrongful act, deliberate or otherwise, in respect of which vicarious responsibility is claimed and to assess the closeness of its connection to the employment in question. If the act is sufficiently closely connected with the employment, there is vicarious responsibility. In such circumstances and bearing in mind Lord Griffiths' reasoning in *Stubbings v Webb* (para 99 above) there is no justification or need, for the purpose of establishing vicarious responsibility, to elide the duty in respect of which the employee's deliberate act is a breach of duty of care delegated or 'entrusted' to him by the employer. The two are quite distinct. Where section 11 is under consideration, it follows that claims for personal injury in respect of deliberate conduct, whether considered in the context of vicarious responsibility or not, are not caught by its provisions. Accordingly, in absence of some provable allegation of systemic negligence of the first defendant, we are of the view that its employee's deliberate abuse does not fall within section 11 and is,

therefore, governed by a non-extendable six year period of limitation rather than an extendable three year period.

This decision may itself be subject to appeal to the House of Lords, who are in any event to consider limitation in child abuse claims in the case of *McDonnell v Congregation of Christian Brothers* [2001] PIQR P28. The circumstances in which time should be extended (where the reason for delay is the difficulty the Claimant has in discussing the abuse) and the mechanism for such extensions remain controversial. The Court of Appeal in the *Bryn Alyn* case gave guidelines in respect of the application of sections 11, 14 and 33 of the Limitation Act 1980 in these cases. However the position remains uncertain and difficult to apply in practice.

In the case of *Ablett & Others v Devon CC & Others (December 2000, unreported)* when the Defendants sought permission to appeal from the decision of Toulson J refusing to order limitation to be heard as a preliminary issue, Sedley LJ described the specific difficulties in respect of abuse claims and stated:

> Inevitably there is a problem of limitation in these proceedings. I say 'inevitably' because it is in the nature of abuse of children by adults that it creates shame, fear and confusion, and these in turn produce silence. Silence is known to be one of the most pernicious fruits of abuse. It means that allegations commonly surface, if they do, only many years after the abuse has ceased.

In the *Bryn Alyn* cases however the Court of Appeal suggested that where possible the Court should strive to hear limitation as a preliminary issue. This may be because the Court envisaged that after their decision the Court would more frequently be asked to consider date of knowledge arguments rather than section 33 discretion arguments. The former may be capable of separate determination, the latter rarely as they depend on hearing all the circumstances of the case.

Limitation Issues in Child Abuse Cases

In considering a potential claim for child abuse it is necessary to consider the following questions:

- Is the client still a child?
  If yes, no limitation problems occur; it is necessary to identify a suitable litigation friend; this may need to be the Official Solicitor.
- Is the Claimant over 18 but under 21 years of age?
  If yes, no limitation problems but a need to issue urgently in respect of a claim in negligence.
- Is the claimant over 21 but under 24?
  If yes, need to consider urgently any potential claim in assault with a 6

year non-extendable limitation period, following *Stubbings v Webb* [1993] AC 498 and *Bryn Alyn*.

- Is the client now a patient within Part 21 CPR, section 1 Mental Health Act 1983?
  If this is a possibility it is necessary to obtain a psychiatric report on this issue. If the Claimant can now be considered a patient it is necessary to identify a suitable litigation friend.
- If the client is now a patient can it be established that the client had been a patient for the entire period since he reached majority?
  Under the Family Law Reform Act 1969 the age of majority was reduced from 21 to 18. Under schedule 3, paragraph 8 of the 1969 Act the change in limitation periods only applied to causes of action which arose after the commencement date of the act. The Act came into force on 1 January 1970.

Therefore for a client reaching 18 after 1970 the age from which he needs to have been a patient is 18; for a client reaching majority before 1970 it is 21.

If there is any possibility of the Claimant being a patient for the entire relevant period since reaching his majority a psychiatrist will need to report. The psychiatrist should have the client's complete medical records, any other contemporaneous records and statements of family/friends who remember the client during that period.

- Was the claim limitation barred before August 1980?
  The Limitation Act 1980 did not come into force until 1 May 1981. Under paragraph 9 of schedule 2 of the Limitation Act 1980 it is provided that:

> Nothing in any provision of this act shall (a) enable any action to be brought which was barred by this act or (as the case may) be the Limitation Act 1939 before the relevant date (being 1 August 1980).

It is therefore necessary to consider whether the client's claim was barred by the Limitation Act 1939 on 1 August 1980.

Causes of action which accrue prior to 1954 have been held to be limitation barred and non-extendable.

See: *Arnold v Central Electricity Generating Board [1988] AC* 288, [1987] 3 All ER 694 at 701;

McDonnell v Congregation of Christian Brothers Trustees [2001] EWCA civ 2095.

- Is there a later date of knowledge pursuant to section 11, Limitation Act 1980?
  Is the court likely to exercise its discretion to allow the action to proceed pursuant to section 33, Limitation Act 1980?
  See: *Various Claimants v Flintshire County Council (the former Clwyd*

County Council) (Mr Justice Scott-Baker 26 July 2000);
Various Claimants v Bryn Alyn Community Holdings Limited and the Royal Sun Alliance plc, Court of Appeal, 13 February 2003.

The Complaints in Child Abuse Cases

Claimants in child abuse litigation have a range of complaints about the way that they were treated whilst in local authority care or in public institutions. These complaints may include:

- Physical assaults including excessive chastisement;
- Sexual assaults varying in severity from inappropriate touching to anal intercourse and rape;
- Bullying;
- Emotional abuse;
- Being subjected to a harsh and uncaring regime;
- Being imprisoned in a secure unit or hospital unit without justification;
- Neglect, including under-nourishment and lack of sufficient clothing;
- Lack of suitable education;
- Failure to provide a suitable home;
- Failure to promote a proper level of family life with the natural family or substitute family;
- Failure to provide a social worker or other means through which to make complaints;
- Failure to provide suitable arrangements for re-integration into the community after being in care or in an institution.

Damages

The claims will be personal injury claims and will require to be supported by medical evidence. Generally the evidence of a psychiatrist will be required, in some cases evidence in respect of physical symptoms of injury will also be required.

General Damages

Usually there are two elements to the injury suffered by the Claimant for which general damages for pain, suffering and loss of amenity will be claimed:

- The pain, suffering and injury incurred at the time of the abuse and as an immediate result of it; for example, bruising or broken bones from physical assaults, pain suffering and bleeding from anal intercourse;
- The long-term psychiatric damage suffered as a result of the incidents of abuse; for example, post-traumatic stress disorder, personality disorder, anxiety disorder, sexual problems.

The importance of distinguishing these two elements of damage was made clear in the *Bryn Alyn* case where the Court of Appeal pointed out that the psychiatric damage suffered by those who had been abused might need to be apportioned to reflect a number of different contributing factors including the Claimant's own family background or abuse in the family home. The physical pain and suffering caused by the abuse itself could not however be subject to apportionment and should be additional to the psychiatric damage.

Special Damages

The most common categories of special damage are:

- Cost of therapy/counselling: this will need to be identified and costed by the psychiatrist unless it has already been obtained when past costs will need to be supported by bills;
- Past loss of earnings;
- Future loss of earnings including vulnerability on the labour market.
- Care costs are rarely claimed but may be relevant to very severe cases of psychiatric damage.

Causes of Action

Theoretically there may be a number of possible causes of action against the responsible public authority including misfeasance in public office. Usually however in practice there are the following possible actions to consider:

- Vicarious liability of the authority for the assaults of its servants or agents.
  See: *L and Others v Hesley Hall Limited* [2001] 2 WLR 1311 HL;
  reversing *T v North Yorkshire County Council* [1999] IRLR 98.
- Negligence of the public authority in the supervision and running of an institution.
  See: *Various Claimants v Leicestershire County Council (Potts J, 2 April 1996);*
  Various Claimants v Flintshire County Council (the former Clwyd County Council) (Mr Justice Scott-Baker 26 July 2000);
  Various Claimants v Bryn Alyn Community Homes Limited and the Royal Sun Alliance plc (Connell J, 26 June 2001) unreported.
- Negligence of a local authority in respect of the placement of a child in care with foster parents.
  See: *Surtees v Kingston-Upon-Thames Borough Council* [1991] 2 FLR 559;
  S v Gloucestershire County Council [2000] 3 All ER 346;
  reversing *H v Norfolk County Council* [1997] 1 FLR 384;
  W v Essex County Council [1998] 3 WLR 534.

- Negligence of the public authority in failing to make suitable or adequate provision for a child placed in local authority care.
  See: *Barrett v Enfield London Borough Council* [1999] 3WLR 79.
- Vicarious liability of the local authority for the negligent acts of its social workers or other employees.
  See: *X (Minors) v Bedfordshire County Council* [1995] 2 AC 633; *Barrett v Enfield London Borough Council* [1999] 3WLR 79.

The Test for Negligence of Public Authorities

The House of Lords considered in *Barrett* the proper test for negligence in respect of the liability of public authorities and Lord Slynn, at page 98, stated that social workers and other staff were entitled to rely on the principle in *Bolam v Friern Hospital Management Committee* [1957] 1 WLR 582. Lord Hutton at page 111 stated that:

> ...I consider where a [Claimant] claims damages for personal injuries which he alleges have been caused by decisions negligently taken in the exercise of a statutory discretion, and provided that the decisions do not involve issues of policy which the courts are ill-equipped to adjudicate upon, it is preferable for the courts to decide the validity of the [Claimant's] claim by applying directly the common law concept of negligence than by applying as a preliminary test the public law concept of Wednesbury unreasonableness (see *Associated Provincial Picture Houses Ltd v Wednesbury Corporation* [1948] 1 KB 223).

With the actions of public authorities being tested by the *Bolam test* it has become necessary to identify expert witnesses to deal with the allegations of negligence raised against social workers, the Director of Social Services or other employees of social services, in order to establish whether in the circumstances the care provided to the child was competent when measured by the standards of the time.

Summary of the Landmark Cases

X (Minors) v Bedfordshire County Council [1995] 2 AC 633

It would not be just, fair and reasonable to impose a direct duty of care on a local authority in respect of its functions relating to removal of children from home. Nor would it be just, fair and reasonable to impose vicarious liability for the acts of its social workers.

Z v UK [2000] 2FCR 245

The children in *X v Bedfordshire CC* were entitled to recover damages from the UK government for breach of Articles 3 (inhuman and degrading treatment) and 13 (no effective remedy) of the European Convention on Human Rights.

Barrett v London Borough of Enfield [2001] 2 AC 550

In respect of a child who has been taken into the care of a local authority the position is different and the local authority owes a duty to keep the child safe from foreseeable injury, whether physical or psychiatric. Social workers and other professionals employed by the local authority also owe a duty of care and the local authority will be vicariously liable for any breach of professional duty measured by the test in *Bolam v Friern Hospital Management Committee* [1957] 1 WLR 582.

The strike-out procedure is not usually appropriate in a developing area of law.

S v Gloucestershire County Council [2000] 3 All ER 346

There is no immunity for local authorities. The critical question is a composite one which embraces the alleged duty of care and its breach in the context of the damage alleged to have been caused; the court has to consider the nature of the actions and decisions of the local authority which are said to have been negligent.

K v Secretary of State for the Home Department [2002] EWCA civ 775:

In English law the decision as to whether it is fair, just and reasonable to impose a liability in negligence on a particular class of would-be defendants depends on weighing in the balance the total detriment to the public interest in all cases from holding such a class liable in negligence as against the total loss to all would-be plaintiffs if they are not to have a cause of action in respect of the loss they have individually suffered. In third agency cases there was to be an additional factor to give the special nexus between the Claimant and the Defendant in order to give rise to the duty.

Conclusion

The common law duty of a public authority to protect children from abuse was considered by the House of Lords on three occasions in the 1990s. In a fourth case the issue of vicarious liability for abuse by employees was considered. The European Convention of Human Rights and the implementation of the Human Rights Act 1998 have led to further scrutiny of the public policy considerations in this area. There are many issues still to be determined in respect of limitation and quantum.

The civil claims for compensation for child abuse now proceeding through the litigation system raise a variety of issues of fact, law and practice, as follows:

- The scope of the direct duty of care owed by any public authority or institution.
- The scope of the vicarious duty owed by any public authority or institution for its employees and the extent to which such employees were acting within the scope of their employment.
- The identity of the authorities, institutions or individuals owing a duty of care at the time of the allegations.
- The identity of the correct defendant to any proceedings, that is authorities, institutions or individuals who may have taken over responsibility for outstanding torts from preceding bodies or institutions.
- The professional standards of teachers, social workers or inspectors at the relevant time.
- The appropriate experts to identify the standards acceptable at the time.
- The extent of any breach of duty measured by the standards of care acceptable at the time.
- The relevant statutory framework governing the authority or institution against which complaint is made.
- The provisions for inspection of schools and homes by the Home Office and Department of Education at the relevant time.
- Causation of damage to the Claimant in a particular regime or by a particular abuser.
- The apportionment of responsibility between institutions, public authorities and/or other individuals who are alleged to have caused injury to the Claimant.
- The extent of the damage suffered: physical, emotional and psychiatric.
- The appropriate experts to identify and substantiate such damage.
- The quantification of the damage for pain suffering and loss of amenity, particularly where there is a lack of comparable cases and the Judicial Studies Board guidelines do not encompass such cases.
- The extent of past and future losses and in particular loss of earnings that can be attributable to the injury sustained.
- Limitation.
- Disclosure of documents; identifying the relevant documents and where they are now stored.
- Identifying witnesses and other evidence.
- Case management particularly in relation to generic actions and group litigation orders.

The Points that now Appear Settled

1 There is no blanket immunity for public authorities in the area of social services or child care.

2 Whether in a particular situation a duty of care is owed and then breached depends on:
   a the application of the principles in *Caparo Industries plc v Dickman* [1990] 2 AC 605 and whether it is just, fair and reasonable to impose a duty;
   b the factual nexus between the parties; or whether there has been a specific assumption of responsibility and reliance;
   c whether the alleged injury is caused by a local authority employee or a third agency;
   d principles of distributitive justice and a balancing of the interests of the potential Claimants and Defendants.
3 A local authority who takes a child into its care will owe a duty to prevent foreseeable risk of harm to the child.
4 An employer will be vicariously liable for acts of abuse by an employee if these are carried out in the course of employment or closely connected to it.
5 In a developing area of law strike out proceedings will not usually be appropriate and an examination of the facts of the case will be necessary.
6 In assessing the conduct of professionals employed by a local authority the *Bolam test* not a *Wednesbury test* will be appropriate.

Outstanding Points of Principle

The following areas still remain particularly unclear;

1 Whether there are situations where a local authority will owe a duty of care to a child placed at home: if so, whether this depends on a special nexus test, an assumption of responsibility or some other test.
2 The impact of the Human Rights Act 1998 and Article 3 (without Article 13) on this area of responsibility.
3 The limitation position.
4 The causation of damage: where there has been abuse by a number of different abusers and psychiatric damage arises, how does the Claimant establish causation: is the test a material contribution (*McGee v National Coal Board* [1993]1 WLR 1)?
5 An apportionment test (*Hatton v Sutherland* [2002]2 All ER 1).
6 Or whether there should be an exception to the usual rules (*Fairchild v Glenhaven Funeral Services Limited* [2002] 3WLR 89).

Notes

1 *X v Bedfordshire County Council* [1995] 2 AC 633. *Barrett v Enfield LBC* [2001] 2 AC 2001. *W v Essex County Council* [2000] 2WLR 601. *Lister v Hesley Hall Limited* [2001] 2 WLR 2011.

2 An article in the *Independent* newspaper, 8 January 2001, identified 98 police investigations in 34 police forces in England, Wales and Northern Ireland into historic child abuse.

3 *Stubbings and Others v the United Kingdom* (paragraph 56 at 119G).

4 *Stubbings v Webb* [1992] QB 197 (Russell LJ at 866).

Chapter 4

Child Abuse Tort Claims against Public Bodies in Italy

*Roberto Caranta**

Preliminary Remarks

There are no Italian cases stemming from facts similar to those of *X (Minors) v Bedfordshire County Council*[1] and *Barrett v Enfield London Borough Council*.[2] This paper will offer a tentative explanation to account for this noteworthy difference.

Attention is drawn to an important feature of the Italian legal order at the outset: as a rule, decisions concerning care for children in distress are taken by magistrates and courts; this means that they are taken by way of judicial procedure even though the competent courts partially comprise lay people (decisions are taken by the *Tribunale per i minorenni*).[3]

This feature has not been altered in any significant way by the quite recent legislation, legge 28 marzo 2001, n.149, which has, in some respects, changed the provisions laid down in legge 4 maggio 1983, n.184, the most significant piece of legislation concerning adoption and temporary placement.[4]

Brief Introduction to Italian Law on Adoption and Temporary Placement

The most important changes brought about by legge 28 marzo 2001, n.149, concern its general approach to the problems of children in distress. It spells out a child's right to live with his or her natural family. At present, the basic principle is that regional and local authorities must strive to help families to cope with their difficulties and so keep their child. It is doubtful, however, whether this will have any significant impact, as the duty placed upon public authorities is expressly linked to the resources they have allocated to the same tasks.[5]

Reference to the text of legge 4 maggio 1983, n.184, as amended by the new statute, will be made in this paper as and when appropriate. It should be noted however that the legislative environment relating to adoption and temporary care has not changed recently in any significant way. In respect of the issues of liability dealt with in this paper, actions against public bodies have been made neither easier nor more difficult.

---

* Università degli Studi di Torino Law Faculty.

Dealing first with the issue of temporary placements, Article 4 of the legge 4 maggio 1983, n.184, provides for the temporary placement of children outside their natural family. If those exercising parental care agree on the necessity of temporarily placing the child outside his/her family, the decision is taken by the social services and approved by a magistrate exercising the functions of ward supervisor in the district where the child lives (Sec. 1). If they do not agree, the decision is taken by the court following a procedure in which the public prosecutor and all concerned parties can make their voice heard (Sec. 2). In each case, the child itself is heard when he/she is more than twelve or even less depending on his/her discerning capacities. Legal aid is available for the parties who cannot meet their costs in defending a point which is not *prima facie* devoid of any merit. The decision about the temporary placement must be reasoned; it has to lay down the arrangements governing the placement; further, it has to appoint a social authority charged with the overview of the arrangements taken.[6] The social authority must immediately report any relevant event to the ward magistrate or to the court; every six months it has to submit a detailed report to the ward magistrate, which must include an updated appraisal of the situation of the natural family; it must indicate whether there is a need for an extension of the temporary placement (Sections 3 and 4).[7]

The temporary placement can be discontinued at any stage, in the event of reports by the social services outlining any situation within the new family which may put at risk the well-being of the child taken in care.[8]

Similar provisions concerning adoption are to be found in Article 7 and those directly following it. Here again courts take the decisions leading to the adoption; when necessary they act following the initiative of the public prosecutor (Article 9); courts also take the decision to hold a child to be in a state of non-temporary neglect (Article 8); the social services are under a duty to refer to the public prosecutor details of any neglected child they hear about (Article 9.1).

Decisions are taken after hearing all concerned parties; the minor and his/her parents are entitled to be assisted by their own legal counsel (Articles 8.4 and 10.2); alternatively, counsel are nominated for them by the court (Article 10.2).

The courts decide which families are fit to adopt; they place children in pre-adoption placements with a chosen family, the one they think will best fulfil the needs of any given child (Article 22); surprisingly it is the court itself which is charged with overviewing the placement during this period, it can obtain assistance from both the ward magistrate and the social services (Article 22, Sec. 8);[9] one year after the pre-adoption placement, it is the court which rules on the final adoption (Article 25).

The fact that decisions concerning children in distress are taken by courts in accordance with judicial procedure, results in decisions of a higher quality than might otherwise be the case. This could partially account for the absence of liability cases. It also however greatly complicates the issue of liability, and so provides further explanation for the current position.

There are additional other reasons which also help to explain the absence of any such liability cases and these are given below.

Brief Introduction to Some Major Features of Governmental Liability in Italy

Civil courts usually hear liability cases arising as the result of the performance of operational tasks and the provision of services to the general public.[10] The fact that the defendant public authorities may enjoy discretionary powers does not, as a rule, result in civil courts striking out actions as inadmissible.[11]

Under Article 28, an action can be brought against both the public servant and/or the relevant public body; the public body is said to be directly rather than just vicariously liable for acts and omissions of its servants; vicarious liability plays a role only in cases of criminal acts or omissions which, although made possible or simply easier by the official status of the wrongdoer, are in no way linked to the duties bestowed upon him/her. As a general rule, liability actions are brought against the public bodies, whose solvency is not in doubt.[12]

Then faced with liability claims, Italian civil courts apply the general provisions of tort liability laid down in Article 2043 et seq. of the Civil Code. More specifically, Article 2043 provides for a general principle of negligence liability (different standards apply with respect to the liability of professionals charged with difficult tasks, such as surgeons: Article 2236). The provision is quite open-ended, following as it does the model laid down in Article 1382 of the *Code Napoléon*. Intentional or negligent actions or omissions unlawfully harming others give rise to a right in damages. The condition that is least straightforward is that concerning 'unlawfulness'. Nonetheless, as the law stands today, it is a condition easily met by claimants. It is sufficient for them to show that some relevant interest of theirs has been infringed without any legal justification.[13] With respect to public bodies' liability, the distinction between acts and omissions has no role to play. Indeed, Italian public authorities are simply held to be under a legal duty to perform the tasks assigned to them.[14]

Liability actions must be brought within five years from the day the harm suffered has become apparent (Article 2947 Civil Code); if the act or omission also amounts to a crime, the limitation period for civil action runs from the day when the limitation period to bring a criminal proceeding against the tortfeasor has finally expired (Article 2935 Civil Code); the sole fact that the victim is a minor has no affect upon the limitation period, although the period is stayed for as long as the minor has no legal representative (Article 2947 Civil Code), that is, until he or she is made a ward of the court.

The provisions mentioned above apply by way of general rule. However, those that specifically concern liability of magistrates (which includes lay people sitting in *Tribunali per i minorenni*) are much stricter. These cases are ruled by a specific statute: the legge 13 aprile 1988, n.117 (redress for damages caused by the exercise of judicial functions and civil liability of magistrates).[15]

In accordance with Article 13 of legge 13 aprile 1988, n.117, magistrates can be directly sued for damages only in so far as the relevant acts or omissions also amount to crimes. Alternatively, the claimant may choose to sue the State. Under Articles 2 ff, claims for damages involving non-criminal wrongdoing may be brought against the State only. If the claim is substantiated in court, the

State will seek an indemnity from the magistrate.[16] The most significant exception to the general rule applicable to tortious liability of public bodies is to be found in the requirements that need to be met by claimants. The State can be held liable if and only if the magistrate is guilty of gross negligence. Article 2, Sec. 2, of the statute further stipulates than no liability can be attached to the construction of a legal provision, to assessments of the relevant facts or to evaluations of the evidence submitted to the court. This provision is clarified and possibly qualified by Sec. 3 of the same Article. Under Sec. 3, gross negligence is to be found in four instances: when, without any reasonable excuse, *a*) the law is gravely breached; *b*) a fact is said to exist, the non-existence of which is plain from the circumstances of the proceedings, and, conversely, *c*) a fact, the existence of which is plain from the circumstances of the proceedings, is denied; further, *d*) when personal freedom has been restricted beyond those circumstances permitted by law and/or without giving any reason.

Probably not surprisingly, Italian courts have been quite willing to further qualify the conditions to be met to prove liability as set out by the legge 13 aprile 1988, n.117. Such conditions have been read in a restrictive way with only the most aberrant constructions of the law being held to give rise to liability (notably this is in theory only, as it was held *obiter*);[17] the fact that the least convincing construction of the many possible interpretations of a given provision was adopted in a given case was also not enough to make the State liable.[18] In relation to factual assessments, it has been held that liability cannot arise simply as the result of insufficient care and/or neglect capable of criticism; what is needed is a total failure to appreciate and assess the relevant facts as they were laid in front of the court.[19]

In accordance with Article 3, liability can also arise in the case of a refusal or delay to hand over a decision when the time for taking the decision has expired; if this occurs, a specific request has to be addressed to the magistrate concerned and a further period laid down by the statute (in principle, it is 30 days, although the term can be extended) has to elapse without any decision being taken.

Article 5 lays down a filter procedure; it is a device quite exceptional by Italian standards. Nonetheless, it has been extensively applied by courts, further hindering liability actions.[20]

Not surprisingly, tort actions against magistrates are quite rare and to date, only two have been successful. The most recent of the two was a difficult case concerning a judge who had abused his powers to blackmail the claimant; the criminal courts had already held the judge guilty; the only question was whether the State could be held liable for acts committed by a magistrate in pursuit of his/her private and self-interests; the *Corte di cassazione* decided in the affirmative, thus conforming with a well established case law involving public authorities' liability for the acts or omissions of their servants.[21]

The earlier case concerned arrest warrants for financial crimes (namely, false statements and related documents in the budget of a corporation) against two persons who, as it was plain from the evidence the police had submitted to the public prosecutor, held no position whatsoever in the corporation at the time the crime was allegedly committed.[22]

Child Abuse Tort Claims Against Public Bodies

Turning our attention to the main topic of this paper, the net effect of the statutes on the civil liability of magistrates is to limit significantly public bodies' liability for child abuse.

Most decisions concerning children in need are taken by courts; these decisions, however, can lead to liability under only the most restrictive conditions. An easier option therefore, albeit limited, might be to sue the social services. In theory at least, there exists the possibility of a claim in respect of the discharge of their duties under the general rules laid down in Article 2043 of the Civil Code (negligence liability). An example could be the case where social services fail to report promptly to the public prosecutor, the ward judge, or the court, children suffering ill-treatment and/or those in a condition of general neglect.

Further, it is the social services who are responsible for implementing the decisions taken by courts. The *Scozzari and Giunta* case, decided by the European Court of Human Rights, illustrates how at times the social services are prepared to approach court decisions with considerable flexibility.[23] The social services would be liable for abuses committed by their servants and also where these servants failed to properly address the needs of the children placed in their care; a standard of care similar to that developed by English courts in the *Bolan v Friern Hospital Management Committee*,[24] would be probably be applied in this instance.[25]

In the currently hypothetical examples above, the acts and omissions by the social services could even amount to a crime under Italian law. This would clearly be the case where public servants were concerned. Under Article 329 of the Criminal Code, officials can be found guilty if they fail to discharge their duties in matters concerning, *inter alia*, the physical integrity of the citizenship. The existence of a margin of discretion as to the way officials may discharge their duties does not provide a blanket defence of immunity in criminal (or civil) cases. The courts will assess whether discretionary powers were exercised with the care appropriate to each case.[26]

In such cases the limitation period would be extended considerably, thus making liability actions easier against both public servants and the social services. As Article 28 of the Constitution provides for civil liability to 'extend[s]' from the civil servant to the public authority, the longer limitation period will apply also to the latter.[27]

A further and possibly more important advantage of proceeding against social services from the claimant's point of view is the possibility of bringing his or her liability case in front of the same criminal court hearing the criminal case. This option is always available under Articles 74ff of the Criminal Procedure Code. Under Article 85, those who are vicariously liable for the wrongdoings of a third party having committed a crime can also be sued before the criminal court; the social services could therefore be sued with the officials liable for criminal acts and the claimant could utilise the results of the investigative activities performed by the police on the public prosecutor's behalf.[28]

A more difficult case would be that of an incompetent presentation to the court by the social services of the child's case; the presence of the public prosecutor, and more generally the appeal procedure, is normally adequate to correct any such mistake; when it is not, the causal contribution of the social services' actions would be rather marginal, the entire system having gone wrong. Be that as it may, to date no liability cases have been brought against Italian social services and their servants by abused children.

Heads of Recoverable Damages

Were some claimant able to establish liability, compensation afforded by courts would be full and fairly generous.

Under Article 2059 of the Civil Code, redress for moral harm is recoverable only when the tort committed also amounts to a crime. This kind of harm was recently held recoverable in the legal aftermath of the *Icmesa* or *Seveso* case. Icmesa s.p.a. had a chemical manufacturing plant in the Seveso area. In 1974 a major breakdown occurred, the consequence of which was the release of huge quantities of dangerous substances into the environment; the breakdown was linked to breaches of the applicable security rules and as such amounted to a crime. The *Corte di cassazione* held that those who had suffered no physical harm as a consequence of the breakdown were nonetheless entitled to recover damages for the stress induced by the fear of having contracted any major illness and for the inconvenience of having to undergo check ups and other medical tests over a long period of time.[29]

In the past twenty years or so Italian courts have tested their ingenuity in widening the heads of damages recoverable in tort actions. Initially they distinguished from both physical and moral harm a *tertium genus* termed *danno biologico*, a concept encompassing harm to the physical and/or the psychological integrity of a person. Italian courts have also been fairly quick to find harm to the psychological well-being of tort victims; one recent case concerned the psychological distress suffered by a conscious but mortally wounded motorcyclist, during the four hours from the moment he was harmed, to the moment he died; the *Corte di cassazione* held that the mother and a number of the deceased's siblings were entitled to recover damages, also under the specific head of the suffering of the dead motorcyclist.[30]

A popular claim today is that of *danno esistenziale*. This further concept of harm resembles that which flows from a diminished ability to enjoy life at its best.[31] The leading case, which was affirmed at the highest judicial level, concerned prejudice flowing from delayed payment of money due by a father for the maintenance of his natural son; the *Corte di cassazione* held the father liable for breach of the fundamental constitutional rights of the child; it further held that such a breach, which amounted to a crime, entitled the child to be compensated for more than just the pecuniary damages (capital and interests had already been paid), and consequently included lump sums to compensate the lost chance to fully develop his personality.[32]

Although the case involved a crime, and as such could have easily been decided by relying upon the traditional notion of moral harm under Article 2059 of the Civil Code, the court based its decision upon different grounds, referring instead to the general rule of negligence liability laid down in Article 2043 of the code; uncertainty now exists as to the actual sphere within which *danno esistenziale* is recoverable;[33] a case in point, significant for not involving any criminal wrongdoing, concerned an unsuccessful vasectomy and the resulting birth of a baby; a first instance court awarded the parents both patrimonial damages for the upbringing costs and *danno esistenziale* for having to change their habits to adjust to the newcomer.[34]

So far no (proven or otherwise) abused child has claimed under such a potentially available panoply of redress; much less no such child has obtained compensation from a public body.

Conclusion

One could ask why, when in theory the possibility of success exists, the procedure can be so claimant-friendly and compensation so high, no liability actions have been brought before Italian courts. Some sociological enquiry might be of some use in offering an explanation. It might prove that the overall Italian system dealing with children in need, works adequately. The fact that a digital database search spanning the last twenty years or so showed no reported criminal cases dealing with abuses against temporarily placed or adopted children, could be evidence of this. Further evidence might be the fact that there exists no known pressure to set up any statutory compensation scheme for abused children.

The facts of the case of *Scozzari and Giunta* are of relevance to this discussion. In this case a paedophile working with the social services, charged with helping a troubled family, had repeatedly abused a young boy the parents had placed with him during the weekends.[35] Given the fact that it was the parents and not the social services who had arranged the placements, it is doubtful whether a head of public body liability could accrue in such a case under Italian law. Liability cannot however be ruled out in principle, as the law proves generous in holding public authorities liable for the acts of their employees.

The complaint, when brought to the European Court of Human Rights, did not however deal with the abuses suffered by the child. Rather, it dealt with the excessive limits placed upon the rights of the parents to see their children once they had been temporarily placed elsewhere by the social services. It further dealt with the limits on the parents' say on the ways the placement was arranged, particularly as since the arrangement modalities were at best questionable even if they did not lead to any further abuse).[36] The facts of this case support the conclusion that a system for dealing with children in need *that works*, is the best way to solve liability problems – by not having any.

Nevertheless no system, not even one that relies heavily upon court procedures, can be watertight. The total absence of such cases in Italy may possibly be due to both the extreme difficulties in establishing judicial liability and, in respect of social services, a limited awareness on the part of potential claimants of potential claims.

Notes

1 [1995] 2 AC 633 (HL).

2 [1999] 3 All ER 193 (HL); P. Craig and D. Fairgrieve, '*Barrett*, Negligence and Discretionary powers' [1999] PL 626.

3 E. Urso, *La famiglia*, in P. Cendon (ed.), *Il diritto privato nella giurisprudenza*, Torino, UTET, 2001, 22.

4 A detailed analysis of the old statute is to be found in E. Urso, *La famiglia*, in P. Cendon (ed.), *Il diritto privato nella giurisprudenza*, Torino, UTET, 2001. It is unclear whether a situation as the one denounced by the ECHR decision in the *Scozzari and Giunta v Italy* case, REF00001707, (decided on July 13, 2000), could again take place today; the decision was reported in part in *Famiglia e diritto* 2001, 5, notes A. Sonaglioni and N. Paschetti, 'Scarsa vigilanza del Tribunale per i minorenni sull'operato dei servizi sociali e sui soggetti affidatari: severa condanna della Corte di Strasburgo'.

5 See e.g. Art. 5.4.

6 The duties imposed upon the social service are further spelt out in Article 5, Sec. 2 of the statute:
Il servizio sociale, nell'ambito delle proprie competenze, su disposizione del giudice ovvero secondo le necessità del caso, svolge opera di sostegno educativo e psicologico, agevola i rapporti con la famiglia di provenienza ed il rientro nella stessa del minore secondo le modalità più idonee, avvalendosi anche delle competenze professionali delle altre strutture del territorio e dell'opera delle associazioni familiari eventualmente indicate dagli affidatari.

7 According to Article 4:
(1) L'affidamento familiare è disposto dal servizio sociale locale, previo consenso manifestato dai genitori o dal genitore esercente la potestà, ovvero dal tutore, sentito il minore che ha compiuto gli anni dodici e anche il minore di età inferiore, in considerazione della sua capacità di discernimento. Il giudice tutelare del luogo ove si trova il minore rende esecutivo il provvedimento con decreto.
(2) Ove manchi l'assenso dei genitori esercenti la potestà o del tutore, provvede il tribunale per i minorenni. Si applicano gli articoli 330 e seguenti del codice civile.
(3) Nel provvedimento di affidamento familiare devono essere indicate specificatamente le motivazioni di esso, nonché i tempi e i modi dell'esercizio dei poteri riconosciuti all'affidatario, e le modalità attraverso le quali i genitori e gli altri componenti il nucleo familiare possono mantenere i rapporti con il minore. Deve altresì essere indicato il servizio sociale locale cui è attribuita la responsabilità del programma di assistenza, nonché la vigilanza durante l'affidamento con l'obbligo di tenere costantemente informati il giudice

tutelare o il tribunale per i minorenni, a seconda che si tratti di provvedimento emesso ai sensi dei commi 1 o 2. Il servizio sociale locale cui è attribuita la responsabilità del programma di assistenza, nonché la vigilanza durante l'affidamento, deve riferire senza indugio al giudice tutelare o al tribunale per i minorenni del luogo in cui il minore si trova, a seconda che si tratti di provvedimento emesso ai sensi dei commi 1 o 2, ogni evento di particolare rilevanza ed è tenuto a presentare una relazione semestrale sull'andamento del programma di assistenza, sulla sua presumibile ulteriore durata e sull'evoluzione delle condizioni di difficoltà del nucleo familiare di provenienza.

(4) Nel provvedimento di cui al comma 3, deve inoltre essere indicato il periodo di presumibile durata dell'affidamento che deve rapportabile al complesso di interventi volti al recupero della famiglia d'origine. Tale periodo non può superare la durata di ventiquattro mesi ed è prorogabile, dal tribunale per i minorenni, qualora la sospensione dell'affidamento rechi pregiudizio al minore.

(5) L'affidamento familiare cessa con provvedimento della stessa autorità che lo ha disposto, valutato l'interesse del minore, quando sia venuta meno la situazione di difficoltà temporanea della famiglia d'origine che lo ha determinato, ovvero nel caso in cui la prosecuzione di esso rechi pregiudizio al minore.

(6) Il giudice tutelare, trascorso il periodo di durata previsto, ovvero intervenute le circostanze di cui al comma 5, sentiti il servizio sociale locale interessato ed il minore che ha compiuto gli anni dodici e anche il minore di età inferiore, in considerazione della sua capacità di discernimento, richiede, se necessario, al competente tribunale per i minorenni l'adozione di ulteriori provvedimenti nell'interesse del minore.

(7) Le disposizioni del presente articolo si applicano, in quanto compatibili, anche nel caso di minori inseriti presso una comunità di tipo familiare o un istituto di assistenza pubblico o privato.

8 Such a case was probably the one decided at the highest level by the *Corte di cassazione*: Cass. Civ., Sez. I, 28 dicembre 1998, n.12849, *Fracasso e altro* c. *Proc. gen. Potenza*, in *Giust. civ. Mass.* 1998, 2650; as far as it can be said by the summary of the decision, a child was temporarily placed with some relatives, but the man behaved violently (it is not clear whether with his own natural family only or with the placed child too; the latter is more probable); the summary of the decisions states that 'Il provvedimento di affidamento di un minore a soggetti appartenenti alla sua famiglia (nella specie, i prozii paterni) cessa, oltre che per il venir meno della situazione di temporanea difficoltà della famiglia d'origine, tutte le volte in cui la prosecuzione dell'affidamento possa, comunque, arrecare pregiudizio al minore stesso, pregiudizio da accertarsi all'esito di una indagine sulla idoneità mostrata, in concreto, dai coniugi affidatari nell'allevarlo in un ambiente familiare sano ed armonioso (Principio affermato dalla S.C. in relazione ad una vicenda di revoca dell'affidamento di un minore conseguente all'accertamento di una situazione familiare caratterizzata da tensione e paura, nella quale, in particolare, la prozia affidataria appariva completamente succube delle continue violenze esercitate dal marito nei confronti suoi e dei suoi figli)'.

9 (8) Il tribunale per i minorenni vigila sul buon andamento dell'affidamento preadottivo avvalendosi anche del giudice tutelare e dei servizi locali sociali e consultoriali. In caso di accertate difficoltà, convoca, anche separatamente, gli affidatari e il minore, alla presenza, se del caso, di uno psicologo, al fine di

valutare le cause all'origine delle difficoltà. Ove necessario, dispone interventi di sostegno psicologico e sociale.

10 R. Caranta, 'Public Law Illegality and Governmental Liability', para. I 3(*b*).

11 R. Caranta, 'Public Law Illegality and Governmental Liability', para. I 3(*b*) and II 3.

12 M. Clarich, 'The Liability of Public Authorities in Italian Law' in J. Bell and A.W. Bradley, *Governmental Liability: a comparative study* (UKNCCL London 1991) 207, 233ff.

13 Cass., Sez. un., 22 July 1999, n.500; the decision has been reported and commented in most Italian law journals (and there are many of them); here is just a selection of journals: in *Foro it.* 1999, I, 2487, with observations by A. Palmieri e R. Pardolesi, in *Foro ital.* 1999, I, 3201, with notes by R. Caranta, 'La pubblica amministrazione nell'età della responsabilità'; F. Fracchia, 'Dalla negazione della risarcibilità degli interessi legittimi all'affermazione della risarcibilità di quelli giuridicamente rilevanti: la svolta della Suprema corte lascia aperti alcuni interrogativi'; A. Romano, 'Sono risarcibili; ma perché devono essere interessi legittimi?'; E. Scoditti, 'L'interesse legittimo e il costituzionalismo. Conseguenze della svolta giurisprudenziale in materia risarcitoria'; in *Giorn. dir. amm.* 1999, 832, with note by L. Torchia, 'La risarcibilità degli interessi legittimi: dalla foresta pietrificata al bosco di Birnam'; in *Riv. it. dir. pubbl. comunitario* 1999, 1108, with note G. Greco 'Interesse legittimo e risarcimento dei danni: crollo di un pregiudizio sotto la pressione della normativa europea e dei contributi della dottrina'; in *Giur. cost.* 1999, 3217, with note by F. Satta, 'La sentenza n.500 del 1999: dagli interessi legittimi ai diritti fondamentali', and in *Giur. cost.* 1999, 4045, with annotations by F.G. Scoca, 'Per un'amministrazione responsabile', and by G. Azzariti, 'La risarcibilità degli interessi legittimi tra interpretazioni giurisprudenziali e interventi legislativi. Un commento alla sentenza n.500 del 1999 della Corte di cassazione'.

14 R. Caranta, 'Public Law Illegality and Governmental Liability', para. II 5.

15 An updated text of the statute can be read at http://www.giustizia.it/cassazione/leggi/l117_88.html; a full analysis of the statute is to be found in M. Graziadei and U. Mattei, 'Judicial Responsibility in Italy: A New Statute', 38 (1990) *Am. Jour. Comp. L.* 103.

16 A full indemnity is possible in cases of criminal acts only.

17 No liability arises for departing from the case law of the highest court: Cass., 30 luglio 1999, n.8260, in *Foro ital.* 2000, I, 2671, obs. C.M. Barone; it is to be remembered that Italian courts not bound by the *stare decisis* rule.

18 Cass., 20 settembre 2001, n.11859, in *Foro ital.* 2001, I, 3556, note G. Scarselli, 'La responsabilità del giudice nei limiti del principio di indipendenza della magistratura'.

19 Again Cass., 20 settembre 2001, n.11859, *cit.*

20 E.g. Cass., 20 settembre 2001, n.11880, in *Foro ital.* 2001, I, 3556, note G. Scarselli, 'La responsabilità del giudice nei limiti del principio di indipendenza della magistratura'; the author points out that the sphere of application of Article 5 has been undluly extended (ibid., 3559).

21 Cass., 24 novembre 2000, n.15192, in *Responsabilità civile e previdenza* 2001, 620, note by S. Marinucci, 'Brevi osservazioni relative alla corresponsabilità dello Stato per il reato compiuto dal magistrato'.

22 Trib. Brescia, 29 aprile 1998, in *Danno e responsabilità* 1998, 1020, note by A.M. Benedetti, 'L prima condanna dello Stato per grave negligenza di un magistrato'; the court held that the mass of documents composing the file and the complexity of the case was no excuse given the particular severity of the consequences attached to an arrest warrant.

23 *Scozzari and Giunta v Italy* case, REF00001707 (decided on July 13, 2000); see particularly points 178 f. of the judgment: '178. Therefore, in the circumstances of the present case, the Court finds it unacceptable that social services should be able, as they have been in this instance, to alter the practical effect of judicial decisions establishing that contact will, in principle, take place. Given their limited number and irregular occurrence (there have been only two in almost three years), the visits arranged to date have for all intents and purposes been sporadic and make little sense when viewed in the light of the principles established under Article 8. 179. It is apparent from the case file that since the first visit social services have played an inordinate role in the implementation of the Youth Court's decisions and adopted a negative attitude towards the first applicant, an attitude for which the Court finds no convincing objective basis. In reality, the manner in which social services have dealt with the situation up till now has helped to accentuate the rift between the first applicant and the children, creating a risk that it will become permanent. The information contained in social services' latest report only goes to confirm that trend (see paragraph 96 above). Faced with that evolution in the situation, the Youth Court, which should in principle supervise the implementation of its decisions, approved the action being taken by social services, without conducting any thorough review.'

24 [1957] 1 WLR 582.

25 The standard is the same as the one applied by the House of Lords in *Barrett v Enfield London Borough Council* [1999] 3 All ER 193 (HL) 212 (per Lord Slynn).

26 C. Franchini, *Il controllo del giudice penale sulla pubblica amministrazione* (CEDAM 1998), pp. 46 ff.

27 There is no case in point; an opposite decision was taken concerning a case not involving a public authority: Cass., 23 maggio 1975, n.2071, *unrep*.

28 Concerning public bodies liability two such cases are Cass., Sez. un., 23 November 1985, n.5813, in *Giust. civ.* 1986, I, 734; Cass., 11 February 1995, n.1540, in *Dir. proc. amm.* 1997, 358, con nota di D. D'orsogna, 'Danno 《da reato》 e comportamento illegittimo dell'amministrazione: verso l'《ingiustizia》 dei danni derivanti da lesioni di interessi legittimi'.

29 Cass., Sez. un., 21 febbraio 2002, n.2515, in *Responsabilità civile previdenza* 2002, 384; *ibid*, 726, note by D. Feola, 'Il prezzo dell'inquietudine: il caso 《Seveso》 torna in Cassazione'.

30 Cass., 2 aprile 2001, n.4783, in *Responsabilità civile previdenza* 2001, 555, note by P. Ziviz, 'Attesa consapevole della morte e danno psichico'; the case was referred back to the lower court for the assessment of the damages due.

31 See M. Franzoni 'Il danno esistenziale come sottospecie del danno a persona'; E. Navarretta, 'Il danno alla persona tra solidarietà e tolleranza'; M. Rossetti, 'Il danno esistenziale tra l'art. 2043 e l'art. 2059 c.c.', and P. Ziviz, 'Equivoci sul danno esistenziale', all in *Responsabilità civile previdenza* 2001, 777 ff.

32 Cass., 7 giugno 2000, n.7713, in *Responsabilità civile previdenza* 2000, 923, note by P. Ziviz, 'Continua il cammino del danno esistenziale'.

33 Contrast Trib. Roma, 7 marzo 2002, and Trib. Napoli, 12 febbraio 2002, both in *Responsabilità civile previdenza* 2002, 797, note by P. Ziviz, 'Chi ha paura del danno esistenziale'; both cases concerned car accidents; the two courts diverged as to the question whether *danno esistenziale* is something else from a new fancy name for *danno morale*; the latter court awarded both *danno esistenziale* and *danno morale*, while the first refused to do so.

34 Trib. Busto Arsizio, 17 luglio 2001, in *Responsabilità civile previdenza* 2002, 441, note by F. Bilotta, 'La nascita non programmata di un figlio e il conseguente danno

esistenziale'; *ibid.*, 590, note by A. Demori, 'Fallimento di intervento di sterilizzazione maschile e 《wrongful birth》: profili di responsabilità medica e problemi di liquidazione del danno'.

35 *Scozzari and Giunta v Italy* case, REF00001707 (decided on July 13, 2000); see particularly points 14ff. of the judgment.

36 *Scozzari and Giunta v Italy* case, REF00001707 (decided on July 13, 2000); see particularly points 14ff. of the judgment, quoted *supra*, ft.; see also point 208 '[...] In the Court's view, such a failure to communicate is not compatible with the duties incumbent on States to act fairly and to provide information when taking serious measures interfering in a sphere as delicate and sensitive as family life. Unless full and pertinent explanations are given by the authorities concerned, parents should not be forced, as they were in the instant case, merely to stand by while their children are entrusted into the care of a community whose leaders include people with serious previous convictions for ill-treatment and sexual abuse. The situation was compounded by the following two sets of circumstances ...'; the court also expressed reservations as to how the placement was arranged.

Chapter 5

Child Abuse Tort Claims against Public Bodies in South Africa

*Rosalind English**

No case in the South African law reports raises precisely the same issues as the *X v Bedfordshire* litigation.[1] This is not a reflection of the seamless operation of social services in South Africa, nor does it indicate that neglected or unwanted children do not risk abuse or violence; sadly both are high on the agenda in South African social life. The absence of any such cases is due rather to the fragmented responsibilities of government departments and local authorities, and the lacunae in common law and statutory liability regimes.

This paper will assess the current situation and then investigate the extent to which the Bill of Rights in the Constitution[2] is being developed by the Constitutional Court to widen the boundaries of liability and define the areas of government responsibility so that an action against public authorities by abused children may be possible one day in the future. It is worth pointing out at the outset that this will be achieved not via the somewhat fuzzy range of civil and socio-economic rights themselves, but as a consequence of the Constitutional Court's attempts to render these rights workable by focusing them through the lens of the common law of delict.

An overview of the legal devices currently available to potential claimants goes some way towards showing why such devices have rarely been deployed against the public authorities; but the real weaknesses in the system, explored later in this paper, are structural rather than juristic; these are the serious – if unsexy – issues such as the lack of defined responsibilities for local government, combined with social crises such as poverty, illegal immigration and the AIDS pandemic, which leave most 'street' children well outside the loop of litigation available to the well-advised claimants in the Bedfordshire case.

Common Law

Liability in Delict

South African common law is a patchwork of judicially developed norms and actions derived from Roman law, combined into a system called Roman-Dutch

* Barrister, One Crown Office Row.

law. Under this system delictual liability is divided into three categories; the first two are actions derived directly from Roman law (*actio legis Aquiliae* and *actio iniurarium*), and the third is the closest to negligence in English law, the action for pain and suffering. This action is the means by which compensation for injury to personality as a result of the wrongful and negligent impairment of bodily or physical-mental integrity is claimed. Aquilian liability used to be only applicable to certain physical infringements of corporeal legal interests, although by now it has been developed by South African courts to cover any wrongful or culpable act, which causes patrimonial damage, and this includes impairment of the personality. In both the *actio legis Aquiliae* and the action for pain and suffering damages are not limited to physical pain or suffering. Protection is also given to emotional shock, shortened life expectancy, amenities of life and health. The second form of action, the *actio iniurarium*, is a 'wrongful act' *designedly* done in contempt of another, which infringes his dignity, his person and reputation. As a tort requiring intent, it does not concern us here.

The relationship between wrongdoer and victim is based not on neighbourhood but on the concept of obligation. The wrongdoer has an obligation to compensate for the damage suffered, the person prejudiced has a corresponding right to claim compensation, and as a result an *obligatio* between the two parties is created.

For liability to be established the following requirements must be met:

1 an act;
2 wrongfulness;
3 fault;
4 harm;
5 factual causation;
6 legal causation.

Omissions

Liability for an omission is generally more restricted than liability for a positive act. In terms of the law of delict a person does not act wrongfully where he/she fails to act positively to prevent harm to another. Liability only follows if the omission is wrongful and there existed a *legal duty* on the defendant to act positively to prevent harm from occurring.

The concept of 'legal duty' should not be confused with the English common law concept of 'duty of care'. In South Africa the test for negligence is configured as a 'reasonable man test', namely, *whether the reasonable man would have foreseen and guarded against the damage*. It is only in assessing the wrongfulness of the act complained of, that the test of 'legal duty' is applied. The rationale is that the law does not generally demand altruistic behaviour. There is no recognition in South African common law of the existence of a legal duty to act positively to prevent harm, physical or otherwise, to someone else.[3]

'Legal Duty'

In cases where the alleged wrongdoer is in a position of control over the claimant, by statute or otherwise, the question is not – as it is normally formulated in South African delict law – whether the claimant's *subjective right* has been infringed, but whether the defendant had a *legal duty* to prevent that loss.

Sometimes the office held by a person places a legal duty on him to conduct himself in a particular manner in relation to the public; also when one party acts in reasonable reliance on the impression created by another party that the latter will protect the person or property of the former, a legal duty rests on the party creating that impression to prevent prejudice to the party acting in reliance on that impression.

So, for example, where someone fixed with the requisite knowledge and authority has failed to rescue a child at risk of abuse, there is no assumption that the former owes the latter a 'duty of care.' In the absence of clear legal norms founding liability for this particular type of omission, it has to be established whether a legal duty rested on that person. In Roman-Dutch law the question is whether in the light of all relevant circumstances the person's omission constitutes conduct which the community regards as wrongful for the purposes of the law of delict – this is called the concept of *boni mores*.

Although South African delict law does not require a special relationship between the claimant and the defendant as an absolute pre-requisite for the existence of a duty of care, the existence or absence of such a relationship are usually a relevant and often a decisive factor in the inquiry. So for example where schoolchildren have suffered injury whilst under the supervision of the school authorities it was held that the latter should,

> like parents ... observe towards their charges the standard of care that a reasonably prudent man would observe in the particular circumstances.[4]

The potential for a private action for breach of statutory duty by a child exposed to abuse is explored below.

'Boni Mores'

To show that the act of the defendant is 'wrongful', in the delictual sense, the Court applies the general criterion of reasonableness, which is determined according to the *boni mores*, or moral convictions of the community. The determination involves policy considerations, and the Court has to evaluate and balance the conflicting interests of all concerned parties, with due regard to the social consequences of recognising or denying the existence of liability in a given case.[5] In respect of a child at risk a balancing process must take place between the interests of the social worker (or any other responsible party) and the interests of the child. On the one hand there is the need to avoid taking into care children who may not be at risk and to respect sensitive relationships with other agents acting in this field, as well as the parents. On the other hand there is the need to prevent serious violation of the child's personality interests and his physical integrity and those of the child's parent or guardian (mental distress and financial cost brought about by any serious injury to the child, psychological or otherwise).

As will be seen from the discussion below, the Bill of Rights in the South African Constitution[6] now informs and influences the determination of *boni mores*. This seepage of public rights into private law is a process of osmosis that has only just begun on the South African legal landscape and therefore it is too early to assess its impact on private law relationships. The most this paper seeks to do is to speculate on future possibilities as part of this trend.

Statutory Duty

The case law suggests that positive duties are sometimes found to exist under statute even when not expressly specified within the legislation itself. So for example, legislation governing the police[7] stipulates that it is one of the functions of the police to prevent crime. Although the Act in question does not anywhere indicate that it was the intention of the legislature that the failure of the police to prevent crime would also be wrong in delict and give rise to a liability, the case law over the years has shown an inclination by the courts to regard such a provision as an indication that a delictual liability might be found, in certain somewhat limited circumstances.[8]

Unless the statute provides otherwise, the claimant will have an action in private law for breach of statutory duty if the statute protects the interests of a group or class of persons of which the claimant is a member.[9] However, where a statute is enacted in the public interest and not for the protection of individual interests, the courts tend to deny a private law action for the recovery of damages.

The lack of cases brought by children alleging breach of statutory duty against public authorities responsible for allocation of social services suggests that it is generally assumed that the relevant legislation (discussed below) does not envisage such private claims to be within the scope of its protection.

Remedies

There are two forms of remedies in Roman-Dutch delict law: compensation for damages or '*skadevergoeding*', the object of which is to eliminate as fully as possible the person's past as well as future injury; and '*genoegdoening*' or 'satisfaction' which is relevant where the damage is incapable of being compensated because money cannot be a true equivalent of the impaired interest. Satisfaction implies the reparation of damage in the form of injury to personality by effecting retribution for the wrong suffered by the claimant and satisfying the claimant or the community's sense of justice. In this sense it is arguably analogous to the concept of 'just satisfaction' under Article 41 of the European Convention on Human Rights and Fundamental Freedoms 1950 as incorporated by Section 8 of the Human Rights Act 1998.

Again, any detailed discussion of the remedies available to a successful child claimant in an '*X*'-style would be premature if not totally academic, given the hurdles of liability and causation to be crossed first.

Children

The General Picture

The demographic profile of South Africa sits in stark contrast to that of the United Kingdom. In South Africa, 15% of the total population is aged 5 years or younger; a further 21% is aged from 6 to 14 years, and children under 18 form nearly half the population. About 40% of all South African households live in poverty. The situation in South Africa is exacerbated by its refugee problem: the child and youth care system has not yet come to grips with addressing the problems of 'illegal aliens', prohibited persons or refugee children who are flooding into the country from war- and famine-torn countries to the north of South Africa.[10] Another problem peculiar to South Africa, which grafts an essentially Judaeo-Christian system of Western law on to African culture, is the extent to which any future child legislation which seeks to improve upon the existing position should overrule customary and religious practices[11] in order to protect children from abuse.

The South African Law Commission noted recently that:

> Family life is under a great deal of pressure in South Africa due to economic factors, the lack of household food security, unemployment, alcohol and drug abuse, communication and relationship problems, parenting problems, family violence, and a lack of support systems. All these factors, alone or in combination, can put families at risk and lead to family breakdown. Community violence and natural disasters are additional sources of stress and trauma. Most South African families and children live in unhealthy, unsafe communities where overcrowding, a lack of sanitation and recreation facilities and of public transport are features of daily life. Growing numbers live in informal settlements and on the streets.[12]

In 1998 there were about 29,000 children in residential care in South Africa – including places of safety, schools of industry, reform schools and children's homes – and about 74,000 children in foster care.[13]

This welfare system is not only groaning under the load imposed on it by the social situation described above, but it is further weakened by the degree to which responsibility for the implementation of social legislation has been delegated to voluntary welfare organisations. As the Law Commission has noted, this has resulted from a policy, dating back to the 1930s, to the effect that government's role in welfare should be limited, and that responsibility should rest in the first place with the individual and then with the family and the community. In accordance with this policy, the previous South African Government has, where possible, subsidised community groups to undertake approved social services rather than providing them directly. Hence an extraordinarily partitioned social service system has developed, as the availability of services was dependent upon community initiative from and for particular groups, and whether or not they could manage to obtain state and/or private sector support, rather than being based on any plan to ensure that everyone had access to the necessary services. Social services relating to child witnesses in the criminal courts, and to children coming before the children's courts, into substitute care, into the juvenile justice system, into statutory drug rehabilitation programmes, and into any form of statutory provision for the physically or mentally disabled, are split among a vast array of voluntary as well as state structures. This fragmented system continues under the Government of National Unity.

As this picture demonstrates, lines of liability are difficult, if not impossible, to establish. All that one can say with any degree of certainty is that the Department of Social Development maintains overall responsibility for control of statutory social services.

Legislation

The array of legal rules affecting children is made up of a blend of Roman-Dutch principles, which, with the relevant judicial interpretation, comprise the common law body of rules generally known as the 'law of parent and child', together with numerous statutory provisions. Chief amongst the latter of these is the Child Care Act 74 of 1983[14] ('the 1983 Act').

This Act contains numerous civil law provisions and some criminal law provisions designed to protect children from ill-treatment or neglect. Although there does not exist an offence called 'child abuse' in South African law, provisions in the 1983 Act, other legislation such as the Sexual Offences Act, 1957, and the common law, prohibit various criminal acts such as rape and assault that can be classified under the umbrella term 'child abuse'. In terms of section 50(1)(a) of the 1983 Act, for instance, any parent or guardian of a child or any person having the custody of a child who ill-treats that child or allows him or her to be ill-treated, is guilty of an offence. An offence is also committed by 'any other person' who ill-treats a child. 'Ill-treatment' is not defined in the Act and appears to include ill-treatment by omission.[15]

The most important provision for the purposes of this paper is the one imposing a broad-ranging 'reporting obligation'. Section 42(1) imposes a duty on any member of the public with regular contact with children – teachers, medical personnel, social workers – who suspects that a child has been ill-treated or deliberately injured or suffers from a nutritional deficiency disease, immediately to notify the Director-General, who may then order the removal of the child concerned to a hospital or a place of safety. Failure to comply with these reporting obligations constitutes an offence, punishable upon conviction by a maximum fine of R4,000 (based on R11.53 to the £) or imprisonment for a maximum period of one year, or both. These 'obligated' reporters are exempt from all liability, civil and criminal, in respect of any notification given in good faith in accordance with section 42. So far no prosecutions have been brought under this section.[16]

The sections of the 1983 Act dealing with powers to remove children at risk into alternative care are as follows:

Section 11(2) grants a power to all courts to grant a place of safety order. The courts depend upon the reporting obligations imposed by section 42 to initiate the necessary inquiries into children's welfare;
Section 12 allows any policeman, social worker or authorised officer to remove a child without a warrant from a commissioner for child welfare if the 'delay in obtaining a warrant will be prejudicial to the safety and welfare of the child';
Section 14(4): The physical, emotional or sexual abuse or maltreatment of a child by a parent or guardian constitutes a ground for finding a child in need of care, and therefore a ground for removal;
Section 15 deals with situations where alternative care is necessary, whether by fostering, or if that is unavailable or unsuitable, in a children's home which is the responsibility of the Director-General of Social Development. Sometimes children are placed in 'schools of industries', run by the Department of Education (rather than the Department of Social Development, which is responsible for the other institutions);
Pending removal of a child to the category of placement that has been directed by a children's court, the child may be kept in a place of safety under Section 15(3).

The main shortfall in this legislative regime is that it gives no guidance as to who is legally obliged to provide such prevention and early intervention services, when such services should be supplied and what form they should take. There is nothing in the 1983 Act equivalent to Section 17 of the UK Children Act, 1989.[17] Nor is there any liability placed on officials who remove children without a warrant in non-emergency situations. For example, officials working under the authority of the Minister of Welfare are not under any obligation to place the child at all; section 37 of the 1983 Act gives them the discretion simply to discharge the child – in other words, they are not compelled to implement the alternative care placement order of the children's court. This is not some careless omission on the part of the draftsmen – the provision takes into account the situation on the ground, particularly the lack of vacancies in residential care. However its inclusion in the Act has been criticised as the

> legislative admission of a welfare system that is breaking down, and a condonation of inefficiency that erodes what should be a basic right on the part of needy children to receive care in appropriate institutions.[18]

The system of residential care constitutes what is generally called a 'continuum of care' which runs from the least restrictive options, such as adoption, foster care, shelters, children's homes, through the more restrictive schools of industry, to the most restrictive secure care facilities and youth correctional facilities.

Ministry of Social Development officials have the power to amend children's court orders by shifting children between foster care, children's homes and schools of industries. One unfortunate feature about this 'continuum of care' system is that places of safety for children are often court-ordered reception centres used both for young people charged with violent crimes, and for those who are destitute or require protection from abuse or neglect.

Research in 1996 led to the conclusion that punishment of children in many residential care facilities was 'unduly harsh' and that the situation endured by many children was not therapeutic. It was noted that children at residential care facilities were sometimes abused by other children or staff.[19]

It also remains the case that protection of children's rights is still not triggered where there is no care inquiry which results in a careful assessment of their situation and their enrolment in this so called 'continuum of care'. Given factors such as the AIDS pandemic, it may be envisaged that increasing numbers of children will remain on the margins or beyond the machinery of care provided by the 1983 Act.

Despite all these shortcomings, no successful action through the courts has been recorded which might have forced the responsible government departments to tighten up their procedures for protecting children in need. In theory, the abused child with a statutory claim could employ the action *legis Aquiliae* against any member of the public or professions who had failed to take action to report the risks of abuse under section 42 of the 1983 Act. In order to establish such a claim, the claimant child would have to establish evidence to satisfy a court on the balance of probabilities that the following constituent elements were present in the defendant's actions:

1 The defendant's conduct was voluntary;
2 The conduct was unlawful in that it infringed section 42 of the 1983 Act and there was no justification for failure to report;
3 The defendant's capacity was undiminished;
4 The defendant omitted to report their suspicion of abuse, knowing full well that they had such a duty (fault);
5 The injuries suffered by the child were the direct result of the abusive treatment and would have been prevented if the defendant had reported (causation);
6 The claimant suffered loss of amenities of life as a result of the assaults (loss).

Even these factors together would be insufficient to get an '*X v Bedfordshire*' action off the ground. The following requirements would have to be satisfied for an Aquilian action for damages for breach of duty to succeed:[20]

1 The statute must have been intended to give a right of action;
2 The claimant must be one of the persons for whose benefit the duty was imposed;

3 Legislature must have intended to protect the interests of a group of whom the child claimant was a member;
4 The defendant's conduct consisted of a breach of the duty;
5 The breach of duty materially contributed to the damage.

As was mentioned above, the paucity of any such claims indicate that legal advisers and those responsible for providing public funding for litigation have discouraged attempts to mount such an action, most probably on the prediction that the courts will not find that the 1983 Act contemplates any form duty owed to individuals.

In the absence of any specific duty under the 1983 Act, it is worth exploring other legislative responsibilities, which might conceivably provide grounds for an action for breach of statutory duty.

Local Authorities

In Schedule 4B of the Constitution 'child care facilities' are listed as 'functional areas of concurrent competence' involving, expressly, local government as well as higher levels of government. However 'child care facilities' as referred to in Schedule 4B of the Constitution are not defined. Without further legislation and/or judicial development this provides a flimsy basis for any claim for breach of statutory duty.

Section 155 of the South African Constitution refers to Schedule B in section 155(7), stating the following:

> The national government, subject to section 44, and the provincial governments have the legislative and executive authority to see to the effective performance by municipalities of their functions in respect of matters listed in Schedules 4 and 5.

Therefore both national and provincial authorities have extensive power to direct the performance by the municipalities of their Schedule 4 and 5 tasks. But again, absent more precise specification of what these tasks are, it would be difficult for a child claimant to locate the true defendant for an action – the municipality? the provincial government? government department? – or all three?

Section 152(1) in setting out 'the objects of local government' includes duties to promote social and economic development and a safe and healthy environment. Commentators[21] analysing this part of the Constitution claim that it supports the involvement of local government authorities in promoting the welfare of children; this is probably an overoptimistic assessment of the view that the domestic courts might take if the point were tested.

Children's Rights under the Constitution

Under section 28(1)(c) of the Constitution, the child has the express right to care of a certain nature or quality under this section in 'appropriate care when removed from the family environment'. The care that the State provides must therefore be of such a nature and quality that it approximates family or parental care.

Section 28(1)(b) also imposes an obligation on the State to respect existing family or parental care and limits its interference in such existing care to cases where it is justified. It has been suggested that the provision in the 1983 Act regarding the manner in which a removal decision can be taken and implemented is open to criticism because it does not provide sufficiently for participation of the child or parents in the decision to take the child into care, nor does it provide sufficiently for measures through which the cohesion of the family may be maintained while the child is in state care.

Section 28(1)(d) of the Constitution imposes an obligation on the State to protect children from 'maltreatment, abuse, neglect and degradation'. The children's courts are directly tasked with implementing the Constitutional right of every child 'to family care or parental care, or to appropriate alternative care when removed from the family environment'.

Several clauses in the children's rights section in Chapter 2 of the Constitution incorporate second generation, or socio-economic rights, such as the right to housing[22] and health care, food, water and social security.[23] While generally the State is bound to realise socio-economic rights progressively within its available resources, with respect to the socio-economic rights in the children's rights clause, the State is committed to core obligations (such as basic nutrition, basic health care, etc). The right to education is set out in a separate section of the Constitution.[24]

These are not exhaustive of the rights that children enjoy under the Constitution, section 12 of which obliges the State to protect all members of the public from acts of violence. In the light of developments in South Africa, this constitutional protection of freedom from violence remains for many a worthless paper guarantee. The question is to what extent this provision may be relied upon as an enforceable obligation on the State to take reasonable steps aimed at preventing violation of that right, not only by public authorities but by private parties.[25]

The Constitutional guarantee of freedom from violence has been considered by the South African Constitutional Court in the decisions of *Baloyi*[26] and *Christian Education.*[27] In the case of *Baloyi*, it was held that the provisions contained in section 12(1)(c) oblige the state 'directly to protect the right of everyone to be free from private or domestic violence'. In *Christian Education*, it was stated that the provisions oblige the State to 'take appropriate steps to reduce violence in public and private life'. In this ruling the Constitutional Court declared that corporal punishment – the defence of reasonable chastisement in South African common law – was unconstitutional. However, this judgment left untouched the rights of parents to impose corporal correction in the home, and by implication, the rights of carers in *loco parentis* to do the same.

There are two recent decisions by the Constitutional Court that deserve detailed consideration since they are of direct relevance to this paper. The *Grootboom*[28] case, which dealt with the scope of children's rights under the Convention, and then the *Carmichele*[29] case, which has gone further than all the others in extending the boundaries of tortious liability so as to open the way for an action under ordinary common law principles for a claimant without the resources to commit to the uncertainties of rights litigation.

Grootboom

Here residents of a squatter camp applied for an order directing the government to provide adequate basic housing to them and their children, basing their claim on the social and economic rights section in the Constitution. The central issue that the Constitutional Court was obliged to consider was the relationship between everyone's right to housing in section 26 of the Constitution, and children's right to shelter as provided for in section 28(1)(c) of the Constitution. The lower court[30] had held that section 28(1)(c) imposes an obligation upon the State to provide shelter for children in the event that their parents are unable to do so. The Constitutional Court, however, proceeded to analyse the rights concerned by pointing to the evident overlap between the rights in sections 26 and 27, which create the right of access to socio-economic rights for *everyone*, and those in section 28(1)(c), which concern the rights of *children alone*. Because of this, and because the Constitutional Court was of the opinion that viewing the right to housing and the right to shelter as being distinct would render the 'carefully constructed constitutional scheme' for the progressive realisation of socio-economic rights nugatory, it was found that section 28(1)(c) did not create a 'direct and enforceable' claim upon the State by children.

The Court was consequently of the view that section 28(1)(b) must be read together with section 28(1)(c),[31] the former defining those responsible for giving care to children, whilst the latter lists various aspects of the care entitlement (the right to basic nutrition, to shelter, to basic health care services and to social services). The judgment suggests clearly that the right in section 28(1)(b) is primarily of horizontal application (that is, between individuals), as the obligation for fulfilment of the rights enumerated in section 28(1)(c) was regarded as lying primarily upon parents.

This judgment also established several other subsidiary principles of relevance to this investigation. First, the Court elaborated upon the nature of the State's obligation in relation to section 28 rights. Yacoob J stated that where children are in parental or familial care, the State's obligation would normally entail passing laws and creating enforcement mechanisms for the maintenance of children and for their protection from abuse, neglect or degradation.[32] The State would, the Court conceded, incur such primary obligation where children are removed, or lack a family environment, such as where they have been orphaned or abandoned. It is therefore implicit that insofar as children *are* removed, abandoned or orphaned, the State does in fact bear a primary responsibility to provide for those children's basic material needs. It is therefore arguable that street children, and all children in alternative care settings, such as children in foster care or those residing in children's homes, may be able to rely on this consitutional provision to argue that a legal duty rests on the State. The principle established by the *Grootboom* case is that legislative and other steps must be taken in order to ensure that the State does meet its commitments in this regard.

The view has also been put forward that the *Grootboom* judgment recognises that children's right to protection from abuse, neglect, maltreatment and degradation in section 28(1)(d) is a right that is directly enforceable against the State. Given the links between parental poverty and child abuse, it may be argued that the State is obliged, where children's neglect stems from poverty alone, to adopt meaningful preventive measures, which must include some level of financial allocation for family preservation.

Carmichele

Here the Court explored the impact of the provisions in the Bill of Rights on liability in delict of public authorities. It will be remembered from the earlier discussion that South African delict law not only does not recognise a positive duty to rescue, but also draws on English principles to the effect that in the absence of some special relationship between the party who owes the legal duty and the person to whom the duty is owed, there is no reason to impose a duty. So when the Supreme Court came to determine *Carmichele*, it concluded that there was no cause of action. This finding was borne out in a similar case called *Van Eden v Minister of Safety and Security*,[33] the Transvaal Provincial Division holding that, due to the lack of such a special relationship between the police and members of the public, the police owed no duty to prevent harm to a claimant who was raped by a man who had escaped from police custody, despite the police admitting negligence in this respect.

Now *Carmichele* may have tipped the balance against the victim in such a situation. Here the applicant was assaulted by an individual who had been released on bail after the police had made a positive bail recommendation. The applicant's claim in delict was based first on the allegation that the police and prosecutor owed her a legal duty to prevent the assault happening; to ensure, in her words, that she enjoyed her constitutional rights of *inter alia* the right to life, the right to respect for and protection of her dignity, the right to freedom and security, the right to personal privacy and the right to freedom of movement.

She placed particular reliance on section 8 of the Interim Constitution (then in force), which granted the right to equality, and equal protection of the law, and section 215 of which read: 'The powers and functions of the Service shall be–(a) the prevention of crime . . . '. She based these claims on section 39(2) of the Constitution which provides that when developing the common law, every court must promote the spirit, purport and objects of the Bill of Rights. Section 7 makes the Bill of Rights binding on the judiciary as well as the executive and the legislature.

The common law position was based on the leading case of *Kadir*[34] which said that in determining whether there was a legal duty on the police officers to act, the courts should strike a balance between the interests of the parties and the conflicting interests of the community.[35] *Kadir* dictated that the refashioning of the common law entailed 'policy decisions and value judgments' which had to 'reflect the wishes, often unspoken, and the perceptions, often but dimly discerned, of the people'. In *Carmichele* the Constitutional Court said that these 'policy decisions'

> might well have to be replaced, or supplemented and enriched by the appropriate norms of the objective value system embodied in the Constitution. *Following this route it might be easier to cast the net of unlawfulness wider because constitutional obligations are now placed on the state to respect, protect, promote and fulfil the rights in the Bill of Rights, and, in particular, the right of women to have their safety and security protected.*[36]

The Constitutional Court thus concluded that the common law delictual duty to act was inadequate in this case to protect the applicant's constitutional rights. The State was obliged by the constitution and international law to prohibit all gender-based discrimination and that had the effect of impairing the enjoyment by women of fundamental rights and freedoms, and to take reasonable and appropriate measures to prevent the violation of those rights. Thus the recommendation by the police in this case that the applicant's assailant be released in clear knowledge that he had in the past perpetrated crimes of a sexual nature should amount to wrongful conduct giving rise to liability for the consequences.

The Court in this case effectively suggested that the best route was to widen the boundaries of the common law legal duty, and to allow the elements of fault and remoteness of damage to play the greater role in *limiting* liability. The case demonstrates very clearly the so called 'indirect radiating effect' of the Constitution[37] on existing concepts that are open to such influence, particularly the test of what the legal convictions of the community demand where the Courts are determining whether liability should be imposed. From now on, a court's conclusion as to whether or not a legal duty exists in the circumstances must be compatible with the constitutional norms and values.

But it is perhaps unwise to read too much into *Carmichele*. The establishment of a duty or liability in this case means only that police and prosecutors who know that an accused person has threatened violence against someone are liable, and that those who have no such specific knowledge are not going to be liable in delict. Commentators have remarked that 'the vast majority of cases will probably still be subject to principles similar to those espoused in *Hill v Chief Constable of West Yorkshire* [1988] 2 All ER 238'.[38] This case probably articulates the general rule still applicable in South African common law and it is only where the nature of the group of potential victims is such as to create a special relationship, as in the case of *Carmichele*, that liability will arise. *Carmichele* has not created an automatic assumption of a legal duty where a statutory duty exists.

The crucial question, central to this inquiry, is whether *Carmichele* has dealt with the delict point in a way that leaves the door open for abused or neglected children to claim that a legal duty is owed to them by the social services by virtue of section 28 of the Bill of Rights, to prevent them from neglect and abuse.

In general, even after *Carmichele*, liability only follows where the other essential elements of delict can also be proved: see *Moses v MSS* 2000 (3) SA 106 (C) where the duty to prevent harm was found but negligence could not be shown. A breach of duty would exist where it is reasonable to expect protection to be provided; a causal connection will be established when it is reasonable to conclude that the harm ensued as a result of the failure to act; and fault (usually in the form of negligence) will be present if the persons who should have taken action to prevent the harm, did not do so when it could reasonably have been expected that they should act. The trick in every case is to determine what reasonableness demands, and who must prove it.

Conclusion

The full impact of the decision of the Constitutional Court on the delictual liability of public authorities has yet to be explored, and it is unlikely that any future claimant in the position of the appellants in *X v Bedfordshire CC* will find it easy to identify a responsible body, in the current situation where responsibility for social services is so fragmented. However, taking both *Carmichele* and *Grootboom* at face value, it would seem that section 28 of the Constitution may now be relied upon to establish the State's primary obligation towards children in foster care, children in institutional settings, abandoned and orphaned children and children living on the street, and from that obligation to derive a legal duty that would found a liability for failure to fulfil that positive obligation. But it also has to be recognised that it does not necessarily follow that the success of any future action, and the founding of a more generalised delictual duty in this context, will be in the interests of underprivileged children in South Africa. As a commentator has recently noted,[39] this new liability

> ... may well require a veritable army of social workers, providing State services to the ever-increasing numbers of children without adult caregivers, as well as sharp increases in State subsidisation of foster care and institutions for orphaned and abandoned children... As this option accords little or no priority (or fiscal commitment) to families and parents attempting to support their own children, it would impel social workers to remove children whose neglect or abuse stems from parental poverty.

The novel and generally beneficial paradigm of supervening law imposed by the Constitution is not, sadly, backed by practical measures of implementation. It may therefore be the case that courts in the future will seek to limit liability, not by denying that such an action falls outside the law of obligations, but by defeating claims on grounds of remoteness and causation, a route made all the more possible by the plethora of private and volunteer agencies involved in child services in South Africa.

Notes

1 *X (Minors) v Bedfordshire City Council* [1995] 2 AC 633.
2 Constitution of the Republic of South Africa Act 108 of 1996, Chapter 2.
3 *Minister van Polisie v Ewels* 1975 (3) SA 590 (A) at 596–597.
4 *Rusere v The Jesuit Fathers* 1970 (4) SA 537 (R).
5 *Natal Fresh Produce Growers' Association v Agroserve (Pty) Ltd* 1990 4 SA 749 (N) 753.
6 Constitution of the Republic of South Africa Act 108 of 1996, Chapter 2.
7 South African Police Service Act 1995 section 5.
8 *Nkumbi v Minister of Law and Order* (1991) 3 SA 29 (E); *Kadir v Minister of Law and Order* (1992) 3 SA 737 (C) 739.
9 *Da Silva v Coutinho* 1971 3 SA 123(A) 134.
10 One of the problems vexing the Law Commission, currently working on a statute to replace the Child Care Act of 1983, is whether displaced foreign children should fall under a future children's statute or whether immigration legislation should apply to them: see Discussion Paper 103 (Project 110) *Review of the Child Care Act* (2001–2002).
11 Such as circumcision of teenage boys as part of the 'initiation' ritual.
12 Review of the Child Care Act – First Issue Paper July 31 1998, para. 42.3.
13 These various institutions are discussed further in the following section.
14 Supplemented by the Child Care Amendment Act 96 of 1996, the Welfare Laws Amendment Act of 104 of 1997 and the Child Care Amendment Act 13 of 1999.
15 *S v Maree* 1990 (3) SA 365 (C) at 370D-E; *S v B en 'n Ander* 1994 (2) SA 237 (EC).
16 This reporting obligation has come up for criticism. As the Law Commission observed, in a context where there is a serious lack of backup resources, mandatory reporting can increase the vulnerability of children, and set them up for secondary abuse.
17 Which provides that 'Every local authority shall take reasonable steps, through the provision of services under Part III of this Act, to prevent children within their area suffering ill-treatment or neglect'.
18 Zaal and Matthias, 1996 Acta Juridica 60.
19 See Inter Ministerial Committee on Young People at Risk in *In Whose Best Interests? Report on Places of Safety, Schools of Industry and Reform Schools* (20), at 14.
20 *Da Silva and Another v Coutinho* 1971 (3) SA 123 (A).
21 'Local Government and the Provision of Child Care Services: An Essential Area for Legislative Reform', Noel Zaal and Carmel Mattthias, SALJ Vol 119 part 1 (2002) 138.
22 Section 26.
23 Section 27.
24 Section 29.
25 Gretchen Carpenter has pointed out that, to the extent that private law protects physical integrity as a subjective right, the values protected by s 12(1)(c) have always entailed horizontal obligations ('The right to physical safety as a constitutionally protected human right' in Gretchen Carpenter (ed) *Suprema Lex: Essays on the Constitution presented to Marinus Wiechers* (1998) 139 at 142).
26 2000 (2) SA 425 (CC).
27 (2000) (4) SA 757.
28 *The Government of the Republic of South Africa v Grootboom* (2001) 10 BHRC 84.
29 *Carmichele v Minister of Safety and Security* (2002) 12 BHRC 60.

30 See *Grootboom v Oostenberg Municipality and Others* 2000 (3) BCLR 277 (C).
31 Paragraph 76 of the judgment.
32 Paragraph 78.
33 2001 (4) SA 646 T.
34 *Kadir v Minister of Law and Order* (1992) 3 SA 737 (C).
35 This is not dissimilar to the 'fair just and reasonable' requirement in *Caparo*; to quote Lord Browne-Wilkinson in *Barrett v Enfield LBC* [1999] 4 LRC 473: 'the decision as to whether it is fair, just and reasonable to impose a liability in negligence on a particular class of would-be defendants depends on weighing in the balance the total detriment to the public interest in all cases from holding such a class liable in negligence as against the total loss to all would-be claimants if they are not to have a cause of action in respect of the loss which they have individually suffered'.
36 Ackermann and Goldstone JJ, paras 56–57.
37 Referred to in *Du Plessis v De Klerk* 1996 (3) SA 850 (CC) para. 110.
38 'The Impact of the Constitution on the Law of Delict: Carmichele v Minister of Safety and Security' Leinius and Midgely, (same SALJ p 17).
39 See Julia Sloth-Nielsen, 'The child's right to social services, the right to social security, and primary prevention of child abuse: Some conclusions in the aftermath of Grootboom' (2001) 17 SAJHR 210 at 230.

Chapter 6

Liability for Government Actions: A Comparative Study of English and American Law

*Helene M. Goldberg**

The governments of both the United Kingdom and the United States touch the lives of their inhabitants in a myriad of ways. From some of the most significant aspects of a person's life to some of the least significant, government plays a role. Government decisions can dramatically affect one's healthcare, lifestyle, ability to earn a living – even one's most intimate family life. Because of the great scope and reach of government activities, it is an essential element of the democratic nature of the two countries that a fair and effective mechanism exists for seeking redress for government decisions that cause harm. The ability to obtain meaningful relief from wrongful government actions lies at the heart of the relationship between a government and its inhabitants.

Both countries meet this need with legal avenues for challenging the legality of government actions in order to halt or alter practices that are not in accordance with law and for obtaining monetary damages for harm suffered by wrongful government actions. This paper will examine the legal framework for the latter of these remedies – monetary damages from the government. It will discuss the source of law governing tort claims against the government and the defences to these claims. It will then compare cases in both countries dealing with the government's liability for harm to children and will conclude with some comparative observations about discretionary decisions and the separation of powers.

* Formerly Director, Constitutional and Specialised Tort Litigation, U.S. Department of Justice; Atlantic Fellow in Public Policy. The views expressed in this article are those of the author and do not represent the position of the United States Department of Justice.

Liability of Public Authorities in England[1]

General Framework

English courts have long recognised a cause of action in tort against public authorities. The general principle is that the common law of torts governs the liability of public authorities just as it does of private individuals.[2] The ordinary rules of vicarious liability apply, and plaintiffs must establish the same basic elements of the torts alleged. Sovereign immunity does not pose a barrier to tort claims, as local public authorities and other statutory bodies have never been entitled to claim the immunity, and the Crown Proceedings Act of 1947 expressly subjects the Crown to the same general liability in tort as a person of full age and capacity.

This general rule is subject to some significant exceptions, however, as even in the absence of a claim of sovereign immunity, the courts must take into account the unique attributes of governmental actions. Thus, for example, if harm is necessarily caused by the proper execution of an Act of Parliament, no liability is created.[3] More problematic are cases in which the plaintiff's claim arises from the exercise of discretion by government officials in the performance of their statutory powers and duties. British courts have shown a marked preference for considering such claims within the framework of traditional tort law, rather than as a breach of statutory duty or a failure to exercise a statutory power.

The Human Rights Act of 1998 superimposed upon the common law jurisprudence an additional source of liability for public authorities. Although the United Kingdom had long been a party to the European Convention of Human Rights (ECHR), the Convention could not be enforced in British courts until it was incorporated into domestic law by the Human Rights Act. The Act came into force in England, Wales and Northern Ireland on 2 October, 2000, having previously become effective in Scotland by virtue of the Scotland Act of 1998.

The Human Rights Act effected dramatic change in British public law, requiring statements of compatibility with Convention rights for all new legislation,[4] making it unlawful for any public authority to act in a way that is incompatible with Convention rights,[5] and allowing violation of Convention rights to be litigated in British courts.[6] This litigation can occur in a variety of contexts – judicial review, defence to criminal proceedings or claims for damages. Although the courts cannot strike down primary legislation, they can issue a declaration of incompatibility, placing the onus upon Parliament to amend the legislation.[7] Judges are instructed 'so far as it is possible' to read legislation as compatible with Convention rights,[8] and are required to 'take into account' the jurisprudence of the European Court of Human Rights.[9] Thus, among other things, by granting judges the ability to review executive and legislative actions for compliance with Convention rights, the Human Rights Act significantly shifted the balance of power among the branches of government, a development that was widely decried prior to the effective date of the Human Rights Act, but has not attracted much attention since.[10]

Section 8 of the Human Rights Act provides that courts may order a wide array of remedies for violations of Convention rights, including the award of damages. Again, judges are mandated to 'take into account' European Court of Human Rights Article 41 jurisprudence on damages.[11] In order to award damages, the court must conclude – taking into account all of the circumstances, including the availability of other relief – that 'the award is necessary in order to award just satisfaction'.[12]

The availability of damage remedies for violation of Convention rights adds a layer of public liability for rights-based causes of action to the existing common law liability for duty-based torts.

Recent Developments

The starting point in any study of English public tort law is the seminal case of *Dorset Yacht Co. Ltd v Home Office.*[13] In that case, youths in the custody of government authorities had escaped and attempted to leave the island on which they had been detained by stealing a yacht. In the process the yacht was damaged, and the owners sued the government authorities, alleging that the officers were negligent in failing to supervise the youths. The House of Lords found liability, but their Lordships reached that result through different analytical paths. Lord Morris and Lord Pearson expressed the majority approach. Those judges had determined that the government officers were under a common law duty of care to take reasonable precautions to control the youths under their charge in order to avoid foreseeable damage to the plaintiff's property. The statutory duty provided a measuring stick by which to judge the extent of the common law duty, but significantly it did not provide either the basis for the liability or a defence to a claim for a common law breach of duty of care. Lord Diplock likewise held that the *Dorset Yacht* plaintiff could state a common law duty of care, but he premised his holding on the reasoning that the officers' conduct could be shown to be so unreasonable as to be outside the discretion granted to them, and hence *ultra vires.* Thus, implicit in his holding is the rule that an erroneous but not patently unreasonable action or omission taken within the scope of discretion granted by statute could not form the basis for a common law cause of action.

In a series of cases since *Dorset Yacht*, the courts have struggled to formulate a workable rule that would fairly and effectively govern situations in which government officials are exercising discretion in areas that have no, or at most an attenuated, analogue in relationships between private individuals. It now seems clear neither a breach of statutory duty nor a careless failure to exercise a statutory power, standing alone, will provide a cause of action. Rather, the courts will require a plaintiff to demonstrate a parallel private cause of action.[14] Thus, as a starting point, a plaintiff must meet the three-fold test, first enunciated in *Caparo Industries plc v Dickman,*[15] for extending a duty of care into new areas: (1) was there foreseeability? (2) was there proximity? and (3) would it be fair, just and reasonable to impose a duty of care?

In *Stovin v Wise,*[16] the House of Lords confronted the question of when liability in tort could be premised upon a public authority's failure to act. Lord

Hoffman, writing for the majority, found no duty of care on the part of a highway authority to undertake action to correct a known hazard. He reasoned that (1) although the authority had the power to take the action, it was under no public law duty to do so; (2) even assuming that the highway authority ought to have done the work, there was no particularised basis or reliance which would justify awarding compensation for damages that arose from its failure to do so, and (3) that even if the failure were considered irrational (and presumably hence *ultra vires*), granting compensation would intrude upon the highway authority's exercise of discretion in allocating its resources and would foster defensive practices.

Lord Nicholls, writing in dissent, provided the analysis that may yet carry the day. As Lord Nicholls recognised, foreseeability is rarely the issue, and in any case, is not markedly different for public authorities than for private individuals. Rather, the crux of the matter lies with the intertwined issues of proximity and whether the imposition of a duty would be fair and reasonable. Lord Nicholls' speech is significant for two reasons. First, he recognised that proximity and the fair and reasonable test are but two sides of the same coin. As he explained,

> Proximity is convenient shorthand for a relationship between two parties which makes it fair and reasonable one should owe the other a duty of care.[17]

Second, he stated that a concurrent common law duty to act should be engrafted onto a statutory power when the common law duty would impose no greater obligation to act than that already imposed by its public law obligations. He acknowledged, however, that:

> Some statutory powers are less susceptible to a concurrent common law duty than others. As the part played by broad discretionary considerations in the exercise of the power grows, the less readily will a common law duty be imposed, and vice versa.[18]

Significantly, Lord Nicholls did not believe that the mere existence of fiscal considerations should rule out the imposition of a common law duty. Rather, he believed that fiscal considerations should be incorporated into the standard for determining breach:

> The standard of reasonableness is to be measured by what may reasonably be expected of the defendant in his individual circumstances. Where action calls for expenditure, the court if necessary will have regard to the financial resources of the defendant. The law does not always shrink away from such an investigation and regard itself as unable ever to make an assessment of competing demands for money.[19]

English courts continue to strive to develop cohesive standards for liability of public authorities. Their efforts focus upon the need to articulate a principled standard for determining when the courts should refrain from imposing liability because the matter is properly within the discretion of the public authority. At various times, the courts have considered basing this determination upon whether the act is considered *ultra vires*,[20] is policy based rather than operational,[21] and whether the matter would require an allocation of scarce resources.[22] This is one of the areas in which English law can be expected to undergo yet more refinement in the near future.

The wild ride of English public tort law is best illustrated by two recent cases: *X and Others v Bedfordshire County Council*,[23] considered by the European Court of Human Rights as *Z and Others v UK*,[24] and *Barrett v London Borough of Enfield*.[25] In analysing these cases, it is important to stress that they were determined on strike-out motions, which are to be granted only 'where the statement of the case discloses no reasonable basis for bringing the claim'.[26] Thus, affirmance of a strike-out order would amount to a holding that there was no conceivable set of facts upon which the plaintiff could recover on the claims alleged.

In *X*, the local authority failed for a period of approximately five years to take any significant protective action for five siblings, despite being alerted on several occasions that the children were living in 'horrific' conditions – dirty, uncared for and hungry. After their eventual placement in foster care, they sued the local authority (through the Official Solicitor as next friend) for breach of statutory duty and common law negligence. The House of Lords affirmed the dismissal of the action on a strike-out motion, holding (1) that the relevant child protection legislation did not create a private cause of action on behalf of the children and (2) that it would not be fair, just and reasonable to impose a common law duty of care on the local authority.

In an expansive examination of the claims, Lord Browne-Wilkinson, joined by a majority of the House, distilled the essence of prior cases dealing with liability of public authorities, dividing the claims into four categories. As an initial matter, he observed that:

> A breach of statutory duty does not, by itself, give rise to any private law cause of action. However, a private law cause of action will arise if it can be shown that, as a matter of construction of the statute, that the statutory duty was imposed for the protection of a limited class of the public and that Parliament intended to confer upon the members of that class the private right of action for breach of the duty.[27]

Noting that private rights of action for breaches of statutory duties had been implied only rarely and in cases where the statutory duty was very limited and specific, Lord Browne-Wilkinson found no such private right of action was conferred by the relevant legislation in this case. Although the legislation was enacted for the protection of children at risk (a limited class), Lord Browne-Wilkinson found that the duties imposed by the statutes were much too general and discretionary to provide a basis for an implied private right of action.[28]

Lord Browne-Wilkinson's rejection of a cause of action for even the careless performance of a statutory duty was based upon his reading of the seminal case of *Dorset Yacht Co. Ltd. v Home Office*.[29] From this, Lord Browne-Wilkinson concluded in *X*:

> In order to found a cause of action flowing from the careless exercise of statutory powers or duties, the plaintiff has to show that the circumstances are such as to raise a duty of care at common law. The mere assertion of the careless exercise of a statutory power or duty is not sufficient.[30]

Next confronting the question of whether the local authority owed the children in *X* a duty of care, Lord Browne-Wilkinson avoided placing full reliance on the doctrine of *ultra vires*. Instead, he treated a showing by the plaintiff that the conduct at issue was outside the ambit of statutory discretion as a necessary, but not sufficient, precondition to liability. According to his analysis, allegations that a public authority acted outside the scope of its authority premised upon an allegedly wrongful weighing of policy issues (such as allocation of scarce resources or the balancing of competing social values) are non-justiciable. 'Therefore a common law duty of care in relation to the taking of decisions involving policy matters cannot exist.'[31]

Allegations of carelessness in the practical or operational performance are justiciable, however, and should be decided by applying the ordinary principles of negligence. Thus, with regard to such allegations the court must determine foreseeability, proximity and, particularly critical to public authority cases, whether it would be just and reasonable to impose a duty of care.[32]

Lord Browne-Wilkinson emphasised that

> a common law duty of care cannot be imposed on a statutory duty if the observance of such common law duty of care would be inconsistent with, or have a tendency to discourage, the due performance by the local authority of its statutory duties.[33]

It was on this basis that he concluded that it would not be fair and reasonable to impose a common law duty of care on the local authority. Among the factors weighing in his decision were the multi-disciplinary nature of child protection activities, the difficulty and delicate nature of the decisions that must be made, the tense relationship between social workers and parents. Under these circumstances, introducing a cause of action would lead to defensive practices, delays in taking protective action for children at risk, and the diversion of resources from the children whom the local authority was statutorily directed to serve.

Disappointed with their inability to get relief from the English domestic courts, the plaintiffs in *X* took their case to the European Court of Human Rights in Strasbourg. From the time of the House of Lords decision in 1995 to the Strasbourg court's decision in 2001, English public tort law underwent dramatic change. The trigger for this upheaval was the Strasbourg court's decision in *Osman v UK*.[34] *Osman* was brought by a mother and son. The son was injured and the father killed by one of the son's former teachers who had developed an obsession with the son. The Osmans sued the police in English courts for negligence in failing to take action to prevent the assaults in the face of repeated complaints about the teacher's behaviour. The Court of Appeals dismissed the Osmans' claim, holding that claims of negligence in police investigations were barred on the grounds of public policy.[35]

In the European Court of Human Rights, the Osmans asserted violations of Article 2 of the ECHR (failure to protect right to human life), Article 6 (right to a hearing by neutral tribunal in the determination of civil rights), Article 8 (right to respect for physical integrity and family life), and Article 13 (right to an effective remedy notwithstanding that the violation has been committed by persons acting in an official capacity). The Strasbourg court rejected the Osmans' claim of a violation of Article 2, for breach of the positive obligation to protect human life, because they failed to carry their burden of establishing that the authorities had not done all that could *reasonably* be expected of them in the circumstances to avoid the risk. For many of the same reasons, the court held that the police authorities had not breached Article 8.

The Osmans' claim with regard to Article 6 formed the controversial basis of the court's decision. The Osmans had argued that the police immunity amounted to an illegitimate restriction on their right to a hearing of their negligence claim, or alternatively, that even if the immunity were intended to serve a legitimate goal, its application in their case was disproportionate because it precluded a consideration of what they viewed as the strong merits of their case. The government, by contrast, had argued that Article 6 guarantees a hearing only for civil 'rights' and that, under English domestic law, the Osmans had no such right because the finding of immunity amounted to a failure to establish one of the essential elements of a claim of negligence, namely that it was fair, just and reasonable to impose a duty of care in the circumstances of the case. Beyond this, the government defended the legitimacy of the aim of immunity, asserting that immunity served the valid public policy goal of focusing police resources on suppression of crime rather than litigation and avoiding defensive policing practices.

The Strasbourg court allowed the Osmans' Article 6 claim and their subsumed Article 13 claim. The court's reasoning is strained. It accepted the government's contention that the immunity served legitimate public policy goals,[36] but rejected the immunity as disproportionate, holding that it 'amounts to an unjustifiable restriction on an applicant's right to have a determination on the merits of his or her claim against the police in deserving cases'.[37] With respect to proportionality, the Strasbourg court noted, somewhat incorrectly, that English courts could consider, as they indeed had in specified cases, whether application of the rule was appropriate in individual cases.[38] Despite this, the Strasbourg court appeared to hold that in order to be proportionate, the 'immunity' rule must allow case-by-case balancing of the strength of a plaintiff's claim against the public policy benefit derived from insulating the police from liability. At the heart of the *Osman* decision was a visceral distrust of any procedure that deprived a plaintiff of a fact-finding hearing; the Strasbourg court took no solace in the fact that the English domestic court had accepted as true all facts pled by the Osmans, but held nonetheless that they were not entitled to relief.[39]

This decision met with cries of outrage from English judges, practitioners and scholars. The decision was roundly (and justifiably) criticised as intruding upon the substantive domestic law. The Strasbourg court had repeatedly emphasised in prior cases that:

> Article 6 extends only to *contestations* (disputes) over (civil) 'rights and obligations' which can be said, at least on arguable grounds, to be recognised under domestic law; it does not itself guarantee any particular content for (civil) 'rights and obligations' in the substantive law of the Contracting States.[40]

Despite this restraint, the *Osman* decision seemed to plunge headlong into re-writing the substantive English law of negligence. The Strasbourg court acknowledged that:

> The House of Lords in the Hill case modified that right [to sue for the tort of negligence] for reasons of public policy in order to provide an immunity for police from civil suit for their acts or omissions in the context of the investigation and suppression of crime.[41]

Yet, the Strasbourg court refused to recognise and give scope to this clear statement of substantive English law that plaintiffs after *Hill* had no right to sue in negligence for acts or omissions relating to the investigation and suppression of crime. Instead it held that:

> In its view, it must be open to a domestic court to have regard to the presence of other public-interest considerations which pull in the opposite direction to the application of the rule. Failing this, there will be no distinction between degrees of negligence or of harm suffered or any consideration of the justice of a particular case.[42]

The Strasbourg court's refusal to give effect to the *Hill* decision may have been rooted in its own rules, which do not bind the court to prior precedent. By contrast, an English court was free to consider whether the case before it properly belonged in the category of cases to which the 'immunity' applies. However, under the doctrine of *stare decisis*, in any case fitting within the category described by *Hill*, that is, any case alleging negligence in the conduct of a police investigation, the court was required to follow the House of Lords decision in *Hill v Chief Constable of Yorkshire* and find that it would not be fair, just and reasonable to impose a duty of care. Under domestic law, the judicial refinement of the law in *Hill*, followed by the Court of Appeals in *Osman*, defined the substantive content of the existing civil right just as surely as a statutory restriction could have.[43]

The *Osman* decision also was viewed as a frontal attack on the strike-out procedure, a rule much like American Federal Rule of Civil Procedure 12(b)(6), which allows for the dismissal of claims upon the defendant's motion where the court finds that, accepting all of the facts as pled by plaintiff, the complaint fails to state a claim for which relief can be granted.[44]

Despite the overwhelming judicial criticism of *Osman*, the House of Lords clearly took the case into account in formulating its view of liability for negligence by public authorities. Less than eight months after the *Osman* decision, the House of Lords announced its judgment in *Barrett v Enfield London Borough Council*.[45] In that case, the plaintiff, a young man who had been under a care order from the time he was ten months old until he turned

18, sued the local authority, alleging, *inter alia*, negligence in its serial placements of him in foster homes and failing to place him for adoption. In a stunning departure from the reasoning of *X*, their Lordships reversed the decision of the Court of Appeal and ordered the claim reinstated.

The House of Lords did not explicitly overrule *X*, preferring instead to distinguish it on the grounds that *X* involved the decision whether to take children into care, while *Barrett* dealt with the question of duty of care to a child who had been taken into care. Nonetheless, a reading of the judgments makes clear that *Barrett* represents a fundamental shift in favour of duty of care based upon the careless performance of statutory discretion. In the main judgments in *Barrett*, Lord Slynn and Lord Hutton concluded that the test for determining the existence of a duty of care by a public authority arising from the exercise of its statutory authority was justiciability. Criticising both the existence of discretion and the policy/operational distinction as incomplete tests for determining justiciability, Lord Slynn held that 'each case has to be looked at on its own facts and in light of the statutory context'.[46] On this basis, Lord Slynn rejected strike-out motions as inappropriate, explaining:

> the importance of seeing in each case whether what has been done is an act which is justiciable or whether it is an act done pursuant to the exercise or purported exercise of a statutory discretion which is not justiciable requires in this kind of matter, except in the clearest cases, an examination of the facts.[47]

Lord Hutton was particularly critical of the policy/operational test. He held that only those 'policy' matters involving a weighing of competing public interests or the allocation of limited financial resources would preclude justiciability. Thus, according to Lord Hutton, where, as in *Barrett*, it is not clear from the pleadings that a case involves such issues, it should proceed to trial, when the trial court can consider justiciability along with other relevant issues based upon the evidence presented.

Having decided on the basis of common law principles that the claim should not be struck out, Lord Hutton expressly declined to discuss the implications of *Osman*. Lord Browne-Wilkinson, by contrast, declared the *Osman* decision extremely difficult to understand, and explained, perhaps for the benefit of the Strasbourg court, that a finding that it would not be fair, just and reasonable to impose a duty of care was not an immunity, but rather the failure of plaintiff to establish an essential element of his cause of action. That said, however, Lord Browne-Wilkinson acknowledged that if the House of Lords affirmed the strike-out of Mr. Barrett's claim, he was likely to appeal to Strasbourg, where he would probably meet with success.

The Strasbourg court seems to have absorbed Lord Brown-Wilkinson's lesson. In ruling on the application of the *X* plaintiffs before the European Court of Human Rights, *sub nom Z v UK*, the court found no violation of Article 6, although it did award damages for violations (conceded by the UK government) of Articles 3 and 13. As the Strasbourg court explained:

> The Court considers that its reasoning in the *Osman* judgment was based on an understanding of the law of negligence, which has to be reviewed in light of the clarifications subsequently made by the domestic courts and notably the House of Lords. The Court is satisfied that the law of negligence as developed in the domestic courts since the case of *Caparo* and as recently analysed in the case of *Barrett v Enfield LBC* includes the fair, just and reasonable criterion as an intrinsic element of the duty of care and that the ruling of law concerning that element in this case does not disclose the operation of an immunity.[48]

So where will English law go from here? The Court of Appeal decisions in *S v Gloucestershire County Council* and *L v Tower Hamlets London Borough Council*[49] provide some clues. In *S*, the plaintiff was a young man who had been in care of the local authorities from the time he was 13 until he reached adulthood. When the local authorities took him into care (at the request of his adoptive parents), he was placed in foster care. A few months later, other youths raised allegations of sexual abuse against the foster father. The local authorities immediately removed S from the foster home and placed him in another home. S repeatedly denied that he had been subjected to sexual advances or other abuse. Eighteen months later, however, S told his key worker that the foster father had in fact molested him. Throughout his adolescence, S was involved in a series of petty and then escalating offences, and was moved to a variety of housing situations. At the age of 24, he instituted this suit against the public authorities alleging that they had been negligent in placing him with the foster family in the first instance and then in failing to investigate properly and to provide him with appropriate care and treatment after the allegations of child abuse surfaced.

In *L*, the plaintiff was a woman who as a young child had spent 18 months in foster care. Shortly thereafter, she disclosed that she had been subjected to sexual abuse by the foster father during her stay there. The foster father was later convicted of a number of sexual assaults, including two upon the plaintiff. As a young adult with serious psychological troubles, she sued the local authorities, alleging negligence in placing her with the foster family.

The Court of Appeal addressed these cases in a very thoughtful way, taking advantage of new procedures introduced by the Civil Procedure Rules. Both cases were heard on appeal following strike-out by the lower court. The Court of Appeal rejected the local authorities' attempts to rely upon *X* as establishing that cases alleging harm from child abuse by private individuals were bound to fail. After summarising the principles derived from *Barrett*, Lord Justice May opined:

> In an ordinary case a local authority is unlikely to establish a defence which relies on blanket immunity. There would be a blanket immunity for this purpose if it were decided without reference to particular facts that all cases which have certain basic characteristics were not justiciable; or that in every case with certain characteristics it was not just or reasonable to impose a duty of care.[50]

The need for an examination of the facts did not lead the Court of Appeal ineluctably to require a trial, however. Lord Justice May expressly rejected the notion that Osman required a trial, noting:

> In an appropriate case, a summary hearing can be a fair hearing for the purpose of Article 6. I would add that, in an appropriate case, a defendant is entitled to a fair summary hearing of a case which, when it is properly investigated, has no real prospect of success.[51]

The Court of Appeal utilised the new civil procedure rules to consider the cases on applications for summary judgment and to consider as evidence the contemporaneous notes of the social workers. Noting that the records were silent about the considerations that went into the selection of the foster family in the *S* case, the Court of Appeal held that it was possible that S could establish at trial that it would be just and reasonable to impose a duty of care in this case. By contrast, in *L*, the court reviewed the allegations of negligence against a record of a detailed investigation of the foster family. This investigation, although it contained some reservations about the foster father's maturity, revealed no information that even hinted that the foster father might be prone to sexual abuse. For this reason, the court concluded that L could not establish causation and thus, her claim had no real prospect of success. Accordingly, it dismissed her appeal.

Each of the cases in which a court has found an arguable duty of care involved children actually in care of public authorities. In light of the clear trend toward imposing a duty seen in the more recent cases, the distinction in British law between failing to prevent abuse by custodial parents and negligence after a child is in care may be tenuous. For the moment at least, however, that remains the law in England. In the United States, the same distinction appears to prevail. In *DeShaney v Winnebago County Department of Social Services*,[52] the Supreme Court held that failure of social services to remove a child from his father's custody did not constitute a violation of substantive due process under the Constitution. The majority reasoned that, in the absence of a special relationship such as institutionalisation, the government was under no affirmative obligation to protect individuals from third parties. Thus, where the government neither created the danger nor rendered the individual more vulnerable, a failure to protect a child, even in the face of knowledge of the danger, would not implicate the Constitution. Rejecting an argument that the child protection statutes created a constitutionally enforceable obligation, the majority noted that its holding did not prevent the states from creating a tort cause of action through common law or statute.

More recent cases for the United States Courts of Appeals indicate some discomfort with the strictures of *DeShaney*, at least in the context of child abuse cases. In *Currier v Doran*,[53] the United States Court of Appeals for the Tenth Circuit distinguished *DeShaney* by holding that it did not bar constitutional claims where the state affirmatively acts to remove a child from the custody of one parent to place it with the other. In *Currier*, the Tenth

Circuit held that social workers who had discounted numerous bruises and injuries and nonetheless recommended that the father be given custody had in fact increased the danger to the children and thus could be liable under the state-created danger theory.

Following *Barrett*, the English courts have continued to apply tort theories to expand remedies against public authorities. In *Phelps v Hillingdon London Borough Council*,[54] the House of Lords considered four cases alleging a failure to provide appropriate education to children. The first of these, *Phelps*, was before the House of Lords following a trial in which damages were awarded against the school authority based upon vicarious liability arising from the school psychologist's failure to diagnose dyslexia. The House easily overcame the hurdles of foreseeability, proximity and public policy to declare that there is a duty of care on the part of educational professionals (teachers and psychologists alike) in the delivery of educational services. Lord Nicholls drew a distinction, likely to be very hard to apply in practice, between claims based upon poor quality of teaching and those based upon more specific failures of the educational system:

> It is one thing for the law to provide a remedy in damages when there is manifest incompetence or negligence comprising specific, identifiable mistakes. It would be an altogether different matter to countenance claims of a more general nature, to the effect that the child did not receive an adequate education at the school, or that a particular teacher failed to teach properly.

In *Phelps*, their Lordships noted that in the United States, the weight of the law was against a cause of action for educational malpractice. While this is certainly the case for common law tort claims, some American federal courts have granted monetary damages for breaches of statutory duties by education authorities.[55] The Supreme Court, in *Davis v Monroe County Board of Education*, held that students had a private right of action under a federal funding statute to sue schools who as grant recipients failed to comply with federal regulations precluding discrimination.[56] In *Davis*, the student had been subjected to severe sexual harassment by a fellow pupil, and alleged that the school had evidenced deliberate indifference despite knowledge of the situation.

It is arguable that breach of statutory duties is a more appropriate framework than common law tort within which to consider failures of the educational system.[57] The Education Act at issue in *Phelps* and its successors contain very specific requirements to individual students, stipulating special needs assessments, a statement of those special education needs, and provision for those needs. Both the assessment process and the subsequent education are to be particularised to the individual student. Under these circumstances, it appears that the requirements for implication of a statutorily created private right of action have been met. Adjudicating education claims as alleged breaches of statutory duties would have four clear advantages. First, it would focus the enquiry upon whether the education authority had complied with Parliamentary intent, thus eliminating judicial incursion into a sensitive policy area. Second, by focusing upon whether the education authorities had met the statutory requirements, it would make it much easier to enforce Lord Nicholls' distinction between generalised poor teaching and specific, identifiable mistakes such as misdiagnosis. Third, it would avoid the awkward, and perhaps unsupported, need to find that teachers had undertaken an assumption of responsibility. Finally, it would place domestic statutes on a par with European directives for purposes of damages.[58]

English courts have recently revived the tort of misfeasance in public office. In order to recover for misfeasance, a plaintiff must establish (1) an unlawful act or omission, (2) either knowing or reckless abuse of power, (3) bad faith, (4) standing, and (5) causation.[59] Because the required elements of this tort are much more stringent than those for negligence, it is unlikely to be used in any case where a plaintiff can demonstrate the existence of a duty of care.

Liability of the Federal Government Under American Law[60]

The United States inherited from Britain both its common law tradition and the concept of sovereign immunity. Unlike Britain, however, it has retained much of its sovereign immunity. The United States is immune from suit except so far as it has waived its sovereign immunity. Waivers of sovereign immunity must be express and are strictly construed.[61] Against this backdrop of sovereign immunity, Congress and the Supreme Court have struggled to develop a system of remedies that would compensate for wrongs committed by the federal government but would not stifle the initiative and judgment needed for a vital government.

The Federal Tort Claims Act

Congress enacted the first coherent basis for federal government's liability for its torts in 1946, after two decades of debate. Prior to the enactment of the Federal Tort Claims Act (FTCA), recovery for federal government actions was available only through private legislation or a few isolated statutes allowing *ex gratia* payments. As it currently reads, the FTCA, codified in 28 USC §1346 and 28 USC §§2671 et seq., provides both a limited waiver of sovereign immunity and a procedural framework for pursuing claims against the United States.

The Act waives sovereign immunity for acts or omissions of an 'employee of the government while acting within the scope of his office or employment, under circumstances where the United States, if a private person, would be liable to the claimant in accordance with the law of the place where the act or omission occurred'.[62] The FTCA provides the *exclusive* basis for tort claims against the United States; even tort claims against agencies that have statutory authority to sue and be sued in their own name are strictly governed by the FTCA.[63]

The Supreme Court has consistently held that the source of substantive liability under the FTCA means state common law.[64] Thus, the FTCA does not waive sovereign immunity for claims arising from alleged violations of federal law, including federal constitutional law.[65] As discussed below, however, individual government employees may be sued in their personal capacities for constitutional torts.

There are a number of exceptions to the FTCA, codified at 28 U.S.C. §2680. The objectives of these exceptions were to ensure that important governmental activities would not be disrupted by the threat of damage suits, to avoid exposure of the United States to excessive or fraudulent claims and not to extend coverage of the FTCA for matters for which adequate remedies already existed.[66]

Perhaps the most important of the FTCA's exceptions is the discretionary function exception, which excludes all claims 'based upon the exercise or performance or failure to perform a discretionary function or duty on the part of a federal agency or an employee of the Government, whether or not the discretion be abused'.[67] In enacting this provision, Congress gave statutory support to the notion that separation of powers precludes judicial review of public policy decisions by the executive branch.

Thus, unlike the situation in England, where the courts are relying upon notions of justiciability to limit judicial interference in executive decision-making, the parameters of American courts' jurisdiction to entertain tort claims based upon executive branch decisions are defined by statute. The discretionary function exception covers a broader swath of executive decisions than are excluded by English courts under the rubric of justiciability, and it is an interesting question whether the discretionary function exception would pass muster under Article 6 of the ECHR.

The Supreme Court has examined the discretionary function exception on several occasions, refining and explaining the exception. It is now clear that the discretionary function exception encompasses governmental acts or omissions that (1) involve an element of judgment or choice and (2) are susceptible to policy analysis.[68]

Any permissible exercise of policy judgment is exempt from the waiver of sovereign immunity, but 'when a suit charges an agency with failing to act in accordance with a specific mandatory directive, the discretionary function exception does not apply'.[69] Thus, to use the categorisations discussed by Lord Browne-Wilkinson in *X*, the discretionary function exception would not bar claims based upon a breach of statutory duty, but could exclude claims based upon the careless exercise of a statutory power if the challenged conduct involved an element of judgment that was susceptible to policy analysis.

Although Lord Browne-Wilkinson framed his ultimate conclusion in *X* as a finding that under ordinary negligence law it would not be fair and reasonable to impose a duty of care, the same result could have been reached by an acknowledgement that in fact the day-to-day decisions and actions by the social workers involved policy judgments. In the United States, 'discretionary conduct is not confined to the policy or planning level'.[70] Indeed, as the Court explained in *Gaubert v United States*, a case challenging regulation of a savings and loan association:

> If the routine or frequent nature of a decision were sufficient to remove an otherwise discretionary act from the scope of the exception, then countless policy-based decisions by regulators exercising day-to-day supervisory authority would be actionable. This is not the rule of our cases.[71]

Often, the key to determining the applicability of the discretionary function exception lies in the language of federal laws, regulations or directives governing the government's conduct. By definition, government standards that impose general responsibilities but leave discretion as to how a federal employee is to accomplish his or her task are covered by the discretionary function exception. In order for directives to deprive an employee of discretion and hence render the conduct subject to suit, there must be 'no element of judgment or choice' and the employee must have 'no rightful option but to adhere to the directive'.[72] Thus, because under the Supremacy Clause[73] state law cannot control federal decision-making, only federal directives will be considered for determining whether a federal official possesses the requisite discretion. Nor can the discretionary function exception be avoided by arguing that the agency lacks discretion to breach a duty imposed by state negligence law. As the United States Court of Appeals for the Ninth Circuit explained, 'Such a rule would collapse the discretionary function inquiry into the basic issue of negligence'.[74]

Properly applied, the discretionary function exception serves a vital role, ensuring that government decision-makers are free to balance competing policy considerations without the threat of tort liability based upon judicial second-guessing. Sloppy application of the exception can lead to either the failure to achieve this goal or to the use of the exception as an improper shield against negligence in the administration of government programmes. Key to the correct application of the discretionary function exception is the careful identification of the challenged conduct. The Supreme Court's decision in *Berkovitz v United States* is instructive.[75] The parents of a child who had contracted polio from taking oral polio vaccine sued the United States, alleging that the government had been negligent in licensing the manufacturer to make the vaccine and in approving the release of the lot from which their child was vaccinated. The Court analysed each component of the plaintiffs' claim, finding that claims that the government failed to determine whether the manufacturer had complied with mandatory licensing standards were not barred by the discretionary function exception. A claim that the government had erred in its determination might be barred by the exception, however, if it involved policy judgment rather than merely application of objective scientific criteria.[76] Additionally, the Court held that the plaintiffs' allegation that the release of the vaccine violated the government's policy of testing all lots of vaccine for safety survived a motion to dismiss, allowing discovery and fact development on whether the alleged policy was in fact mandatory.

Thus, in order to determine whether a claim will be barred by the discretionary function test, one must ascertain whether the actions upon which the claim actually is based involved discretionary decisions based on considerations of public policy. In *Fischer Brothers Sales, Inc. v United*

States,[77] for example, Chilean grape growers claimed that the Food and Drug Administration banned import of their grapes based upon negligent laboratory inspection, causing economic losses. The United States Court of Appeals for the Third Circuit held that the losses were caused not by the negligent inspection, but by the discretionary decision to impose the ban, and dismissed the claim.

Other key exceptions to the FTCA include claims arising out of 'assault, battery, false imprisonment, false arrest, malicious prosecution, abuse of process, libel, slander, misrepresentation, deceit or interference with contract rights'.[78] There is, however, an exception to this 'intentional tort' exception for claims arising out of assault, battery, false imprisonment, false arrest, abuse of process, or malicious prosecution by investigative or law enforcement officers.

Nowhere is the interplay between the Supreme Court and Congress more dramatically displayed than in the area of claims against individual government employees. In *Westfall v Erwin*,[79] the Supreme Court slashed the immunity of federal employees for common law torts arising out of their official actions. Prior to the *Westfall* decision, it was widely understood that federal employees enjoyed absolute immunity from common law tort claims as long as they were acting within the scope of their employment.[80] In *Westfall*, however, the Supreme Court held for the first time that absolute immunity was available only if 'the challenged conduct is within the outer perimeter of an official's duties and "is discretionary in nature"'.[81]

By adding the requirement that a federal employee's actions be 'discretionary in nature,' the Court significantly restricted the previously recognised scope of absolute immunity for common law torts. At the same time, however, the Supreme Court invited Congress to review by legislation the standard it had adopted. The Court stated that 'Congress is in the best position to provide guidance for the complex and often highly empirical inquiry into whether absolute immunity is warranted in a particular context'.[82] The Court added that 'legislated standards governing the immunity of federal employees involved in state law tort actions would be useful'.[83]

Within 10 months, Congress responded to the Court's invitation by enacting legislation to overturn the *Westfall* decision. The legislation is officially titled the Federal Employees Liability Reform and Tort Compensation Act of 1988 but is known, for obvious reasons, as the Westfall Act. The Westfall Act restores the absolute immunity of government employees for common law torts arising from acts within the scope of their employment by requiring claimants in such cases to proceed exclusively against the United States under the FTCA. It is important to note, however, that this provision does not apply to claims alleging constitutional violations against government employees.

Damage Remedies for Constitutional Violations

As noted above, the United States has not waived sovereign immunity for constitutional violations, and thus cannot be sued for damages for such violations. Nor is there a general statutory authorisation for liability of individual federal government employees for violations of constitutional rights.[84] Although a party may seek injunctive relief to protect against continuing prospective constitutional violations, there may be cases where individuals have suffered serious constitutional deprivations for which injunctive relief provides no remedy. It was in precisely such a case, *Bivens v Six Unknown Federal Narcotics Agents*,[85] involving a warrantless and destructive search of the claimant's home, that the Supreme Court recognised for the first time a right to recover money damages from government employees personally for the violation of one's constitutional rights. In a decision reflecting the sharp disagreement over the role of the courts, the majority held that federal courts' jurisdiction over questions of federal law carried with it the ability to fashion a damage remedy for the violation of constitutional rights. The dissenters (Burger CJ, Black J, Blackmun J) argued strenuously that the creation of such a remedy was a matter for congressional determination beyond the power of the Court, with Chief Justice Burger going so far as to propose a remedial scheme for Congressional consideration.[86]

Although *Bivens* arose in the context of the Fourth Amendment, nothing in the opinion limits the availability of a damages remedy for constitutional violations of the Fourth Amendment, and indeed the Court has extended the damages remedy to violations of the due process clause of the Fifth Amendment,[87] the Eighth Amendment,[88] and implicitly the First Amendment.[89] Governmental actions can give rise to both common law and constitutional claims. The courts have made clear, however, that artful pleading may not transform mere negligence into a constitutional violation. As the Supreme Court explained in *Daniels v Williams*:

> Our Constitution deals with the large concerns of the governors and the governed, but it does not purport to supplant traditional tort law in laying down rules of conduct to regulate liability for injuries that attend living together in society.[90]

The *Bivens* Court did recognise two important exceptions to the right to recover money damages for violations of constitutional rights, however. A money remedy should not be inferred where there are 'special factors counselling hesitation' or an 'explicit congressional declaration' that money damages may not be awarded.[91] These 'escape valves' have provided fertile ground for the ongoing debate regarding the role of the courts in creating remedies for constitutional violations, and not always with logically consistent results.

There is no direct parallel between constitutional tort actions in the United States and damages claims in England under common law and the Human Rights Act. In part, this is because the American Bill of Rights is phrased in the negative, as a restriction upon government power, rather than as conveying positive rights.[92] Nonetheless, the Supreme Court's determinations of when it will imply a constitutional cause of action are relevant both to the justiciability issue so crucial to English public tort law and to the question of when damages are thought necessary to provide just satisfaction for violations of Convention rights.

In *Carlson v Green*,[93] the Supreme Court determined that the existence of a statutory remedy under the FTCA was not a 'special factor counselling hesitation' against creation of a damages remedy for actions claimed to be in violation of a prisoner's Eighth Amendment right to be free from cruel and unusual punishment. In 1974, following the Court's decision in *Bivens*, Congress amended the FTCA to allow recovery for common law claims for intentional torts by law enforcement officers.[94] Reading the legislative history of this amendment as indicating that Congress intended to create a parallel remedy, the Court held that the availability of relief complemented but did not replace the *Bivens* remedy. The majority found support for its holding in four factors: the deterrent effect of a *Bivens* remedy, the presumed availability of punitive damages against individual defendants,[95] the availability of a jury trial in a Bivens action,[96] and the dependence of an FTCA remedy upon state law.[97] Thus, concluded the Court, the 'FTCA is not a sufficient protector of the citizens' constitutional rights, and without a clear congressional mandate we cannot hold that Congress relegated respondent exclusively to the FTCA remedy.'[98] In dissent, Chief Justice Burger railed:

> Until today, I had thought that *Bivens* was limited to those circumstances in which a civil rights claimant had no other effective remedy. Now it would seem that the implications of a *Bivens*-type remedy is permissible even though a victim of an unlawful official action may be fully recompensed under an existing statutory scheme. I have difficulty believing that the Court has thought through, and intends the natural consequences, of this test; I cannot escape the conclusion that in future cases the Court will be obliged to retreat from the language of today's decision.[99]

Indeed, only three years later the pendulum had begun to swing back. In *Bush v Lucas*,[100] the Court refused to infer a *Bivens* remedy for alleged constitutional violations arising out of the federal employment relationship, which is protected by a comprehensive system of statutory safeguards. In reaching this conclusion, however, the Court seemed to engage in a legislative type decision-making:

> The question is not what remedy the court should provide for a wrong that would otherwise go unredressed. It is whether an elaborate remedial system that has been constructed step by step, with careful attention to conflicting policy considerations, should be augmented by the creation of a new judicial remedy for the constitutional violation at issue. The question obviously cannot be answered simply by noting that existing remedies do not provide complete relief for the claimant. The policy judgment should be informed by a thorough understanding of the existing regulatory structure and the respective costs and benefits that would result from the addition of another remedy for violations of employees' First Amendment rights.[101]

In *Schweicker v Chilicky*,[102] the Court went even further, holding that Congress, in enacting the comprehensive Social Security review system, provided the only permissible remedies for wrongs resulting from the denial of Social Security benefits. Writing for a 6–3 majority in an opinion that sparked strong dissent, Justice O'Connor noted:

> The concept of 'special factors counselling hesitation in the absence of affirmative action by Congress' has proved to include an appropriate judicial deference to indications that congressional inaction has not been inadvertent. When the design of a government program suggests that Congress has provided what it considers adequate remedial mechanisms for constitutional violations that may occur in the course of its administration, we have not created additional Bivens remedies.[103]

Thus, under this decision, even where a statutory remedy provides undeniably incomplete relief, a *Bivens* damage remedy may not be inferred. The majority did not discuss the apparent incongruity between this holding and the ruling in *Carlson v Green*, eight years before.

In its most recent decision addressing the applicability of *Bivens, Correctional Services Corp v Malesko*,[104] the Supreme Court has completed the circle. In a sharply divided 5–4 decision, the Court refused to apply *Bivens* to provide a remedy for constitutional violations against a private corporation running a prison under contract with the federal Bureau of Prisons. The philosophical divide of the Court is demonstrated clearly by the framing of the question. The majority characterised the decision as a refusal to extend *Bivens* to new contexts, and held that such an extension would not serve the deterrent function of individual liability. By contrast, the dissent stated that 'the question presented in this case is whether the Court should create an exception to the straightforward application of *Bivens* and *Carlson*, not whether we should extend our cases beyond their "core premise"'.[105]

The *Malesko* decision may well reflect a fundamental hostility to any damages remedy for constitutional violations. Justice Scalia, joined by Justice Thomas, noted in his concurrence,

> Bivens is a relic of the heady days in which this Court assumed common-law powers to create causes of action – decreeing them to be implied by the mere existence of a statutory or constitutional prohibition.[106]

At this juncture, however, the basic principle of individual liability for violations of constitutional rights is so well entrenched in the nation's jurisprudence that any change in the law is likely to be seen only at the margins.

Thus, at a time when English courts are opening the courthouse doors to claims for damages based upon a far broader range of government decisions, the United States Supreme Court is clearly signalling its desire to pull back from the implication of causes of action, both in the constitutional sphere and in the interpretation of statutes.[107]

Striving for Balance: Separation of Powers and Deference

At the crux of the debate over damage remedies against public authorities lies a fundamental issue of separation of powers. Although the doctrine of separation of powers is not as explicit in British legal tradition as it is in the United States, there can be no doubt that both countries subscribe to the notion that legislators should make the law, the executive should administer and enforce the law, and the judiciary should interpret and apply the law in accordance with the expressed intent of the legislature.[108] Within this broad structure, however, there is room for many gradations of judicial involvement. The key element of the balance between the branches of government must be an assessment of whether the judiciary should be involved at all, that is, whether the question is justiciable, and if it is, what deference should be given to the discretion of the legislative and executive branches.

Until the passage of the Human Rights Act, the concept of parliamentary sovereignty clearly cabined the courts' role in reviewing legislation. Lord Irvine of Lairg described the situation as being one in which 'the courts approach all legislation on the well-founded presumption that Parliament intends to legislate consistently with [the] principles [of the common law]'.[109] Under the Human Rights Act, English courts still cannot invalidate legislation, but they are expressly instructed to interpret legislation in conformity with Convention rights 'so far as possible'. In the course of this 'writing down' of legislation, it is inevitable that courts will be called upon to make policy judgments. Indeed, one of the most frequent objections in the debates upon the Human Rights Act was that the act would give unelected judges unprecedented powers to shape the law on fundamental issues.[110]

Despite the very serious concerns voiced prior to the effective date of the Human Rights Act, there has been little negative comment about the actual performance of the judiciary in interpreting and applying the Convention rights. This may be due in part to the fact that the House of Lords has adopted a deferential standard of review. Applying an objective test, courts will look to see if the decision-maker could reasonably have determined that the interference with a Convention right was necessary to achieve one or more of the legitimate aims recognised by the Convention and, if so, whether the action taken was proportionate.[111] The first arm of this test is similar to the traditional *Wednesbury* unreasonableness: it requires only that the decision-maker could reasonably have believed that the interference was necessary to the fulfilment of a legitimate aim. The second arm of the test, proportionality, is more far reaching; it may require the court to look beyond the rationality of the decision to assess the balance struck and the relative weight given to the factors under consideration. As Lord Bingham has stressed, however, this is not a shift to merit review, merely a more searching enquiry.[112]

Just as in the United States many cases are arguable as both constitutional and common law claims, so in England, many cases may be arguable as both Human Rights Act and common law tort claims. The Supreme Court underscored the distinction between common law torts and constitutional violations by holding that a claimant's allegation that an employer acted with malice in providing a negative reference that impinged upon the employee's ability to find suitable employment.[113] As the Supreme Court explained in *Baker v McCollan*, 443 U.S. 137, 146 (1979):

> Section 1983 imposes liability for violations of rights protected by the Constitution, not for violations of duties of care arising out of tort law. Remedy for the latter type

of injury must be sought in state court under traditional tort law principles. Just as medical malpractice does not become a constitutional violation merely because the victim is a prisoner, false imprisonment does not become a violation of the Fourteenth Amendment merely because the defendant is a state official.

An interesting example of the intersection of rights-based claims and duty-based claims arises in the context of prisoners' suits challenging the conditions of confinement. In the United States, common law claims that the prison authorities were negligent in housing an inmate with another inmate known to pose a particular risk of violence are routinely dismissed as falling within the discretionary function exception of the FTCA.[114] The very same facts, however, may well state a cause of action for violation of the Eighth Amendment's prohibition against cruel and unusual punishment if the claimant can demonstrate deliberate indifference to a substantial risk of harm.[115] The Supreme Court has defined deliberate indifference as requiring a showing that the government official was subjectively aware of the risk.[116]

In England, a prisoner confined under lawful authority cannot recover for segregation or other conditions of his confinement on grounds of false imprisonment, although it may be possible to recover for negligence if a breach of the duty of care is established.[117] Article 3 of the ECHR secures the right to be free of inhuman and degrading treatment, and suits based upon conditions of confinement are precisely the type of case for which the Human Rights Act was intended. The Strasbourg court has incorporated some duty-based concepts into its Article 3 jurisprudence, however, holding that:

> For a positive obligation [to protect life] to arise it must be established that the authorities knew or ought to have known at the time of the existence of a real and immediate threat to the life of an identified individual from the criminal acts of a third person and that they failed to take measures within the scope of their powers which, judged reasonably, might have been expected to avoid that risk.[118]

The Strasbourg court has recognised that there should be level of gravity in order for governmental actions to implicate the ECHR. For example, 'ill-treatment must attain a minimum level of severity if it is to fall within the scope of Article 3'.[119] Similarly, not every nuisance involving the home should trigger Article 8.[120] Although one may argue over whether the line has been drawn in the right place, the Supreme Court's admonition in *Daniels v Williams* is equally apt when considering the balance between common law torts and Convention rights. The Human Rights Act is intended to protect fundamental rights, not to substitute for traditional tort law in regulating 'liability for injuries that attend living together in society'.

Judicial deference has two faces in the context of common law tort claims against public authorities in England. The first is seen in the somewhat ill defined concept of justiciability. While judges have not hesitated to criticise the policy/operational distinction as a basis for determining whether a duty of care should be implied, the attempted substitution of the concept of justiciability as a limiting principle is not without its problems. The courts have been unable to define in any concrete fashion the characteristics that will render a matter non-justiciable, although a number of judges have referred to matters involving a weighing of competing social or fiscal concerns. It is unclear how the concept of justiciability differs in substance from the much maligned policy/operational distinction, and for this reason, it is subject to the same criticisms.

Inherent in the concept of justiciability is a notion of judicial restraint imposed by the separation of powers. It is precisely because matters involve the weighing of competing social and fiscal concerns that they lie within the province of Parliament, or the executive departments charged with carrying out the mandates of Parliament. Whether courts will continue to exercise this self-imposed restraint in common law torts when, under the Human Rights Act, they are re-assessing the balance struck by the legislative and executive branches remains to be seen.

The second aspect of judicial deference lies in the substantive test applied to those cases deemed justiciable. Again, the tests employed by English courts allow a reasonable amount of deference. In negligence claims, deference comes into play both in determining the existence of a duty of care and in determining breach if a duty of care is found. In the first instance, even after *Barrett*, the *Caparo* tests of foreseeability, proximity and whether implication of a duty would be fair, just and reasonable allow for consideration of such issues as the delicacy and complexity of the decision and the potentially chilling effect of the spectre of litigating such complex decisions.

The case of *Palmer v Tees Health Authority*,[121] is instructive. The plaintiff sued the health authority, alleging negligence in its treatment of a mentally ill individual who subsequently raped and murdered the plaintiff's daughter. The Court of Appeal held that *Osman* precluded its determination on a strike-out motion that it would not be fair, just and reasonable to imply a cause of action, but that it was still free to consider the issue of proximity on strike-out. As part of that consideration the court thought it relevant to ask what the defendant could have done to avoid the danger. Finding that the plaintiff's daughter was not identifiable as a likely victim and that there did not appear to be any legal and reasonable action that the authority could have taken to minimise the risk to the child, the court held that there was no duty of care because of a lack of proximity.

The logic of the Court of Appeal in concluding that it could not consider one aspect of the *Caparo* test on a strike-out, but could consider another is questionable. In light of the Strasbourg court's retrenchment in *Z v UK*, the distinction, if it ever existed, is irrelevant. Nonetheless, the *Palmer* decision, taken together with the innovative approach utilised in *S v Gloucestershire County Council*, indicates that English courts will use appropriate procedural methods to reach an early termination of cases in which the record indicates that there is no real prospect of success.

With regard to the question of breach, the standard itself incorporates a measure of deference. Under the *Bolam*[122] test, the duty of care is only the exercise of ordinary skills of an ordinary competent person in similar circumstances. Proper application of this test should ensure that liability is not imposed based upon mere second-guessing or differences of opinion.[123]

This is all to the good. While England does not suffer from the glut of litigation that engulfs American courts, there can be no doubt that requiring a trial in cases which meet the standards of Civil Procedure Rule 3(1) is a waste of resources for both parties and the courts. This is particularly true given the lack of clarity inherent in the justiciability standard. For the most part, English courts appear to have struck a sound balance that allows plaintiffs a remedy in appropriate cases without unduly constricting the efficient operation of government.

Federal courts in the United States face a somewhat different picture with regard to common law tort claims. Because the source of law for common law torts under the FTCA is state law, federal judges adjudicating claims against the federal government are not at liberty to expand upon the substantive law they are applying. Moreover, Congress, in enacting the discretionary function exception, stipulated that the courts lacked jurisdiction to entertain cases based upon a discretionary function or duty. While certainly there may be a question of whether a particular claim is based upon a discretionary function or duty, those cases which do are beyond the courts' purview. Despite these restrictions, FTCA judgments against the government in 1999 totalled $332 million.

In the constitutional arena, the courts have greater latitude. As we have seen above, the Supreme Court's view of its proper role in creating remedies for constitutional violations has varied over time. Clearly, the current Court takes a more narrow approach than some of its predecessors. The *Bivens* case, which first recognised a damage claim for constitutional violations was decided in 1971, when the majority of the Supreme Court held a more expansive view of its role. At the time, the majority doubted that the courts would see many such claims. Contrary to the *Bivens* majority's belief,[124] Justice Blackmun was indeed correct in predicting that the Court's creation of a damages remedy for constitutional torts would 'open [..] the door for another avalanche of new federal cases'.[125] In the thirty years since *Bivens* was decided, many thousands of federal employees have been subjected to suits based upon claims of constitutional violations. Significantly, only about 100 of these suits have resulted in final judgments against individual government employees.

Suits against individual federal employees are particularly disruptive of government operations. As the Supreme Court explained:

> Claims frequently run against the innocent as well as the guilty at a cost not only to the defendant officials, but to society as a whole. These social costs include the expenses of litigation, the diversion of official energy from pressing public issues, and the deterrence of able citizens from acceptance of public office. Finally, there is the danger that fear of being sued will 'dampen the ardour of all but the most resolute, or the most irresponsible [public officials], in the unflinching discharge of their duties'.[126]

Thus, in order to balance the rights of those who have genuinely been deprived of constitutional rights by government employees with the need to protect government employees from unfounded and disruptive suits, courts have developed immunity doctrines specially adapted to constitutional tort litigation.

Most government employees are protected by a qualified immunity from suit. As originally formulated, the qualified immunity defence required a showing of both 'objective' and 'subjective' good faith. In *Harlow*,[127] the Supreme Court held that the subjective element of the good faith test was incompatible with the precept that insubstantial suits against government employees should not proceed to trial. An employee's subjective intent could easily be cast as a disputed fact question, thus precluding disposition of the case by summary judgment. Moreover, as the Court noted:

> Judicial inquiry into subjective motivation... may entail broad-ranging discovery and the deposing of numerous persons, including an official's professional colleagues. Inquiries of this kind can be peculiarly disruptive of effective government.

In order to maintain the proper balance between claimants' rights and the proper functioning of government, the Supreme Court formulated a new test based solely upon objective factors. Under this new test, government employees performing discretionary functions generally are shielded from liability for civil damages insofar as their conduct does not violate clearly established statutory or constitutional rights of which a reasonable person would have known.[128]

The Court stressed that reliance upon the objective reasonableness of an official's conduct, measured by reference to clearly established law, should permit the resolution of insubstantial claims on summary judgment. Indeed, the Court instructed that discovery should not be allowed until the threshold issue of immunity is resolved.[129]

As the Supreme Court explained in *Anderson v Creighton*,[130] '[t]he operation of this [qualified immunity] standard... depends upon the level of generality at which the relevant "legal rule" is to be identified'. Reasoning that the 'clearly established rights' standard would be meaningless if it were applied on a general, abstract level, the Court held that a claimant may overcome an official's qualified immunity only if, in light of pre-existing law, the unlawfulness of the specific action upon which the claimant's claims are based was apparent. To do otherwise

> would destroy 'the balance that our cases strike between the interests in vindication of citizens' constitutional rights and in public officials' effective performance of their duties' by making it impossible for officials 'reasonably [to] anticipate when their conduct may give rise to liability for damages'.[131]

The operation of the qualified immunity standard is well demonstrated by the Supreme Court's opinion in *Wilson v Layne*.[132] In that case, representatives of the media accompanied federal law enforcement officers who, pursuant to warrant, searched the petitioners' home for their son, a dangerous fugitive. The Wilson's son was not at their home, and after a protective search of the home, the officers departed. During the course of the search, media photographers took several photographs, which were never published. The Wilsons sued the law enforcement officers, alleging that the officers' actions in bringing members of the media to observe and record the attempted execution of the arrest warrant violated their Fourth Amendment rights.

In ruling on the defendants' defence of qualified immunity, the Court explained:

> A court evaluating a claim of qualified immunity must first determine whether the plaintiff has alleged the deprivation of an actual constitutional right at all, and if so, proceed to determine whether that right was clearly established at the time of the alleged violation.[133]

The Court weighed the strong privacy interest in the sanctity of one's home against the proffered justifications for inclusion of the media – good public relations for the police and the need for accurate reporting on police issues. Finding the reasons insufficient for the intrusion, the Court held that it is a violation of the Fourth Amendment to bring members of the media or other third parties into a home during the execution of a warrant when the presence of the third parties is not in aid of the execution of the warrant.[134]

The Court then turned to the qualified immunity analysis. Surveying the body of law addressing this issue, the Court found that there were no cases of controlling authority in the petitioners' jurisdiction nor was there a consensus of persuasive authority such that a reasonable officer would have believed that taking members of the media along was unlawful. Rather, the law on the issue of 'media ride-alongs' was at the time of the incident 'at best undeveloped'.[135] Moreover, the court noted that between the time of the incident and its decision a split had developed among the federal courts of appeal. 'If judges thus disagree on a constitutional question, it is unfair to subject police to money damages for picking the losing side of the controversy'.[136]

Accordingly, the Court held that the law enforcement officials were entitled to qualified immunity. The case was then remanded for action on the FTCA claim for the common law claim for invasion of privacy, which was ultimately settled. This resolution reveals the complex interplay between constitutional and common law torts. The Supreme Court clarified substantive Fourth Amendment law, but did not penalise the individual police officers involved for taking action that was not clearly illegal at the time, and the plaintiffs were compensated by the government for their common law claims.

The concerns underlying the qualified immunity doctrine do not appear to carry much force in England. In *Barrett*, for example, Lord Hutton quickly dismissed the fear that potential liability could cause public authorities to adopt cautious and defensive practices.[137] One significant reason for the difference in approach may lie in the existence of public authority's vicarious liability, a protection which is unavailable to American government employees in constitutional cases. The more direct parallel may be seen in English cases seeking exemplary damages for misfeasance in public office, which require proof of subjective malicious intent.

Conclusion

The United States and England share a closely linked legal heritage, as is reflected by the similarities in basic elements of governmental liability. The law of the two countries is diverging somewhat as England opens its courts to more claims of negligence by public authorities. At the federal level in the United States, no such liberalisation is occurring, although on a municipal level there is a movement to broader liability. Although there are clear benefits to the English approach in terms of deterrence of careless practices and the fairness of compensating those who have suffered loss, some of the recent decisions may leave the door open to a diversion of public resources, as public authorities devote increasing time and money to litigation.

Notes

1 The legal systems of Scotland and Northern Ireland are separate, and in many respects different, from that of England and Wales. The vast majority of cases dealing with liability of public authorities have arisen in English courts, and hence this paper focuses upon liability of public authorities in England. The substance of the common law issues involved is essentially the same in all three systems, and the Human Rights Act 1998 applies to all three systems. Under the terms of the Scotland Act 1998, legislation enacted by the Scottish Parliament that is found to be incompatible with Convention rights can be invalidated, but as explained below legislation enacted by the Parliament of the United Kingdom cannot.
2 *Mersey Docks and Harbour Board Trustees v Gibbs*, [1866] LR 1 HL 93.
3 See, for example, *Hammersmith Railway Co v Brand*, [1869] LR 4 HL 171.
4 HRA {19.
5 HRA {6.
6 HRA {7(1)(b).
7 HRA {4(2).
8 HRA {3.
9 HRA {2.
10 See, for example, *Guardian*, 'Power Shifts to the Judges,' Sept. 11, 2000.
11 HRA { 8(4).
12 HRA { 8(3).
13 [1970] AC 1004.
14 See *Barrett v Enfield LBC* [1999] 3 WLR 79; *Phelps v Hillingdon LBC* [2000] 3 WLR 776, discussed *infra*.
15 [1990] 2 AC 605.
16 [1996] AC 923.
17 Ibid at 932.
18 Ibid at 938.
19 Ibid at 933.
20 *Lonrho plc v Tebbit*, [1991] 4 AER 973 (High Court); affirmed [1992] 4 AER 280.
21 *Anns v Merton LBC*, [1978] AC 728, 754.
22 *Hill v Chief Constable of West Yorkshire* [1989] AC 53.
23 *X and Others v Bedfordshire County Council* [1995] 2 AC 633.
24 ECtHR, May 10, 2001.
25 [1999] 3 WLR 79.

26 Civil Procedure Rules, Part 3, Rule 3.4(2)(a).
27 *X and Others v Bedfordshire County Council* [1995] 2 AC 633, 731.
28 Ibid at 747–48.
29 [1970] AC 1004.
30 *X*, 2 AC at 734–35.
31 *X*, 2 AC at 738.
32 See *Caparo Industries plc. v Dickman*, [1990] 2 AC 605, 617–18.
33 *X*, 2 AC at 739.
34 *Osman v UK* [1999] 29 E.H.R.R. 245.
35 *Osman v Ferguson* [1993] 4 A.E.R. 344, citing *Hill v Chief Constable of West Yorkshire* [1988] 2 AER 238.
36 Ibid. at para. 150.
37 Ibid. at para. 151.
38 Ibid. at para. 138.
39 Somewhat surprisingly, the Strasbourg court did not base this ruling on Article 13, which by its terms appears to undermine a claim of immunity by requiring an effective remedy notwithstanding that the violation has been committed by persons acting in an official capacity. Instead, the court merely held that the Article 13 claim was subsumed into the Article 6 claim.
40 *James and Others v UK*, A 98 (1986) para. 81.
41 *Osman* at para. 135.
42 Ibid. at para. 151.
43 Cf. *Powell & Rayner v UK*, A 172 (1990).
44 *United States v Gaubert*, 499 U.S. at 327.
45 [1999] 3 AER 193.
46 Ibid. at 573.
47 Ibid. at 574.
48 Ibid. at para. 100 (citations omitted).
49 [2001] Fam. 313.
50 [2001] Fam. at 338.
51 [2001] Fam. at 340.
52 489 U.S. 189 (1989).
53 242 F.3d 905 (10th Cir. 2001), *cert.* denied 122 S.Ct. 543 (2001).
54 [2001] 2 AC 619.
55 See, for example, *WB v Matula*, 67 F.3d 484 (3d Cir. 1995); *Walker v District of Columbia*, 969 F.Supp. 794 (D.D.C. 1997).
56 526 U.S. 629 (1999).
57 For an alternative view, see Markesinis and Stewart, 'Tortious Liability for Negligent Misdiagnosis of Learning Disabilities: A Comparative Study of English and American Law', 36 TxILJ 427 (2001).
58 See *R v Secretary of States for Transport ex p. Factortame Ltd* [2001] AC 524 (government liable for breach of Community directive where the directive was intended to confer benefits upon individuals, breach is sufficiently serious, and there is a direct causal link between breach and damages).
59 *Three Rivers DC v Bank of England* [2001] AER 513.
60 This paper only addresses liability of the federal government. State law is discussed only tangentially based upon its incorporation as the choice of law under the Federal Tort Claims Act.
61 *Smith v United States*, 507 U.S. 197, 203 (1993).
62 28 USC 1346 (b).
63 28 USC §2679(a); *FDIC v Meyer*, 510 U.S. 308 (1991).

64 See, for example, *United States v Muniz*, 374 U.S. 150, 153 (1963).
65 *FDIC v Meyer*, 510 U.S. 471 (1994).
66 *Kosak v United States*, 465 U.S. 848, 858 (1984).
67 28 USC §2680(a).
68 *Gaubert v United States*, 499 U.S. 315, 325 (1991).
69 *Berkovitz v United States*, 486 U.S. 531, 544 (1988).
70 Ibid. at 325.
71 *Gaubert*, 499 U.S. at 334.
72 *Gaubert*, 499 U.S. at 322.
73 United States Constitution, Article VI, cl 2.
74 *Kennewick Irrigation District v United States*, 880 F.2d 1018, 1030 (9th Cir. 1989).
75 *Berkovitz*, 486 U.S. 531.
76 Ibid., 486 U.S. at 544–45.
77 46 F.3d 279 (3d Cir. 1995) (en banc).
78 28 USC §2680(h).
79 484 U.S. 292 (1988).
80 See for example *Barr v Matteo*, 360 U.S. 564 (1959) (plurality opinion). See also *Howard v Lyons*, 360 U.S. 593 (1959).
81 484 U.S. at 296.
82 484 U.S. at 296.
83 Ibid.
84 Title 42 USC §1983 provides a cause of action for constitutional deprivations committed by individuals acting under colour of *state* law, but this does not apply to federal actors. Federal officials may be liable under other civil rights statutes that provide a cause of action for discriminatory actions, but these generally require a showing of class based discrimination. See for example, 42 USC §§1985, 1986.
85 403 U.S. 388 (1971).
86 403 U.S. at 422–23.
87 *Davis v Passman*, 442 U.S. 228 (1979).
88 *Carlson v Green*, 446 U.S. 14 (1980).
89 *Crawford-El v Britton*, 523 U.S. 574 (1999).
90 474 U.S. 327, 332 (1986).
91 *Bivens*, 403 U.S. at 396–97.
92 *See DeShaney v Winnebago County Department of Social Services*, 489 U.S. 189 (1989), discussed *infra*.
93 446 U.S. 14 (1980).
94 28 USC §2680(h).
95 Punitive damages are not available under the FTCA. 28 USC §2674.
96 Under the FTCA, fact findings are reserved to the judge. 28 USC §2402.
97 28 USC §1346(b).
98 *Carlson v Green*, 446 U.S. at 23.
99 Ibid. at 31 (Burger CJ dissenting) (citations omitted).
100 462 U.S. 367 (1983).
101 462 U.S. at 488.
102 487 U.S. 412 (1988).
103 Ibid. at 423.
104 122 S.Ct. 516 (2001).
105 *Malesko*, 122 S.Ct. at 521 (Stevens J dissenting).
106 *Malesko*, 122 S.Ct. at 524.
107 See, for example, *Alexander v Sandoval*, 532 U.S. 275 (2001).

108 See, for example, *In Re S(FC) v In Re S & Others*, 2002 WL 237130 (March 14, 2002).
109 Irvine, 'Sovereignty in Comparative Perspective: Constitutionalism in Britain and America', 76 NYULR 1, 16.
110 See, for example, House of Commons Hansard Debates 16 Feb. 1998, cols. 788–790.
111 *R (Daly) v Secretary of State for the Home Department* [2001] 2 WLR 1622.
112 Ibid. at para. 28.
113 *Siegert v Gilley* 500 U.S. 226 (1991). *Accord DeShaney v Winnebago County Dep't of Social Servs.*, 489 U.S. 189, 203 (1989) (failure to protect from harm caused by third party does not implicate due process); *Brower v Inyo County*, 489 U.S. 593, 596 (1989) (only intentional conduct rises to the level of a seizure under the Fourth Amendment).
114 *Cohen v United States*, 151 F.3d 1338 (11th Cir. 1998).
115 *Estelle v Gamble*, 429 U.S. 97, 106 (1976) (only deliberate indifference to serious medical needs, and not negligence such as the mere failure to provide medical care, implicates Eighth Amendment prohibition against cruel and unusual punishment).
116 *Farmer v Brennan*, 511 U.S. 825, 829 (1994).
117 *R v Deputy Governor of Parkhurst Prison ex p. Hague* [1992] 1 AC 58.
118 *Keenan v UK*, 33 EHRR 38, para. 89.
119 Ibid. at para. 108.
120 But see *Hatton v UK* [2002] 34 EHRR 1; *Marcic v Thames Water Ltd.* [2002] EWCA Civ 64 CA.
121 2000 PIQR P1 CA.
122 *Bolam v Friern Hospital Management Co.* [1957] 1 WLR 582.
123 See *Phelps*, 2 AC at 655.
124 403 U.S. at 391 n.4.
125 403 U.S. at 430.
126 *Harlow v Fitzgerald*, 457 U.S. 800, 814 (1982)(citations omitted).
127 457 U.S. 800, 814 (1982).
128 *Harlow*, 437 U.S. at 818.
129 Ibid.
130 483 U.S. 635, 639 (1987).
131 Ibid. at 639 (citations omitted).
132 526 U.S. 603 (1999).
133 Ibid. at 609.
134 Ibid. at 614.
135 Ibid. at 617.
136 Ibid.
137 2 FLR at 463.

Chapter 7

Antipodean Perspectives on Child Welfare Tort Claims against Public Authorities

*Geoff McLay**

Introduction

Like common law courts, both New Zealand and Australian Courts have had to deal with difficult civil claims arising out of child neglect or abuse.[1] This is especially so when those claims involve allegations that the neglect or abuse was either perpetrated or could have been prevented by those caring for or educating children on behalf of the community. This paper deals with the small proportion of cases that reach the courtroom and the legal theories that courts have employed, or at least might employ, to resolve these cases. In *S v Attorney-General* Blanchard J was hopeful that imposing liability on the New Zealand Government for acts of foster parents might have a beneficial impact on the quality of foster care:[2]

> This result may provide an incentive for the State to take even greater precautions in the future for the protection of children in its care by way of vetting and monitoring of foster parents. We do not see that as likely to affect the Department's trust in people who take on this role to an extent which has an adverse impact on the relationship.
>
> If those efforts are successful even in only a few cases in preventing or limiting abuse of a child, there may well be savings in social costs of the kind to which Ms Cooper drew attention, to which we would add the costs of accident compensation claims by sexual abuse victims now that all emerging cases of child abuse are covered under the current legislation.

One suspects that the real story is elsewhere, and that rather than relying on the tort system to provide the correct incentives to social welfare agencies to prevent harm occurring to children, or to compensate or rehabilitate victims of abuse, the solution to either issue lies outside the courtroom, especially given the reality that the *S* case involved allegations of over 30 years ago. New Zealand and Australian courts have employed similar methodologies, the law of negligence and vicarious liability, but have sometimes reached different

* Senior Lecturer in Law, Victoria University of Wellington.

results to those reached in the United Kingdom and Canada in resolving neglect and abuse cases bought before them. In New Zealand it has been held that it is possible to bring negligence actions against care and protection agencies for failing to protect children, at least in some circumstances, while the New South Wales courts have at least contemplated such actions but have emphasised the difficulty in establishing that such a duty has been breached. New Zealand courts appear to have adopted an expansive view of vicarious liability that perhaps accords with that adopted in Canada and maybe in the United Kingdom while the High Court of Australia has more recently adopted a more sceptical approach to vicarious liability.

A number of antipodean cases have considered the ability of parents to complain about the removal of the children on the suspicion that those children had been abused. Although perhaps a little tangential to the main topic of this book, the paper will outline the holding of the High Court of Australia in *Sullivan v Moody*,[3] which essentially denies that welfare authorities owe affected parents a duty of care. While there is some similarity between the litigation being conducted in Australia and New Zealand there are, of course, a number of important differences. In Australia, much debate over the obligations of the Federal Government has related to claims brought by the 'stolen generation' of aboriginal children who were taken from their own communities to be placed in government-sponsored schools. Much of those cases depended upon the validity of the measures under which these removals were made. Somewhat bleakly, Australian courts have acknowledged the general validity of what was done (or at least accept that the actions were made within the relevant decision-maker's discretion), and have been unable to award compensation for what many perceived the principal wrong of having removed children in the first place. The *Enever*[4] doctrine under which the Federal Crown cannot be made liable for discretionary decisions of those granted a statutory discretion, has also been employed to hold that the Crown cannot be liable for the actions of appointed officials. In *Cubillo*, O'Loughlin J described the doctrine as follows:[5]

> As the law presently stands, the independent discretion rule represents a limitation upon the vicarious liability of the Commonwealth at common law for the torts of its servants. If an officer or employee of the Crown, acting in the course of his or her service under the authority of the Crown, commits a tort, the Crown will, *prima facie*, be liable, unless the officer or employee was exercising or fulfilling an independent duty or power. This principle of independent discretion, as originally enunciated in *Enever*, applies to any public officer with a discretion in the exercise of an independent legal duty. However, the employee does not have that necessary independent discretion if the employee is subject to the control of the relevant Minister.

Allegations of abuse cases like these, as *Williams*[6] and *Cubillo*,[7] often appear to be ways of getting around the general validity of what was done in the Commonwealth Government's name (and at least *Cubillo* was marred by the failure to plead the Government's obligation to prevent abuse).

Government Liability Downunder

Courts in both countries appear to be more willing to recognise that government bodies owe duties in exercising some, but certainly not all, discretionary powers or duties than Courts in the United Kingdom. Neither country followed the rather hard English line of early and mid-nineties cases such as *Murphy*[8] (if indeed that is properly treated as a government liability case), *Bedfordshire*,[9] or *Stovin*[10] that appeared to leave little scope for a general law of government liability.

New Zealand has been at the forefront of extending government liability, at least in relation to the liability of local councils for building inspections. The major feature of New Zealand courts' approach to government liability, at least under the leadership of Lord Cooke and even subsequently under Sir Ivor Richardson, was the development of common law duties that run parallel to statutory obligations. New Zealand Courts apparently do not see much merit in an independent tort of statutory duty.[11] At least in relation to Government inspection cases there appeared to be what was described by Lord Hoffmann in *Stovin* as a theory of 'general reliance'.[12] As the famous cases of *Hamlin*[13] established, New Zealanders are entitled to rely on their local councils to correctly inspect houses. Before the last year or so it might have been possible to argue that the principle was one of general application, but more recently we have been told by the Court of Appeal that the building cases are *sui generis* and that they do not stretch to such things as ship inspections.[14]

In Australia the story is similar, although not identical. In the last five years the High Court of Australia has produced an extraordinarily lengthy jurisprudence on the liability of government authorities, which has clearly established at least some instances where public authorities can be liable when exercising discretion. For example, in *Pyrenees Shire Council v Day*,[15] failure to properly enforce relevant fire prevention bylaws gave rise to a duty of care when the inevitable fire happened, since the neighbour had to rely on the Council doing its job. In *Brodie*,[16] the High Court of Australia, by majority accepted that the old common law rule which rendered immune roading authorities liable for failing to repair a road (nonfeasance) no longer ought to apply. In *Crimmins*,[17] the High Court of Australia accepted that an agency responsible for regulating waterfront employment owed a duty of care to stevedores employed to unload ships carrying asbestos.

While it is difficult to neatly summarise what the basis of Australian government liability is, there has been a recent focus at least in the High Court of Australia on citizens' peculiar vulnerability. But vulnerability and the Government's ability to protect citizens may be necessary requirements but are not sufficient to impose liability. In *Ryan*,[18] the High Court rejected the attempt to make the Government of New South Wales and a local council liable to those who had eaten oysters infected with hepatitis, even though both had reason to have foreseen that the oysters might have been polluted and had the ability to regulate for better safety checks.

What is common about the New Zealand and Australian law is that common law negligence has been employed to back fill the gap created by the non-recognition of rights created by statutes as enforceable private rights. The courts of neither country have been able to articulate a convincing justification imposing or not imposing liability on the Government. In *Prince*,[19] it was alleged that government social workers had failed to follow through statutory duties that required them to protect a child at risk. The majority of the New Zealand Court of Appeal held the social workers might owe a common law duty of care to the affected child. The Court analogised that since private sector professionals would be responsible for failure to live up to their duties, so ought public sector professionals. Richardson P wrote for the Court:[20]

> Like lawyers and doctors, social workers are professionals. At that triggering step (and at other steps) they should be expected to have shouldered willingly a standard of reasonable skill and care that their private sector counterparts were expected to discharge. And in the absence of any data as to potential claims based on the roles and responsibilities of the department and social workers under the 1974 Act, which was replaced eight years ago by a very different legislative scheme, it would be unwise to give any particular weight to the resource implications of allowing for a common law duty of care.

While private social workers clearly do provide a range of social services analogous to some of the things that public sector social workers do, they seldom exercise, at least in New Zealand, the kinds of intervention decisions that the New Zealand Court of Appeal found would potentially give rise to liability.

Accident Compensation – The New Zealand Peculiarity

Actions for Compensatory Damages for Abuse

Since 1975 all claims for compensatory damages resulting from personal injury by accident have been barred in New Zealand and been compensated to a greater or lesser extent by a State agency, the Accident Compensation Commission until 1982 and thereafter the Accident Compensation Corporation. The effect of an event being classed as personal injury by accident is twofold. First, it prevents an action for compensatory damages being brought. Second it entitles the victim to claim a number of benefits. In particular, an accident victim is entitled to treatment and rehabilitation for his or her injuries as well as income-related compensation (which can amount to 80 percent of a person's pre-accident-income). For most of the scheme's life, except for the years 1993 to 2001, victims were also entitled to lump sum payments in accordance with a schedule based on the seriousness of the impairment.

While sexual abuse does not easily fall within the common meaning of accident, New Zealand courts have consistently held that whether an incident was an accident was to be considered from the perspective of the victim and hence could include intentional actions of third parties. In *G v Auckland Hospital Board*,[21] the New Zealand trial court held a woman who had been raped by a hospital orderly was barred from suing the Hospital Board. The finding, of course, meant that the victim could access statutory benefits regardless of whom the original criminal had been. Mere neglect however would probably not be considered to be personal injury.

Claims for compensation as a result of sexual abuse have been a controversial part of the administration of the Accident Compensation scheme. Such claims have became such an established feature of the scheme that when compensation for purely 'mental injury' which was not consequential on a physical injury was removed from the scheme by the 1992 Act, the Act expressly included mental consequences of various sexual offences. Abuse victims could still access income related compensation, a small independence allowance and perhaps more importantly private counselling. There has also been a public but rarely substantiated fear that making such claims is simply too easy. When the 2001 Act reintroduced lump sum payments there was great public controversy when a Christchurch law firm openly touted for sexual abuse victims' business in a national mail out, claiming that they would assist such victims in claiming for the reinstated lump sum payments.[22] While there is a maximum of $NZ100,000 (around £33,000) that might allure claimants, the reality that the sliding scale used for calculating entitlements requires very significant impairment before pay-outs are significant and claimants have a hard road to establish the necessary permanent impairment.

Historic Abuse Claims and the Accident Compensation Regime

A number of sexual abuse claims that have come before New Zealand courts have involved alleged abuse that had occurred before introduction in 1975 of the Accident Compensation regime. Normally, if such claims might survive the limitation regime (which as a result of recent judicial flexibility they might possibly do), they would not be caught by the bar on common law actions. However, since the Accident Insurance Act 1998 the legislative policy has seemingly been to include historic sexual abuse claims within the Accident Compensation regime even if the allegations occurred before 1975, presumably so that victims can access the statutory benefits.[23] The mechanism by which this has been done is to deem the time when the claimant first sought medical treatment to be the time of the personal injury.[24] The current provision in the 2001 Act reads:[25]

> 36(1)The date on which a person suffers mental injury in the circumstances described in section 21 [which includes sexual abuse] is the date on which the person first receives treatment for that mental injury as that mental injury.

This can be compared to the normal position where the claimant alleges that he or she suffered mental injury as a result of physical injury:

> 36(2)The date on which a person suffers mental injury because of physical injuries suffered by the person is the date on which the physical injuries are suffered.

The cases *S v Attorney-General* and *W v Attorney-General*, both of which involved claims that social workers had failed to prevent pre-1974 abuse were however commenced under the Accident Rehabilitation, Compensation and Insurance Act 1992,[26] which, while using slightly different language, was held by the High Court judges to have expressed the same fundamental concept – that cover begins at the time that the treatment is sought. In *S* the plaintiff had sought and received treatment and compensation under the provisions of the 1992 Act, and Ronald Young J found it relatively easy to conclude that having done so, he was deprived of the right to sue:[27]

> These factors convince me that it would therefore be wrong to allow compensatory damages to be claimed by the plaintiff. The plaintiff has been in effect fully covered under the Accident Compensation scheme for all his disability arising from PTSD and depression however caused. To now let his claim for compensatory damages proceed would allow him to effectively double-dip. The plaintiff's claims for compensatory damages must therefore fail.

The case of *W* was a little more problematic for Smellie J as while W had claimed that she had not actually received the treatment to which she had been entitled, her Accident Compensation files indicated that she had indeed made a claim. Smellie J concluded that her claim ought to be barred.[28]

The Court of Appeal however reversed both decisions and allowed both plaintiffs to seek compensatory damages. In doing so Blanchard J writing for the Court argued that the drafting of the 1992 Act was significantly different from the subsequent Acts which the Court accepted did bar even pre-1974 actions. The Court interpreted the subsection in the 1992 Act[29] that deemed that the date of the personal injury to occur at the time when treatment was first sought as related to claim administration as opposed to cover since the subsection was contained in a section that dealt with claims administration. Perhaps more importantly the Court focused on section 8(1) that made it clear that the Act only gave cover to personal injuries that occurred after the Act came into effect, rejecting an argument that mental injury occurred at the time the injury became manifest. Most importantly the Court appeared to adopt a restrictive approach to interpretation focusing on the need for clear words to remove 'existing common law rights':[30]

> It is most unlikely that Parliament would have taken the radical step of giving cover for injuries received prior to the first accident compensation scheme, and in the process depriving people of existing common law rights, without making that very explicit, as in fact it did in s.11 which does clearly extend cover under the ARCI Act to gradual process injuries resulting from exposure before 1 April 1974 in the course of employment. Surely if retrospective coverage was also to be given to mental or nervous shock injuries within the description in subs.(3) which had occurred before the accident compensation scheme, that would have been done by a section along the lines of s.11.

This requirement for explicit language to deprive common law rights is a traditional one and has become the common interpretation approach adopted by New Zealand judges to the Accident Compensation regime since the mid-1990s. There was a perception that the 1992 Act and its removal of lump sum payment had created a parsimonious regime from which victims would understandably wish to free themselves.[31] The problem with the approach is that *cover* fulfils a dual purpose under the Act. While it serves to bar common law actions, it also allows claimants access to the scheme's statutory benefits. Victims of abuse may possess common law rights, but one suspects that many might be ultimately better off with the certainty of statutory benefits – which the Accident Compensation Corporation had clearly been prepared to recognise as conferred by the 1992 Act. Some of the consequences of the decision to remove cover from those victims might be ameliorated by the Court's indication that the different statutory wording after 1 July 1999 means victims who first sought medical treatment after that date will be covered by the scheme, but there might be a quite legitimate fear that rather than helping most victims by allowing them to sue, the decision has in fact hindered them getting effective compensation.

Actions for Exemplary Damages

Complicating the already confused picture however is that since 1982 the New Zealand courts have interpreted the bar on damages for personal injury actions as only preventing claims for compensatory damages.[32] That means that claims for exemplary damages, based on 'bad faith, deliberate, use of unnecessary force, or high-handed or contemptuous behaviour' (which no one doubts includes sexual abuse) are not barred.

Actions Against Perpetrators of Abuse

Perhaps the greatest controversy over exemplary damages in New Zealand courts appeared in relation to alleged claims of sexual abuse by doctors of their patients when those doctors had been subject to criminal proceedings (or at least a police investigation). For various reasons, the New Zealand Court of Appeal held that both those who had been convicted, as well as acquitted, of criminal charges and who might be potentially subject to such criminal charges could not be sued for exemplary damages.[33] This holding was subsequently confirmed by the Privy Council.[34] However, in the meantime the decision had been effectively overhauled by Parliament which enacted section 395 of the 1998 Act, now section 319 of 2001 Act, which expressly allows exemplary damages in such actions, but the award must take into account whether the defendant has been convicted or acquitted of an offence in relation to the conduct that merits punishment.[35]

Vicarious Liability Actions

For a number of years there was some debate over whether the somewhat sparse case law might allow exemplary damages for vicarious liability,[36] enabling plaintiffs to 'get at' the body employing the perpetrator as opposed to just the perpetrator. However, the New Zealand Court of Appeal has preferred to hold that, in general, exemplary damages are generally unavailable under vicarious liability. In *S v Attorney-General* and *W v Attorney-General* there were allegations of physical and sexual abuse against foster parents. In *S* there had been findings that although there had been abuse there was no negligence on behalf of the social workers responsible – exemplary damages could alone be awarded based on the fault of the abuser not the department. This the Court of Appeal decisively rejected. In its view while there might be compensatory damages awarded vicariously, the Court emphasised the exemplary damages were justified alone by punishing a wrongdoer:[37]

> When it is appreciated that the primary purpose of such damages is to punish a flagrant wrongdoer, not to provide additional compensation (in contrast to compensatory damages awarded on an aggravated basis), it might seem to be quite unfair to inflict a punishment upon someone who has been found not to have been complicit in the wrongdoing. Exemplary or punitive damages would not then be a reflection of the culpability of the defendant. Any 'message of disapproval' would be delivered to the wrong person. It is one thing to require a principal who has without neglect created a situation leading to injury to compensate the injured person; it is quite another to punish the principal for the sins of the agent.
>
> Exemplary damages are not intended, and should not be used, to provide an additional monetary remedy. Where compensatory damages are able to be awarded vicariously against a principal they will provide the full and effective remedy, even in circumstances in which the actual wrongdoer cannot be found or is impecunious. In this country, of course, the accident compensation scheme will ordinarily prevent an award of compensatory damages, but that does not mean that exemplary damages should be allowed to change their character and become a way of providing lump sum compensation if and to the extent that the scheme does not allow for it. There is no warrant for the courts to attempt to make up for any perceived inadequacy in the accident compensation scheme. That would, as counsel for the respondent said, merely undermine the scheme. It would require employers to self-insure against that risk or pay for insurance cover, if available, as well as meeting levies under the scheme.

The Court was prepared to allow only what it saw as a slight crack. Exemplary damages might be available if the actual wrongdoer could not be identified.[38]

The balance may possibly be different in a case in which an official of the State, for example a police constable, has deliberately, recklessly or (in the rare case contemplated by the Privy Council in *A v Bottrill*) in a grossly negligent manner directly inflicted personal injury on the plaintiff, particularly if, as in *Monroe v Attorney-General*,[39] that official has not been able to be identified and so the wrongdoer has not been punished or disciplined. We therefore leave open the possibility that in such a case the Crown may be held vicariously liable.

Exemplary Damages and Negligence

The New Zealand courts have over last five or six years been engaged in a debate over whether exemplary damages be awarded for conduct that is not intentional. While at one stage it appeared that New Zealand courts might be prepared to read down the requirement for exemplary damages to something approaching objective recklessness,[40] the New Zealand Court of Appeal had resolved the debate, we thought, by requiring there be actual subjective recklessness and a minimum to justify exemplary damages. The leading case is *Bottrill*,[41] in which a pathologist had been found by public inquiry to have been completely incompetent in the reading of cervical smears, which had unquestionably led to the death or disfigurement of patients that otherwise might have been easily cured. Bottrill's defence was that he had simply been so bad that he had not realised the scope or extent of his errors. The Court of Appeal wrote:[42]

> Considerations in this country weigh heavily in favour of confining the remedy to those cases where the defendant is subjectively aware of the risk to which his or her conduct exposes the plaintiff and acts deliberately or recklessly taking that risk.

If the Court of Appeal's rejection of objective recklessness had remained in place it may have provided an effective barrier to claims against public authorities for failing to take proper care to protect the children in their care unless those in charge were somehow aware of the actual abuse or of the risk of it occurring. This was certainly the view of Ronald Young J in relation to a claim that social workers had failed to prevent abuse occurring to a foster child, although his Honour on the facts of the case had concluded that there had been no negligence.[43] While Ronald Young J thought that while the Department might be vicariously liable for the actions of foster parents, it would take special circumstances before it might be liable for exemplary damages as a result of unauthorised acts of foster parents.[44]

> If the Crown is to be liable here for exemplary damages then the plaintiff will need to show some complicity or blameworthiness on the part of the defendant. For the reasons I have already given the plaintiff cannot do so.
>
> I have rejected the submission that the defendant acted outside the statutory regime or that it did anything which allowed or failed to prevent harm to the plaintiff. I have concluded that Child Welfare officers were faced with a series of choices affecting the plaintiff's life. They made those decisions in what they believed to be the best interests of the plaintiff. Although on reflection some decisions can be properly disagreed with, all were reasonably open to Child Welfare officers. Overall, Child Welfare provided reasonable supervision and care. These are not the actions which exemplary damages are designed to punish. The plaintiff has been unable to categorise the actions of the defendant within those contemplated by exemplary damages claims. I therefore award no damages.

Following Ronald Young J's judgment, the Privy Council rejected the Court of Appeal's apparent foreclosure of exemplary damages in cases where the plaintiff might not be able to show subjective recklessness. Lord Nicholls wrote for the Privy Council:[45]

> However, if experience in the law teaches anything, it is that sooner or later the unexpected and exceptional event is bound to occur. It would be imprudent to assume that, in the absence of intentional wrongdoing or conscious recklessness, a defendant's negligent conduct will *never* give rise to a justifiable feeling of outrage calling for an award of exemplary damages. 'Never say never' is a sound judicial admonition. There may be the rare case where the defendant departed so far and so flagrantly from the dictates of ordinary or professional precepts of prudence, or standards of care, that his conduct satisfies this test even though he was not consciously reckless.

The focus of the Privy Council was simply upon whether the conduct might be described as outrageous. While outrageous conduct would normally involve a deliberate running of risks, it might be that Courts could view evidence of long-standing systemic failure as justifying an award of exemplary damages. Certainly the actual facts of *Bottrill*, which involved systemic failure, seemed in the Privy Council's view to be the kind of case that might merit exemplary damages. In the subsequent case of *W v Attorney-General* Smellie J clearly accepted that the effect of *Bottrill* was that in appropriate cases exemplary damages might be awarded for non-intentional behaviour but that there had to be something more than just negligence. In that case Smellie J had found that a supervising social worker had been negligent in failing to act on an abused foster child's complaint that her foster father was being 'rude', but that by itself did not justify punishment:[46]

> If I could be satisfied that the circumstances of [the foster father's] violation of the plaintiff had been clearly articulated so that [the social worker] could not have failed to understand what was being alleged, I would have had little difficulty in holding her either consciously reckless in failing to act and certainly, as having flagrantly departed from acceptable standards of practice and care.... I do not resile from my holding that [the social worker] was negligent in not picking up the message, taking it seriously and acting to protect the plaintiff. But as I have not heard her explanation I can only speculate as to why nothing was done. It may be that given the imprecise nature of the complaints, the default was towards the error of judgment end of the spectrum and well removed from the flagrant breach of acceptable practice threshold. The consequence is that [the foster father's] violation of the plaintiff never came to the attention of the defendant. Having given this aspect of the case anxious consideration I am not satisfied that that [the social worker's] conduct calls for condemnation by way of exemplary damages. Nor would such damages be warranted on a vicarious basis for [the foster father's] unknown wrongdoing.

The Court of Appeal, despite having expressed concerns over the Department's behaviour, subsequently agreed:[47]

> that while that conduct has deserved a finding of negligence, we are not persuaded that, judged by the standards of the time, it was so grossly neglectful that it ought to be marked by an award of exemplary damages.

The Court noted that the plaintiffs had failed to establish a systemic problem.

Actions for Acts 'Attributable' to the Crown

While the Court of Appeal established in *S* that in general there would be no vicarious liability for exemplary damages, in its companion case, *W*, the Court appeared to carve out a major exception. In *W*, as will be explained below, the trial judge had accepted that a relatively senior social worker had been negligent in failing to pick up on the fact that abuse was occurring. Rather than simply applying the same logic of *S* that there could be no exemplary damages for the acts of servants or recognising that the Crown had owed a direct duty which it had breached and was therefore liable for exemplary damages on its own behalf, the Court preferred an intermediate approach of asking whether the social worker was sufficiently senior to justify the conclusion that her acts could be attributed to the Department. Blanchard J 'adapted to fit the situation' the doctrine of attribution from corporate law, under which the company can be charged with the knowledge and the acts of one of its servants so long as the servant is sufficiently high up the organisational chart:[48]

> Guidance is to be found in the opinion of the Privy Council, though in a vastly different factual setting, in *Meridian Global Funds Management Asia Ltd v Securities Commission* [1995] 3 NZLR 7 at 12, which can be adapted to fit the situation of a government department rather than a trading company. It is necessary to look at the substantive rule – here, that a person is liable for exemplary damages if that person acts in outrageous disregard for the rights of the plaintiff – and then to work out whether it is proper to apply it to a government department, as to which we have no doubt, and, if so, how it is appropriate to apply it. In *Meridian* the Privy Council said that the Court has to fashion a special rule of attribution for the particular substantive rule. This involves determining whose act (or knowledge or state of mind) was *for this purpose*, i.e. attribution of conduct, intended to count as the act etc. of the defendant. Rephrased for the current circumstances, the question in this case would be: for the purpose of attributing outrageous conduct whose act ought to count as the act of the Department?

For the Crown looking to escape from future exemplary damages actions, this need to point to the officials high up the chain of command might provide some respite. Whether in fact it will succeed will depend on how far down the chain the Court is prepared to go. Blanchard J continued:

> It cannot possibly be said that the foster parents acted as the Department so no exemplary damages can on this basis be awarded for their actions. But it is arguable that the position is different in relation to the acts and omissions of Mrs Von Hartitzsch. She was, as a Senior Child Welfare Officer, the person responsible for EW's placement and supervision and the person to whom EW brought, in vain, her

> complaints. She was exercising or able to exercise authority under s.20 of the Child Welfare Act 1925 which provided for placements of children to be made by the Superintendent or 'any officer of the Child Welfare Division authorised by the Superintendent in that behalf'. Mrs Von Hartitzsch evidently had that authority to represent the Department in her dealings with EW. In the circumstances it is therefore arguable that her acts and omissions should be attributed to the Department and that, if her acts and omissions were so bad as to be deserving of being marked by an award of exemplary damages, then an award should be made against the Department. But, for reasons which now follow, we find it unnecessary to reach a final conclusion on that question.

One can easily conceive of future battles over whether a classroom teacher or a member of a religious order has been given sufficient control over a child to trigger this attribution doctrine. Indeed one wonders if the doctrine is in the end going to look much like the vicarious liability for exemplary damages doctrine with which the Court thought it was doing away.

Actions for Failing to Properly Act on Reports of Abuse

Prince and the Rejection of X v Bedfordshire

In New Zealand, as well as perhaps New South Wales, courts had held that social welfare officials may owe a duty of care to act to protect children at risk. In New Zealand this was clearly established by *Prince*,[49] in which the Court of Appeal held that social workers owed a common law negligence duty of care to at least investigate claims of neglect that had been brought to their attention. As I have detailed elsewhere,[50] the majority believed that such a common law duty would reinforce the statutory duty that the Director-General of Social Welfare owed to protect children at risk.

Although the case reached a reverse result to that of *Bedfordshire*, the Court of Appeal believed that it had adopted the House of Lords' general approach in focusing on the statutory scheme as the most important factor determining whether a common law duty ought to be owed. The New Zealand Court could not see how imposing a duty of care would cut across the statutory scheme, which focused on the protection of the interests of the child. In fact such a duty of care would rather reinforce the statutory duty.

Failing to Investigate versus Investigating Negligently

The state of New Zealand law after the decision in *Prince*, which did not go to trial, was greatly complicated by the subsequent decision of the Court of Appeal in *B v Attorney General*.[51] *B* was not a case in which social workers had failed to react to an allegation of abuse but rather involved an allegation that, after the removal of two daughters following an allegation of abuse by one, the social welfare authorities failed to return the daughters to their father after it should have become apparent that the abuse had not taken place. Rather than analysing the case as different from *Prince*, at least insofar as it involved a claim by a father who alleged that he had been deprived of his daughters, the Court purported to limit the application of *Prince* to the initial decision of whether to investigate allegations of abuse. The apparent reason for doing so was that in *Prince* the statement of claim had alleged that the social workers had done nothing on receiving the neglect complaints. As *Prince* had never gone to trial, the Court of Appeal had never had to consider an allegation that the investigation into Prince's neglect had been negligently conducted. Rather than seeing the statement of claim in *Prince* as being a place of departure for possible claims against social welfare officials, the Court of Appeal now saw the statement of claim in *Prince* as essentially limiting the kind of claims that had been approved by *Prince*. The Court referred to the so-called triggering step of beginning an investigation as being the limit of the social worker's liability.

There was nothing in the judgments which necessarily limited this distinction to either the father's or the daughters' cases, or the cases in which there was an allegation that social workers had failed to return children as opposed to failing to intervene to protect them. It may be that the Court of Appeal somewhat itself neglected the children's cause of action.[52]

The Privy Council Restores Prince

The Privy Council, on hearing the appeal from *B* some four years later, rejected the Court of Appeal's distinction. Lord Nicholls wrote that:[53]

> Their Lordships confess to having difficulty with the decision of the Court of Appeal. They respectfully consider it emasculates the scope of the common law duty of care recognised in *Prince*'s case. Their Lordships can see nothing in *Prince*'s case to suggest that the concurrent common law duty is less extensive temporally than the statutory duty imposed on the Director-General by section 5(2)(a) of the 1974 Act.

Lord Nicholls continued that the obligation to investigate must mean more than simply starting the investigation:[54]

> This obligation to arrange a prompt inquiry comprehends a duty to arrange and conduct an adequate inquiry. The Director-General would not discharge his statutory obligation ... by merely 'arranging' for an inquiry, whatever precisely that may mean. He must conduct whatever inquiry is necessary. A duty to set an inquiry by his own officials in motion, but no duty to take reasonable steps to see the inquiry duly proceeded, would be a poor sort of statutory duty.
>
> Nor was the duty to investigate discharged by seeking an interim removal warrant.

That did not end the inquiry or the Director-General's duty in that regard. The grant of urgent interlocutory relief by the court did not mean that the department's obligation to conduct an adequate inquiry was satisfied. Understandably and properly, the department next arranged for D1 and D2 to be examined by a doctor. But that also cannot be regarded as the end of the inquiry. Why should it, especially when the outcome was inconclusive? If, as alleged, material further information thereafter came to hand the Director-General's section 5(2) duty required him to follow up that information. This was so irrespective of whether the information tended to support or undermine the abuse allegation. It cannot be that the department was under a duty to investigate further only if the further information tended to support the allegation.

Similarly the Privy Council rejected the Crown's claim, building on Lord Browne-Wilkinson's decision in *X v Bedfordshire*, that the investigation was by its nature 'interdisciplinary', a decisive factor in denying liability.[55]

> Given that the Director-General's statutory duty under section 5, as distinct from the exercise by him of his discretionary powers, extends thus far, there seems to their Lordships to be no basis on which the concurrent common law duty of care recognised in *Prince*'s case should have a less extensive temporal scope. Substantially the same considerations apply to the conduct of the inquiry at the later stage as at the earlier stage. At the later stage, if not at the outset, other agencies, including the police, would be involved. They were in the present case, more or less from the very beginning. At that time inquiry into sexual offences against children was carried out by a multi-disciplinary sexual abuse team procedure. The police interviewed the father on the same day as the children were first interviewed. But this multi-disciplinary procedure is not inconsistent with the Director-General having a continuing positive statutory duty to inquire, that is, to investigate. That being so, the concurrent common law duty he owed the children continued to exist, reinforcing his statutory duty. Such an investigatory obligation is of course quite distinct from making decisions and assessments on what should be done in the light of what is revealed by the investigation.

However as explained below, the Privy Council preferred to hold that the jurisprudential base of *Prince* did not extend to the father, so that only the children might base a claim on the nature of the investigation.

New South Wales – The Possible Existence of a Duty

The New South Wales courts appear to have recognised the possibility of social workers owing a duty of care when they conduct an investigation into allegations of child abuse.[56] *TC* illustrates the difficulty of establishing that social workers had, in fact, breached a duty of care, or if they had breached a duty of care that their breach caused loss to a child which had been subject to ongoing abuse at the time before social services had been alerted.

This rather complex case involved allegations that the New South Wales Department of Youth and Community Services (YACS) had failed to properly act upon warnings that TC was being abused by his mother. The case was complicated by the fact that the allegations were made by TC's father who had separated from the mother, who herself had spent some of the period during which the abuse occurred at a women's refuge (the trial judge accepted that the child had been abused by an unknown other). On a number of occasions, it was alleged, that YACS staff had failed to act upon warnings that the abuse was taking place. At first instance Studdert J had little difficulty in recognising that YACS owed a duty of care. His Honour believed that cases like *Pyrenees Shire* established that even discretionary powers might be subject to an obligation to exercise them reasonably. His Honour concluded that the then Child Welfare Act effectively created a common law duty to exercise powers reasonably. In particular His Honour focused on the then compulsory reporting provision section 148B, which required medical practitioners and other professionals to compulsorily report child abuse. Importantly section 148(b)(5) provided for a mandatory obligation on the Director in the following terms:[57]

> (5) Where the Director has been notified under sub-section (2) or (3) he shall: (a) promptly cause an investigation to be made into the matters notified to him; and if he is satisfied that the child in respect of whom he was notified may have been assaulted, ill-treated or exposed, take such action as he believes appropriate, which may include reporting those matters to a constable of police.

While his Honour was referred to English authorities such as *Bedfordshire*,[58] *O'Rouke*[59] and to the then English Appeal decisions in *W v Essex*[60] and *Barrett*,[61] his Honour rejected the then apparent conclusion from those cases that there was no private law duty of care as necessarily being the law in New South Wales, finding, as had the New Zealand Court of Appeal in *Prince*,[62] that the statutes involved were different.[63] His Honour did however quote extensively from *Prince* and in particular appeared to compare a mandatory obligation under section 148B to the mandatory obligation in the New Zealand statute on the Director-General under section 5 of the Children and Young Persons Act 1974. His Honour concluded:[64]

> Once again the framework of the legislation in the New Zealand case differs from that in the Child Welfare Act but the sort of policy considerations identified in the extract from the judgment set out above arise for consideration here. Plainly regard must be had to considerations such as those set out in the above extract, and in particular to those matters addressed in the three paragraphs last cited above. Nor can it be ignored that the resources of YACS are limited, and that doubtless many demands are made upon those resources. However, in my opinion contrary considerations do not outweigh those factors supportive of a duty of care, at the forefront of which is the statutory framework itself and the recognition in s.148B of the need to protect the limited class there contemplated, namely children at risk in one or other of the ways identified in the section. The vulnerability of the members of that class is a most important and weighty consideration.
>
> I have reached the conclusion that it is fair, just and reasonable in all the circumstances for the common law to impose a duty of care upon the defendant towards this plaintiff, and accordingly I do conclude that the defendant did owe such a duty towards TC.

On appeal the Court of Appeal agreed however that if indeed the duty had been breached, the breach did not cause any loss. In relation to the possibility of imposing a duty Mason P wrote:[65]

> Much time was spent in the appeal in attacking and defending these conclusions. We were referred to a number of recent cases in Australia, New Zealand and the United Kingdom. I would conclude that the issue is an arguable one in the sense that a statement of claim alleging the particular duty found in the present case ought not to be struck out. At the very least the reasoning of Studdert J demonstrates this... In my view it is unnecessary to go beyond that. The appeal can be disposed of on other grounds. The issue is a difficult one and is best addressed by this Court only when it is necessary to do so and in the light of the latest guidance from the High Court and elsewhere on the issues.

One factor in the judge wanting to leave open the determination of the duty question was the fact that the Child Welfare Act had subsequently been replaced by the Children and Young Persons (Care and Protection) Act 1998 which expressed the obligations of the Director-General in slightly different terms.

What Would Amount to Breach?

It is clear from *Prince* that the failure to investigate anything may be a breach of the duty owed by social workers. Further it is clear after the Privy Council's decision in *B* that at least sometimes Courts might hold an investigation to be negligently conducted, but at the same time the Privy Council warned of the difficulties of establishing negligence. *TC* shows that considerable burdens remain in establishing that such that a breach has occurred. Studdert J held with the exception of two alleged breaches that YACS had not breached its duty of care to the child. The two exceptions involved firstly the failure to properly investigate allegations of neglect where the mother had allegedly tied the infant to its cot before going out for a night 'enjoying herself with men', and secondly the failure to obtain a medical examination in a more timely fashion.

Studdert J deferred to the social worker's reactions to the child's father's principal allegations of the child's inappropriate sexual behaviour. Especially important was expert evidence that while that behaviour might raise concerns, by itself the behaviour was not conclusive of abuse. The two breaches that his Honour did find reflected situations where social workers themselves had not followed through on their own practice as opposed to the Court imposing practice upon social workers. In the Court of Appeal, Mason P showed even great deference to the decisions that social workers had made. His Honour accepted the Department's submissions that:[66]

> Its statutory duty to 'investigate' did not convert it into a detective agency. The judge's conclusion that the mother should have been confronted with the material in the affidavits is said to have been a counsel of perfection. The duty (if it existed) was one of reasonable care. Simply to point to something that might have been done is not to establish that failure to do it constituted breach of duty.

He continued:[67]

> YACS' proper concern was the current welfare of the child. YACS was not a detective agency set up to hunt down and prosecute past misconduct. True, the past could be an indicator of the present, but there were matters of degree.

Mason P accepted that the incident had been investigated to an appropriate degree and that the officer in charge had made a rational decision to investigate no further and indeed the matters were to be subject to a Family Court hearing. His Honour then continued to warn:[68]

> In cases involving negligence by omission it is always pertinent to remind oneself that the legal standard is reasonableness, not perfection.

Causation Problems

Causation is also a difficulty that the New Zealand, or indeed English, courts have yet really to grapple with. What does it mean to say that a social worker, as opposed to the abusers or the child's circumstances, has caused the child harm? This is especially so when the social worker claims that even if the investigation had been properly conducted he or she would have made the same decision, or would have had difficulty in convincing a judge to countenance the removal of the child from what turned out to be an abusive situation. Again the *TC* case shows firstly the finding of a duty or its breach does not suspend the normal law that plaintiffs must establish causation.

In a second decision Studdert J doubted that if there had been no negligence the abuse would not have been prevented. Studdert J found that the second breach – the failure to get a more timely medical report – had occurred after the time at which sexual abuse had in fact occurred and hence could not have contributed to any damage the child was claimed to have suffered as a result of a prior abuse. In relation to the first cot-tying incident, his Honour was sceptical of whether there had been any subsequent sexual abuse after that time, but more importantly considered that even if the incident had been properly investigated that the child would not have been removed from his mother or that any further abuse would have been prevented. His Honour wrote:[69]

> Indeed I think it unlikely, so far as I can make any assessment on the evidence before me. There are a number of circumstances which point away from removal occurring:
> (i) The favourable assessment made of [the mother]....
> (ii) The recency of that assessment compared with the time when the events referred to in the material that required investigation allegedly took place.
> (iii) The perception ... as to the difficulties of assessing the credibility of witnesses outside the court process, which perception might have been expected to influence the decision-making process of the defendant.
> (iv) When ultimately the evidence of those who alleged physical ill treatment and

> neglect was put to the test in court, it was not accepted.
> (v) There is also the circumstance that to effect the child's removal from his mother would have required a court order, and there was the need for the purposes of s72 of the Child Welfare Act to satisfy a magistrate that the plaintiff was a neglected child as defined. ...
> (vi) ... Had YACS consulted ... experts after completing the investigations that should have been undertaken ... it would seem unlikely that they would have then supported an application for the removal of the plaintiff from his mother's care.

As the Judge suggests more attention ought to be paid to causation. Obviously in *TC* it would still have been necessary for the social worker to convince a judge of the appropriateness of removal. In *TC* there was an attempt to persuade the Court that the onus of proving or disproving causation had somehow switched from the plaintiff to the defendant once it was established that the plaintiff had suffered the sort of harm within the defendant's usual duty to prevent. Neither the trial Judge nor the Court of Appeal believed that under the Australian law the proper onus switched from the plaintiff to the defendant. Both Courts emphasised that the causation was naturally a matter of a common sense consideration of facts. Care must though be taken to not effectively excuse liability just because a judge still needed to be convinced of the need to remove the child. There is a danger of requiring too much of plaintiffs in terms of predicting what a judge might do and thereby essentially using causation to always deny liability.

Sexual Abuse by State 'Employees': A Plethora of Theories and a Lack of Legal Certainty

In Australia, a number of claims have been brought against State run, as well as privately run, schools. Even more controversially New Zealand courts have had to deal with claims, as have British Columbian courts, that the Crown is liable for the acts of foster parents. These claims have considerable similarity, of course, to claims against the authorities in general for failing to protect children. At least four different theories have been used by common law courts to analyse such a case:

1. that the school authorities or welfare authorities owe a duty of care in the ordinary way;
2. that school authorities or welfare authorities owe a non-delegable duty to protect children who are within their care;
3. that school authorities or welfare authorities might be seen to be vicariously liable for the acts of the teacher, even though the teacher has committed an intentional tort clearly outside scope or the purpose of his or her employment;
4. that the school or welfare authorities owed a fiduciary duty to protect those within their care from the acts of others.

The strength of division on the High Court of Australia over the correct approach to vicarious liability shows members of that Court to be clearly and perhaps unfortunately evenly divided over the appropriateness of using the concept of vicarious liability as a way of ensuring compensation for the unfortunate victims of the abuser's acts. It is difficult ultimately to know how far the Australian Court was from the Canadian or English approaches. In neither jurisdiction would the fact that a child was abused by a day teacher inevitably lead to the conclusion that there might necessarily be vicarious liability. In contrast the New Zealand Court of Appeal showed a remarkable unanimity in accepting the role of vicarious liability at least in the foster care situation was to achieve compensation for the plaintiffs and near unanimity in approach in providing that compensation. The New Zealand decisions may be quite consistent with more expansive parts of *Lister* and *Bazley* while the majority (if there is one) of the High Court in *Lepore* tends to the more conservative aspects of Lister, or of the majority in the Supreme Court of Canada in *Jacobi*. It may be the real difference between these, the High Court and the New Zealand Court of Appeal is one of attitude.

Fiduciary theory has seemingly been pushed to one side because of an Australian reluctance to extend the fiduciary concept to non-traditional areas, or at least let fiduciary law overwhelm areas that are traditionally protected by tort law – fiduciary actions are clearly possible but advocates need to be careful to separate out what is different or unique that leads to a fiduciary relationship as opposed to one that ought to be governed by the common law.[70] Similarly while the New Zealand Court of Appeal has acknowledged that Government Departments that are entrusted with children might be considered to be their fiduciary, there needs to be some allegation beyond saying that the Department had breached its duty by failing to take reasonable care.

The Australia School Cases: Actions Betwixt and Between Theories

Australian courts and advocates struggled to fit sexual abuse claims against schools within their existing legal framework. Faced with undoubted, if rather old, precedent that Australian law would not allow vicarious liability for deliberate wrongdoing clearly outside scope of someone's employment, in a case where a bartender threw a glass at a disorderly patron[71] advocates seemingly felt unable to plead vicarious liability. Similarly without being able to show that the schools involved had somehow been negligent in the hiring or supervision of the teachers, they were unable to succeed on allegations of common law negligence. Instead advocates in both New South Wales and Queensland employed the rubric of 'non-delegable-duty'. Choosing this label however had two consequences. First, the Courts divided over the issue of whether a non-delegable duty in effect imposes strict liability. The New South Wales Court of Appeal was prepared to allow claims to proceed where negligence on the part of the school had been disproved. The Court of Appeal in Queensland had refused to allow the case to go ahead without allegations of negligence on behalf of the schools. The High Court of Australia has seemingly rejected the non-delegable duty analysis and while it accepted that vicarious liability was the appropriate theory under which to consider the cases, vicarious liability is unlikely to be terribly helpful for plaintiffs in intentional tort cases.

New South Wales – Non-Delegable Duty Recognised as Strict Liability

In New South Wales, the New South Wales Court of Appeal held the State of New South Wales liable for abuse perpetrators in one of the schools.[72] A majority of Mason P and Davies JA was prepared to hold that the state of New South Wales owed a non-delegable duty to the children in its care. No allegation of vicarious liability was made against the State and the allegations had principally been negligent based. Mason P's judgment, although couched in the phraseology of non-delegable duty and relying upon High Court of Australian authority, was in very similar terms to that of the Supreme Court of Canada in *Bazley v Curry*[73] and *Jacobi v Griffith*.[74] The difficulty for Mason P and Davies JA was that at trial the Magistrate had made express findings that the duty had not been breached. The accused teacher was an experienced one against whom there had been no other allegations nor had there been anything which would have alerted the school or the State that he was abusing children.

Mason P supposedly built on a series of Australian cases which have examined non-delegable duty particularly in the context of responsibility for the intentional actions not of teachers but of pupils.[75] While his Honour conceded that what was being asked of his Court was a novel extension of the doctrine, he concluded, 'it is not the law that nothing should ever be done for the first time'.[76] His Honour focused on what he perceived to be the essential justice of the plaintiff's case. As McLachlin J had done in *Bazley*, Mason P argued strongly that if the law compensates for a plaintiff who had lost (as with the fur coat stolen by an employee in the case of *Morris*[77]) it would be simply wrong not to allow the victims of abuse to be able to claim against employers.[78]

That the liability under *Lepore* is to be strict was recognised by Mason P, which appears in his judgment before he begins his exercise of extending the concept of non-delegable duty to cover sexual abuse cases:[79]

> The expression 'non-delegable duty' is somewhat misleading. It implies that a person cannot *delegate* a duty, but the truth is that the person cannot *avoid liability* by relying on the delegation, even to a competent delegate. A non-delegable duty is said to be personal or direct, rather than vicarious, but even this difference is more semantic than substantial.

For Hayden JA, who has subsequently been appointed to the High Court of Australia, all of this was simply going too far. His Honour appeared to doubt, as indeed the majority of the High Court did on appeal, whether in effect the High Court of Australia had intended to create a separate form of strict liability in *Commonwealth of Australia v Introvigne*.[80]

Queensland Rejects Lepore

In contrast to Mason P the Queensland Court of Appeal emphasised in *Rich* and *Samin*,[81] that a finding that schools owed a non-delegable duty did not require that such a duty ought to be strict, and certainly not when the case involved sexual abuse of children at schools. In contrast, the duty was in essence to take reasonable care to safeguard children while at school.[82]

Macpherson JA rejected the approach of the New South Wales Court of Appeal as simply having misconstrued the nature of the obligation that a non-delegable duty places on defendants. The contrast was perhaps strongest in the way that Mason P and Macpherson JA dealt with the case of *Morris*, involving the theft of a coat by employees. Macpherson JA accepted that the case had had some relevant in *Lister*, 'but it was a case of vicarious liability, which professedly this is not'[83] and perhaps more importantly he did not believe the analogy between a stolen coat and abused children was quite complete.

The High Court in Lepore *and* Samin *– A Chorus of Dissenting Voices?*

The confusion in the lower Courts was reflected in the High Court's divided decision in the subsequent appeal.[84] Six different judgments were issued, each expressing a different emphasis, a different view of vicarious liability and sometimes of the nature of non-delegable duty. At the extremes were Callinan J[85] who would not allow vicarious liability for intentional torts at all and McHugh J who appeared to prefer a non-delegable duty analysis that bordered seemingly on strict liability. In between the extremes were a continuum of judgments that suggested liability was unlikely using a legal test that might be possibly scoped around the traditional Salmond test (Gummow and Hayne JJ), and liability being likely at least in *Lepore*, with the test being determined by the kinds of policy factors that were prominent in the Supreme Court of Canada or the House of Lords (Kibry J and perhaps Glesson CJ). Complicating the mix was the novel approach of Gaudron J. Her Honour appeared to accept that risk creation was an important part of the policy behind vicarious liability but who then somewhat curiously went off on her own approach under which vicarious liability was properly seen as a consequence of agency and that liability ought to depend on whether the defendant was estopped from denying responsibility for the conduct of employees. In what might be a key passage she expressed that such an estoppel was unlikely in cases where there was an intentional tort unless there was a 'close connection' between the tort and the servant's job. The situation is hopelessly confused and there will be almost certainly a retrial in the *Lepore* case and a repleading of *Samin* and *Rich* in front of very unlucky trial court judges who will have to fashion a coherent approach.[86]

The 'Test' for Vicarious Liability

In perhaps the leading 'unlikely liability' judgment Gummow and Hayne JJ wrote of the attempt to go beyond the 'Salmond test' to the *Bazley* analysis of whether the risk was created or enhanced as a result of the job.[87]

> Reference to the risk of wrongdoing carries with it a danger in this context that must be recognised. A wrongful act is alleged to have occurred. The risk has come to pass. It follows that an inquiry about the risk of a venture may, in the end, become an inquiry into whether, but for the attributes of the employment (control, authority, trust, access to persons or premises), the wrongful act could have occurred. If the act could not have occurred but for the employment, it will be said that the employer should be held to be vicariously liable because the employer should bear the burden of the risk of wrongdoing. The inquiry would be about *how* the wrongdoer carried out the wrong, regardless of what he or she was employed to do. To adopt this approach would represent a radical departure from what hitherto has been accepted as an essential aspect of the rules about vicarious liability: the requirement that the wrongdoing be legally characterised as having been done in the course of employment.

The focus under Gummow and Haynes JJ's approach was therefore not on the nature of the defendant's business but rather on the nature of the defendant's employee's job:[88]

> What unites those elements is the identification of what the employee is actually employed to do or is held out by the employer as being employed to do. It is the identification of what the employee was actually employed to do and held out as being employed to do that is central to any inquiry about course of employment. Sometimes light may be shed on that central question by looking at a subsidiary question of who stood to benefit from the employee's conduct. But that inquiry must not be permitted to divert attention from the more basic question we have identified.

Many cases in which it is sought to hold an employer vicariously liable for the intentional tort of an employee can be determined by reference to the first of these elements. The act of which complaint is made can be seen to have been done in the intended performance of the task which the employee was employed to perform. Cases of excessive punishment by a teacher may fall within this category. So too will many cases where a store detective wrongfully arrests and detains a person or in that process assaults them. No doubt the examples could be multiplied. This approach enabled Gummow and Hayne JJ to distinguish those cases where an employer had been held liable for an employee's intentional torts. For example in *Lloyd*[89] the employer was held liable for a clerk's fraudulent transaction, as the employer had authorised the clerk to work on that kind of transaction. Similarly the *Morris* case might be explained by the fact that checking the coats was clearly within the scope of the employee's job. In contrast the High Court's own previous decision to deny liability in *Deatons*[90] could be explained by the fact the barmaid who had thrown the glass to quell the disturbance in her employer's bar had been employed to serve drinks as opposed to providing security.

Gummow and Haynes JJ's approach might provide a degree of conceptual certainty that the critics of the *Bazley* judgment decried was missing from *Bazley*. It has the advantage of very clearly resting liability on the employer's decision to entrust the employee with particular functions. It obviously would make the sexual abuse cases easier to deal with since the job a teacher has been entrusted with simply does not involve sexual abuse, but it does not exclude the possibility that schools, on occasion, might be responsible for the teacher's intentional and unauthorised actions. For example, the school might be responsible in the *Lepore* case which might have been one of excessive discipline as disciplining students was within the teacher's job. This appears to be the approach of Gaudron J as well under her estoppel and close connection test, that the State might not be able to deny the connection between the teacher being entrusted with the task of disciplining children and the excessive exercise of that task.

However the conceptual tidiness is, as always perhaps, illusory. As McHugh J argued, the test ultimately depends on the level of generality with which the judge views the employee's job.[91] One wonders if the joint judgment's approach really switches the kind of explicit policy considerations that McLachlin J's approach in *Bazley* required to an implicit consideration of those same factors in assessing the kind of job that the teacher had been employed to do. It may be that Gummow and Hayne JJ's approach merely restates in different words the dilemma that the Supreme Court of Canada found itself in *Jacobi* deciding whether sexual abuse was as connected to the defendant day work job as it had been to the night work of the employee in *Bazley*.

In comparison to Gummow and Hayne JJ's approach, Kirby J described vicarious liability as 'an unstable principle' whose application has been 'uncertain and variable'. In those circumstances Courts ought to resort to policy:[92]

> The principle of vicarious liability, and its application, have not grown from a single, logical legal rule but from judicial perceptions of individual justice and social requirements that vary over time. In any re-expression of the common law in Australia, it is normal now to have regard to considerations of legal principle and policy, as well as any relevant legal authority.

His Honour accepted as persuasive McLachlin J's focus on 'fairness and efficiency':[93]

> Such analysis has its foundations in the argument that profit-making enterprises, which derive financial benefits from an operation, must bear the cost of any particular risks which such operation introduces into the community or exacerbates. At first glance it may seem difficult to accept that non-profit enterprises (such as public schools) should be the subject of such a burden, as the cost to them is not balanced by any financial gain. However, upon closer analysis, 'enterprise risk' can be extended justifiably to such enterprises as public schools, with the result that the community bears the cost. The reasoning is essentially the same as for profit-driven

enterprises. Schools undoubtedly benefit the community, with the education and development services they provide for students. In that way, the broader tax-paying community that 'profits' from the enterprise should also bear the cost of any particular risks which evidence establishes would be closely associated with the functioning of such an institution.

McHugh J and School Liability as a Form of Public Liability

English and Canadian judges have tended to deal with the problem of abuse as one of the application of private law concepts of vicarious liability. The public nature of much education or welfare services is somewhat bypassed. This is not surprising on the facts of the cases before those Courts. The leading Canadian and English vicarious liability cases have involved private agencies, although Children's Aid Foundations clearly exercise public functions as arguably the private boarding school in *Lister* was doing. It might, however, be argued that the State's special regulatory and provision roles in education might trigger responsibilities that might be different from those that are owed by private individuals under traditional private law principles or that the private bodies that provide services in the Government's stead might take the Government's extra responsibilities. Indeed notions of vicarious liability are perhaps inapt when it comes to describe the kind of responsibility that parents and citizens might expect of the Government entrusted with their children.

Lepore and the Queensland cases however directly raised the question of whether government run schools ought to owe their students enhanced duties as a result of the compulsory education. Most of the Australian judges also let this consideration slide by. Mason P's focus on the school's non-delegable duty had aspects of this. But McHugh J's dissenting judgment not only would have imposed liability in both *Lepore* and the Queensland cases, but appeared to do so not just as a reflection of private law liability but of a peculiarly public kind of liability:[94]

> The duty of the school authority does not depend on an implied delegation of authority from the parents of the pupil. In the case of a State authority, the duty arises from exercising governmental power and setting up a system of compulsory education.[95] In the case of a private school authority, it arises from the contractual arrangement between the school and the pupil's parents or guardian. In each case, the duty arises because the school authority has control of the pupil whose immaturity is likely to lead to harm to the pupil unless the authority exercises reasonable care in supervising him or her and because the authority has assumed responsibility for the child's protection.

In his Honour's view, that duty could not be delegated, even if reasonable care was taken in the way that it was delegated.[96]

> In the present case, the State of New South Wales by reason of its compulsory education system had a duty to ensure that reasonable care was taken in supervising

> the activities of the plaintiff and protecting him from harm while he was on the school premises during the times that students were known to be on school grounds. The State purported to perform this duty in a number of ways, one of which was to employ the second respondent, Michell, to teach and supervise the plaintiff during particular school periods. If Michell had failed to take reasonable steps to prevent injury to the plaintiff by another pupil or a stranger, the State would have been liable on the principles laid down by this Court in *The Commonwealth v Introvigne*. Likewise, the State would have been liable if by some negligent conduct on the part of Michell himself, the plaintiff had been injured. It makes no difference that the injury in this case was sustained by an assault even if the assault had sexual overtones.

Kirby J might have agreed had he not thought that the possibility of using vicarious liability negated the need to extend the concept of non-delegable duty. The remainder of the High Court did not accept that because schools might owe a non-delegable duty to supervise the safety of children under their care, that the duty might go beyond taking reasonable care in the hiring or supervision of the staff. In doing so they rejected McHugh J's attempt to distinguish non-delegable duties from absolute liability to protect a child from harm, by emphasising that it required the school to take reasonable care to supervise that had necessarily been breached by the school teacher's alleged abuse. For the majority rather than being a principle of broad application the non-delegable duty doctrine was characterised as a restricted one to deal with a rather peculiar and specific problem. The concept had been employed in *Introvigne*[97] for example to deal with the unusual circumstances to sheet home responsibility to the Commonwealth for the failure to supervise children by the New South Wales teachers whom the Commonwealth had employed to run its Australian Capital Territory schools.

Social Welfare Liability for the Acts of Foster Parents or Other Care Givers

Much controversy in Canada has been caused by the decision of the British Columbia Court of Appeal[98] to hold the province liable for the abuse perpetrated by foster parents. The basis of that liability is somewhat unclear. Finding vicarious liability for the intentional abuse by foster parents presents both similar and perhaps different concerns to impose liability for caregivers and schoolteachers. Vicarious liability requires firstly that there be the requisite connection between the tortfeasor and the defendant (traditionally 'employment') and that the tort be somehow in turn connected to the nature of the relationship between the tortfeasor and the defendant (traditionally whether the tort was in 'the course of employment'). If one adopts a risk creation approach to replace the in 'the course of employment' test, it is obvious that foster children are placed at risk of abuse by their foster parents. But it is not so clear that the relationship between the foster parents and the Department of Social Welfare are necessarily within the traditional sorts of relationships that give rise to that liability. Indeed on one view even if it is possible to replace the 'employee' test with an 'under control' test, foster parents may not be under the sort of control that would justify imposing liability. The better, or at least more traditional, theory might be to rely on negligence in selecting the foster parents.

Ronald Young J in the High Court, in *S v Attorney-General*[99] and Smellie J in *W v Attorney-General*,[100] accepted that social workers might owe a duty of care to prevent foster parents committing abuse, although it was only in *S v Attorney-General* that the judge accepted that there might be vicarious liability for the actions of foster parents. In *S v Attorney-General* an unfortunate child had been subjected to different sources of abuse. First, the child had been sexually abused by his foster brother. Secondly he suffered emotional abuse by the foster parents. Finally after the foster mother had separated from the foster father, the child had been subjected to sexual abuse by the foster mother. The child also sought to strengthen his claim by alleging other forms of abuse such as being forced to work from a young age. *W* was factually a little easier, involving clear allegations of abuse by a foster father, which had been relayed to a senior social worker by the child telling her that the foster father had been 'rude'.

The Court of Appeal has confirmed that the Department of Social Welfare might indeed be vicariously liable for the actions of foster parents.

Vicarious Liability

In an analysis remarkably similar to that of Prowse JA in the British Columbian Court of Appeal, Ronald Young J concluded that policy pointed towards the finding of vicarious liability, even if the actions had clearly been outside those authorised by social workers.[101] His Honour thought that the relationship was similar to employment, even without payment. His Honour considered that not recognising vicarious liability where the State had only formally taken responsibility for the children would result in 'the very ... regime designed to protect children ... be[ing] undermined'.[102] There was, however, a disappointing lack of analysis of the critical factor of control over the foster parent that had featured so much in the British Columbian cases. Similarly there was little examination of the impact that the intentional nature of the abuse might have on vicarious liability. His Honour wrote:[103]

> To return to the abuse analysis the state for the last 100 years or more has accepted responsibility for children whose parents cannot look after them. This is no more than a humane society would expect. There is an economic cost to all taxpayers for this care. The state either through its institutions or though foster care has an economic cost it must carry. There is therefore an analogy with an employer who uses an employee's work and skills for his economic advantage and thus who might reasonably be expected to have a corresponding liability for losses incurred in the course of the same employment.

His Honour was not prepared to accept arguments raised by the Department of Social Welfare that the imposition of vicarious liability would have detrimental effects on the way that they did the job. Ronald Young J clearly saw the common law obligations as essentially forcing the Department to do what it should already have been doing.

The Court of Appeal agreed with Young J's finding of vicarious liability. In doing so the Court did a number of interesting things but perhaps most remarkably instead of focusing on the obvious intentional torts that the foster parents might have committed, the Court focused on the concurrent allegations of negligence as they had obviously not adequately looked after the children. This focus somewhat enabled the Court to sidestep the general debate over whether there might be vicarious liability for the intentional torts and tailor its findings to the particular facts at hand, that there might be vicarious liability for sexual abuse. This vicarious liability was best based in the Court's view on some concept of agency and that the question of whether the Department was liable for the foster parents' actions depended on whether the abuse occurred in the course of the agency, which in turn appeared to be based very much on considerations of what risk the agency had created for the children.

One wonders both whether the focus on parents' failure to take care and then basing liability on agency were the best courses to proceed along. The focus on the foster parent's 'negligence' as opposed to the intentional tort risks removing the puzzle that other Commonwealth Courts have had to deal with – that it is the very intentional nature of the acts that makes it difficult to attribute the acts of a servant, employee, independent contractor to the employer or principal. The difficulty is further enhanced in the *S* case by the Court wanting to draw some sort of distinction between the foster parent's own abuse for which the Crown ought to be liable and their failure to prevent their son from committing sexual abuse, for which the Court concluded somewhat oddly the Crown could not be vicariously liable for. There was no real explanation of why this was so.

There are other problems perhaps with choosing 'agency' as the key, rather undefined concept just as Gaudron J's reliance in the High Court of Australia on the concept makes it difficult to assess what exactly she meant. Blanchard J wrote for the Court about the agency concept:[104]

> It seems to us that the more appropriate characterisation, as Ronald Young J thought, is of an agency. For, while there was certainly no employer/employee relationship, the position of the foster parents was not established by means of any formal contract and they were not undertaking a business venture for profit (or loss). The Superintendent had a duty imposed upon him by statute to take care of the children. He was obliged to fulfil that duty by placing them in suitable private homes where there was supposed to be adherence to practices in accordance with a Departmental manual and continued Departmental monitoring. The Department had a right of inspection and a right to remove any child at any time. The children were said, in the words of the long title to the Child Welfare Act, to be '*specially* under the protection of the State'. That protection cannot have been intended to diminish when a fostering arrangement was made. We think that in this setting it would be quite inappropriate to regard such an arrangement as constituting the foster parents as independent contractors. Because of the continuing statutory duty of the Superintendent to provide for the special protection of each child, the foster

> parents should be regarded as having been made agents of the State, albeit that their agency was of an unusual, indeed unique, nature.

It is clear that the Court was not meaning to say something generally about liability of agents beyond the actual or apparent scope of their authority, but rather to emphasise the special nature of this particular kind of agency. One has to wonder with the concurring judgment of Tipping J whether if the relationship is so unique it is wise to use such a label. Tipping J appeared to agree that the question might be resolved by reference to the particular facts at hand. But there has to be some concern whether his Honour's preferred approach as to what was 'just, fair and reasonable' will give later trial courts sufficient certainty in dealing with the inevitable other cases involving teachers or religious orders. One also wonders if inevitably the use of such general concepts will leak outside the particular context into other areas. Most importantly perhaps both Blanchard and Tipping JJ were a little guilty of conflating the two necessary limbs for vicarious liability (the connection to the tortfeasor and the connection to the tort) in a way that meant they did not properly analyse either limb.

It might have been preferable rather than employing such a well-established legal concept of general application simply to have acknowledged that the Court was imposing direct liability on the Crown, perhaps through some theory of non-delegable duty, perhaps founded on some principle similar to McHugh J's approach in *Lepore* which in turn would have required the Court to consider why liability ought to be imposed on the Crown without showing that it had been at fault. The Court, however, would then have had to confront the problem of the Crown Proceedings Act 1950 that like the English 1947 Act only imposes vicarious liability on the Crown.

Existence of a Duty of Care

Because of the findings on vicarious liability, the New Zealand Court of Appeal did not spend much time examining the possibility of a direct duty on the Department or the Crown, or the lower Courts' finding that the social workers owed a duty to prevent the abuse but that with the exceptions of a senior social worker's failure to act on the child W's complaint that her foster father was being rude, the social workers had not breached their respective duties to guard the children whose care they supervised.

S v Attorney-General

The Source of the Duty

S was not a simple case. It involved a difficult factual matrix from some 30 years previously. But perhaps more importantly the case was complex because of the rather complex nature of statutes that the social workers were administering. Much of the evidence apparently focused on whether various technical requirements of the then child protection statutes had been breached – whether for instance the foster family had been licensed to look after the children, or whether the children should have been left with foster parents so long after it became established that these particular foster parents were not going to adopt the children. Interestingly Ronald Young J discounted the possibility that statutory requirements had arisen under the old statutes, and found that even if they had been breached, there was no corresponding private law duty based on the particular statutory or administrative duties. His Honour, in other words, construed very narrowly the kinds of protections, which had been set up by the Legislature. In any event his Honour was not prepared to say that in these matters the social workers could be said to have breached any statutory duty since they had made decisions in good faith dealing with difficult circumstances.

However, Ronald Young J was prepared to hold that the social workers had owed more general private law duties of care to look after the child while the child was with the foster family. His Honour took an expansive approach, following *Prince*, of the obligation of the Department, even if for various technical reasons the Department had not completed the legal processes by which it would have taken legal guardianship of the children. His Honour wrote generally of the obligation of the Social Welfare services:[105]

> Throughout the defendant's case it was suggested that Child Welfare had no responsibility for these children. Its case was in part that the children were placed with the Ss by the Gs and Child Welfare was really an observer keeping an eye on what went on at the Ss'. I reject that. These children were effectively abandoned by their parents. They became a state responsibility although that did not alleviate the Gs' responsibility (at least, economic) for them. However the state clearly had the responsibility to ensure these children were properly looked after. The fact it chose not to seek a committal order cannot and does not mean the state had no responsibility. Mrs S was nominated by the state to look after the children. She accepted the nomination. The state identified her as a suitable person and the state placed the children with her to look after. The state undertook supervision of her care of the children. Mrs S was at the state's request, undertaking the state's responsibility of care for these 'abandoned' children.

In applying *Prince and Gardner*, His Honour wrote:[106]

> In this case the relationship between the plaintiff and Child Welfare is close. This was a child who was abandoned by its parents at less than one year of age. It was Child Welfare that decided where and with whom the plaintiff could live and it was the Child Welfare in the particular circumstances which undertook the responsibility of oversight of where the plaintiff lived. Child Welfare had been unable to find the plaintiff a family which would in law accept responsibility for him (adoption) and thus it fell to Child Welfare to accept this responsibility. Its agent in these circumstances was Mrs S. It was Child Welfare that decided (at least after 1964) that guardianship issues and Mrs S's status would remain ambiguous through the use of preventive supervision. Child Welfare recognised that there could be damage to the plaintiff by his caregivers. The fact that it monitored the home, considered state wardship, reported on the health and welfare of the plaintiff, discussed the plaintiff's

> conduct with his school and reacted to expressions of concern about the plaintiff's conduct all illustrate the social worker's acceptance of risk of harm. I am satisfied therefore on the facts of this case there is sufficient proximity to justify finding that a duty of care existed.

Were the Common Law Duties Breached?

Although Ronald Young J was prepared to hold that the Department owed duties, at least to prevent the children from being neglected or abused, His Honour seemed after a long trial to have gained a rather favourable impression of the actions of the Department. While things turned out badly for the child, there was little that social workers acting in good faith could have done to prevent the abuse that actually occurred. His Honour dismissed specific allegations of negligence against the social workers as either not having been made out or not having been causative of the abuse that actually occurred. The child, for example, claimed that the informal arrangement with the foster parents had resulted in his not being properly considered for adoption. His Honour accepted however that in making the decision about possible adoption, the social workers had acted reasonably. The child would have been separated from his brothers and it was doubtful in his particular area that he would have been adopted as a five-year-old with limited intellectual ability. In relation to the foster mother's later abuse, which occurred because S shared a bed with her, his Honour accepted that the Social Welfare manual at the time would have required that state wards have their own bedroom, but that requirement was a little beside the point given the poverty of the foster family which would have shifted had there have been another home available.

W v Attorney-General

Similarly in *W v Attorney-General* Smellie J easily found a common law duty where it was alleged that a supervising social worker had failed to act on allegations of abuse, believing that 'the two stage *Anns* approach is appropriate in a case such as this'. The duty reflected the powers of 'guardianship' that were given to the Superintendent under the then operative statutory provisions, section 16 of the Child Welfare Act 1925. His Honour then continued:[107]

> On the second issue of policy considerations there cannot possibly be any reasons telling against the imposition of a duty. On the contrary it would be unthinkable in a civilised society for the reverse to be the case.

As discussed above, Smellie J was prepared to hold that the duty had been breached by the failure of a senior social worker to investigate further after W had complained that her foster father had been rude. His Honour appeared to discount a contention that the comment had to be placed in a context where sexual abuse was not at the forefront of social workers' minds, although he seemed prepared to accept the lack of such awareness as a factor that had led more inexperienced social workers not to be concerned about W potentially being abused.

Claims by Parents Who Have Been Wrongly Accused of Abuse

Introduction

While Australasian courts have been prepared to recognise that a duty might be owed to children by social welfare agencies, there has been a lot less sympathy for claims by parents. In a separate article a colleague and myself had suggested that while there are conflicting interests between social workers' role in protecting a child and safeguarding the interests of the parents, that does not necessarily mean that there should be no duty of care to parents from whom children are removed. One of the great difficulties in *B v Attorney-General* was the failure of the Court of Appeal to appropriately separate out concerns about the father being able to sue from the children's action for wrongful removal. The Privy Council has subsequently confirmed that that there is no duty owed to the parents. The issue has been decisively resolved, perhaps too decisively, by the High Court of Australia in *Sullivan.*[108] *Sullivan* comprised appeals from South Australian decisions denying that a duty might be owed by social workers and other professionals for the wrongful removal of children from parents. The High Court of Australia's decision is interesting on two fronts – first is its contribution to the debate over more conceptual questions of the approach to the duty of care in general and secondly the actual rule which prevents suits by parents.

The Big Duty Question

The High Court in *Sullivan* decisively rejected the English *Caparo*[109] test of imposing a duty of care when it is fair, just and reasonable to do so – not because it was felt to be too conservative, but rather the reverse, it was too liberal. The Court believed that a rather unreflective application of just and reasonableness might simply amount to judges making the law up in cases of moral as opposed to legal claims:[110]

> There is a danger that judges and practitioners, confronted by a novel problem, will seek to give the *Caparo* approach a utility beyond that claimed for it by its original author. There is also a danger that, the matter of foreseeability (which is often incontestable) having been determined, the succeeding questions will be reduced to a discretionary judgment based upon a sense of what is fair, and just and reasonable as an outcome in the particular case. The proximity question has already been discussed. The question as to what is fair, and just and reasonable is capable of being misunderstood as an invitation to formulate policy rather than to search for principle. The concept of policy, in this context, is often ill-defined. There are policies at work in the law which can be identified and applied to novel problems, but the law

of tort develops by reference to principles, which must be capable of general application, not discretionary decision-making in individual cases.

Rather the High Court preferred to look back at the rights defined by the common law. The Court saw negligence not as the creator of rights but as a mechanism by which courts required those who damaged the plaintiff's pre-existing rights to have to compensate the plaintiff. The Court wrote:[111]

> The argument was conducted upon the basis that it was foreseeable that harm of the kind allegedly suffered by the appellants might result from want of care on the part of those who investigated the possibility that the children had been sexually abused. But the fact that it is foreseeable, in the sense of being a real and not far-fetched possibility, that a careless act or omission on the part of one person may cause harm to another does not mean that the first person is subject to a legal liability to compensate the second by way of damages for negligence if there is such carelessness, and harm results. If it were otherwise, at least two consequences would follow. First, the law would subject citizens to an intolerable burden of potential liability, and constrain their freedom of action in a gross manner. Secondly, the tort of negligence would subvert many other principles of law, and statutory provisions, which strike a balance of rights and obligations, duties and freedoms. A defendant will only be liable, in negligence, for failure to take reasonable care to prevent a certain kind of foreseeable harm to a plaintiff, in circumstances where the law imposes a duty to take such care.

This is similar to the approach taken by the English Court of Appeal in *Wirral*[112] and then again in its consideration of the *Newham* case. It is probably not the approach of the European Court of Human Rights.[113] The New Zealand Court of Appeal in *Prince* and *B* in general appeared not to adopt this approach but there had been slight echoes of it in the concurrent adoption cause of action where Gardner had alleged that her rights as the mother had been infringed by misrepresentations made by social workers concerning her ability to unwind adoption if thing when wrong. In a very curious passage Tipping J appeared to acknowledge the strength of the analogy to *Hedley Byrne*, but gave the impression that somehow being deprived of a child was a sort of loss that could not be compensatable by law.[114] The Privy Council in *B* drew the distinction between a child's right to bring an action and the lack of a similar right in the child's parent:[115]

> To whom is the duty of care owed? Clearly the duty is owed to the child or young person in respect of whom the statutory duty to arrange for a prompt inquiry exists in the particular case. In the present case that is D1 as much as D2. If D2's abuse allegation was well founded D1 also was at risk. But their Lordships consider no common law duty of care was owed to the father. He stands in a very different position. He was the alleged perpetrator of the abuse. In an inquiry into an abuse allegation the interests of the alleged perpetrator and of the children as the alleged victims are poles apart. Those conducting the inquiry must act in good faith throughout. But to impose a common law duty of care on the department and the individual professionals in favour of the alleged victims or potential victims and, at one and the same time, in favour of the alleged perpetrator would not be satisfactory.

> Moreover, a duty of care in favour of the alleged perpetrator would lack the juridical basis on which the existence of a common law duty of care was largely founded in *Prince*'s case. The decision in *Prince*'s case rests heavily on the feature that the duty imposed on the Director-General by section 5(2)(a) of the 1974 Act is for the benefit of the particular child. Self-evidently this statutory duty was not imposed for the benefit of alleged perpetrators of abuse. To utilise the existence of this statutory duty as the foundation of a common law duty in favour of perpetrators would be to travel far outside the rationale in *Prince*'s case.

But I wonder whether this approach is the appropriate way of resolving these cases. The methodology of the High Court of Australia in *Sullivan* gives some comfort to those who perceive modern negligence law as being unbounded, but it is not necessarily consistent with the Court's own recognition of negligence being able to compensate for the kinds of damage that the common law had previously not allowed recovery for, such as economic loss,[116] or nervous shock.[117] Whether one likes it or not, the modern law of negligence necessarily involves the recognition of new interests. The Court appears to assert that the common law does not protect a particular interest because it has not done so before, even though everyone would accept that such an interest was real, such as a parent's interest in his or her child. In the subsequent *Ryan v NSW*, a very different Government liability case, Kirby J, who had not taken in *Sullivan*, chided the Court for having rejected the more flexible *Caparo* test, as a way of determining whether a duty was owed. He wrote:[118]

> I relinquish my adherence to the *Caparo* approach with reluctance. It is, after all, the methodology adopted in the major common law legal systems with which Australian judges are familiar. It at least provides a methodology or approach for the determination of a complex question, which a search for the so-called 'salient features' of a case does not. *Sullivan* has been criticised, correctly in my respectful opinion, as involving 'serious error'. This Court has been taken to task for its repudiation of the idea that 'policy' has a dominant role to play in the determination of duty issues. It has been castigated for embracing 'a chimera'.

The logic of *B* is that the *Prince* duty is based on a particular statutory duty to guard a child's as opposed to a parent's interests, but perhaps this might be accused of sometimes treating the statutory protections a little narrowly and that a case might be made that the protections of the Act, at least to some degree are designed to protect the interests of parents. The conflict of interest point however remains strong. Perhaps what really might be hoped for in a New Zealand context is a limited change to the removal proceeding so that parents or at least successful parents, are able to recover their legal costs at the conclusion of the care and protection hearing.

The Rejection of a Duty in This Particular Situation

But rather than just focusing on the lack of a 'legal' interest in other parts of the judgment, the Court was clearly concerned over the potential conflict of interest and doubted that that duty of care could be properly imposed on such a conflict situation. The Court compared the case to defamation, and went on to essentially distance itself from the House of Lords' decision in *Spring*:[119]

> The present cases can be seen as focusing as much upon the communication of information by the respondents to the appellants and to third parties as upon the competence with which examinations or other procedures were conducted. The core of the complaint by each appellant is that he was injured as a result of what he, and others, were told. At once, then, it can be seen that there is an intersection with the law of defamation which resolves the competing interests of the parties through well-developed principles about privilege and the like. To apply the law of negligence in the present case would resolve that competition on an altogether different basis. It would allow recovery of damages for publishing statements to the discredit of a person where the law of defamation would not.

The point then widened into a consideration of conflict of interest and problems of 'coherence':[120]

> More fundamentally, however, these cases present a question about coherence of the law. Considering whether the persons who reported their suspicions about each appellant owed that appellant a duty of care must begin from the recognition that those who made the report had other responsibilities. A duty of the kind alleged should not be found if that duty would not be compatible with other duties, which the respondents owed.
>
> How may a duty of the kind for which the appellants contend rationally be related to the functions, powers and responsibilities of the various persons and authorities who are alleged to owe that duty? A similar problem has arisen in other cases. The response to the problem in those cases, although not determinative, is instructive.

In that conclusion the Court wrote:[121]

> The statutory scheme that formed the background to the activities of the present respondents was, relevantly, a scheme for the protection of children. It required the respondents to treat the interests of the children as paramount. Their professional or statutory responsibilities involved investigating and reporting upon, allegations that the children had suffered, and were under threat of, serious harm. It would be inconsistent with the proper and effective discharge of those responsibilities that they should be subjected to a legal duty, breach of which would sound in damages, to take care to protect persons who were suspected of being the sources of that harm. The duty for which the appellants contend cannot be reconciled satisfactorily, either with the nature of the functions being exercised by the respondents, or with their statutory obligation to treat the interests of the children as paramount. As to the former, the functions of examination, and reporting, require, for their effective discharge, an investigation into the facts without apprehension as to possible adverse consequences for people in the position of the appellants or legal liability to such persons. As to the latter, the interests of the children, and those suspected of causing their harm, are diverse, and irreconcilable. That they are irreconcilable is evident when regard is had to the case in which examination of a child alleged to be a victim of abuse does not allow the examiner to form a definite opinion about whether the child has been abused, only a suspicion that it may have happened. The interests of the child, in

such a case, would favour reporting that the suspicion of abuse has not been dispelled; the interests of a person suspected of the abuse would be to the opposite effect.

Of particular interest to an English audience is the seeming positive citation of *Hill*[122] and of *Bedfordshire*[123] as examples of decisions in which the House of Lords had endorsed such an approach. One wonders if the same logic might be applied when inevitably a child protection case makes its way to the High Court of Australia, or whether the Court might prefer to analyse a child's claim differently.

The Place of Witness Immunity and the Relevance of Judicial Proceedings

Commentators, including myself, have tended to push to one side the doctrine of witness immunity and its potential to stymie actions against public authorities in relation to their failure to properly investigate allegations of abuse. In just about all child protection systems, the ultimate decision to remove a child for any length of time from his or her parents belongs not to the investigating social workers but to judicial officers. Does the prospect of judicial supervision, or of subsequent hearings, mean that investigators enjoy some expansive version of witness immunity, and if not what does the fact of the court hearing mean for liability? In the *Newham* companion case to *Bedfordshire*, Lord Browne-Wilkinson appeared to agree about the immunity of a psychologist who had assisted in the investigation of the abuse that occurred and who prepared reports which were to be used in court proceedings concerning whether the child ought to be removed or not. His Lordship wrote approvingly of Drake J's decision in *Evans v London Hospital Medical College (University of London)*[124] to extend the immunity to a pathologist who had communicated the results of a post mortem to the Director of Public Prosecutions, on the basis that if immunity was not granted to the initial investigation, the immunity granted to the actual testimony could essentially be outflanked:[125]

> My Lords, I find the reasoning of Drake J compelling at least in relation to the investigation and preparation of evidence in criminal proceedings. In my judgment exactly similar considerations apply where, in performance of a public duty, the local authority is investigating whether or not there is evidence on which to bring proceedings for the protection of the child from abuse, such abuse frequently being a criminal offence. In the present case, the psychiatrist was instructed to carry out the examination of the child for the specific purpose of discovering whether the child had been sexually abused and (if possible) the identity of the abuser. The psychiatrist must have known that, if such abuse was discovered, proceedings by the local authority for the protection of the child would ensue and that her findings would be the evidence on which those proceedings would be based. It follows in my judgment that such investigations having such an immediate link with possible proceedings in pursuance of a statutory duty cannot be made the basis of subsequent claims.

Since *Bedfordshire*, of course, witness immunity has been the subject of considerable controversy in the United Kingdom. It may be that, after *Darker*,[126] the ability of those who investigate to claim witness immunity for all aspects of the investigations, so long as they might ultimately be presented to the Court hearing, has passed and courts may prefer what a number of the Lords in *Darker* referred to as a functional analysis, which is more tightly tailored to the purposes of the immunity.

In New Zealand, the Crown had attempted to rely on either witness immunity or some other form of statutory immunity in order to defeat claims brought against social workers. In *Prince* the claimed witness immunity seemed to fail on the fact that the allegation essentially involved that there had been no report of abuse at all. However the Court did give considerable weight in the part of the case that related to the allegation that Prince's mother, Gardner, had been tricked by social welfare workers into adopting Prince out as an infant, if not to witness immunity as such, but rather to the fact the adoption decisions were ultimately made by a magistrate, or later a Family Court Judge. This judicial intervention appeared to go some way in breaking the chain of causation between what social workers had done and the subsequent adoption.

In *B v Attorney-General*, the Court appeared a little sceptical as to the proper application of witness immunity to the situation where social workers were investigating the possibility of abuse. Keith and Blanchard JJ wrote:[127]

> That contention leads into the related submission by the respondents that they were protected by witness immunity. That protection is not limited to evidence actually given in Court but extends to statements and documents made for the purpose of pending or contemplated litigation. That is to say, investigatory and preparatory stages may be protected along with the trial. The proceedings may be criminal or civil or indeed relate to an administrative tribunal, The justification for the protection is the public interest in facilitating full and frank disclosure for the purposes of the litigation. In the absence of this extension of protection, the absolute privilege of a witness giving evidence could be simply outflanked. It follows from the justification that the protection may be available even although proceedings are not brought and, if they are, even although the person giving the information does not give evidence .... There are plainly limits to this protection...

Tipping J left open the issue in concurrence:[128]

> These then are the two bases upon which I agree that none of the plaintiffs has a tenable cause of action against any of the defendants. As this is sufficient to dispose of the appeal, I prefer to leave open the question of the so-called witness immunity. Normally such immunity is invoked for statements, whether written or oral, made as a witness or preparatory to giving evidence. In order to reflect the rationale for the immunity there must be a testimonial dimension. It is difficult to see investigatory conduct, even with a greater or lesser degree of likelihood of giving evidence, as being sufficiently testimonial to qualify. After all, the policy reason for the immunity is to enable witnesses, actual or potential, to speak frankly and fearlessly without the risk of being sued for what they say. The judicial process is thereby assisted and enhanced. I make these observations because in this case the 'witnesses' are the social

worker and the clinical psychologist. The plaintiffs are trying to sue them as much for what they did not do as for what they did.

However, while the Court did not seem to want to use a witness immunity (or privilege) doctrine to deny liability, one of its expressed reasons for denying liability on either social workers was that after the initial decision to remove the two daughters, a removal order had been sought and granted by the Family Court. Keith and Blanchard JJ described the importance of this judicial intervention in the following way:[129]

> By that time there was in addition the prospect of the Court assessing the validity of the allegations and the evidence given in support of them – as happened at length in this case, as we have noted. The Court, with the assistance of those most directly involved, their counsel and their witnesses, would have been in a much better position to make those assessments than were the departmental officers and others involved at the preceding stage. There is also the distinction that at that stage only preliminary assessments were required (involving reasonable belief or reasonable grounds for suspicion). By contrast orders could be made at the end of the hearing only if the s.27 ground is 'proved' (s.31). Findings and orders were also subject to appeal and review (Part VI).
>
> [Counsel for the plaintiff] frankly acknowledged that the statement of claim made no attack on the obtaining of the warrants or the filing of the complaints. There was no allegation of negligence in what the departmental officer put to the Court. Nor was there any question of suing the judicial officer or challenging the warrant. We are not saying that the bringing of those legal processes prevents all possibility of action by, in effect, regularising any earlier failings, although such processes would raise major problems about causation. There would remain for instance the possibility of actions for malicious prosecution or of professional disciplinary proceedings. Rather, to repeat, the statutory scheme cuts across a common law duty of care once the triggering step to the 'prompt inquiry' is completed and the officials are moving beyond that initial obligation and are assembling relevant information before considering whether to exercise their statutory powers.

Keith and Blanchard JJ went on to conclude in relation to the witness immunity claim, that the substance of witness immunity claim was already been incorporated within the way in which the Court of Appeal considered whether there was a duty of care.[130]

> That is that in the circumstances of this case. Those more general arguments for witness privilege (a word that seems more apt in the current context) are subsumed within the more specific arguments arising from the terms and scheme of the 1974 Act which we have already held exclude liability in the present case; the legislation 'covers the field to the exclusion of the common law'.[131]

This treatment of the Court proceeding as, in effect, being a *novus actus interveniens* means that those who investigate sexual abuse claims may well be immunised if they can point to this intervening Court proceeding. The difficulty with this is, of course, that the quality of the judicial determination is dependent on competency with which the social workers had conducted the investigation. Perhaps more significantly, it ignores the reality that social workers and others who work with them fulfil a number of different functions, the preparing of evidence for the tribunal only being one, and that treating all those decisions as effectively being overtaken by the Court's decision. If everything about an investigation is always immunised by a Court proceeding, it may leave both parents and children without an effective remedy.

On appeal, the Privy Council clearly preferred, despite very strong submissions from counsel for the psychologist who had advised the Department to leave witness immunity to trial.[132] From the way that Lord Nicholls phrased his observations about assertion of immunity, it might be suggested that days of blanket assertions are numbered:[133]

> This submission gives rise to a difficulty which not infrequently arises in striking out applications. Their Lordships do not have sufficient factual information to reach a firm decision on this issue. Their Lordships lack background information about how the sexual abuse team procedure worked in practice and the role of the psychologist. Further information would also be desirable on the detailed sequence of events in the present case, including full details of all aspects of the psychologist's involvement, together with a copy of her report or reports. Without this evidence too much is left to conjecture. This is not a satisfactory basis for attempting to form a view on whether the link between the psychologist's report and the court proceedings was sufficiently close to attract witness privilege. This is an issue on which the facts should be investigated and found at trial before a decision can properly be made.

But perhaps even more importantly the Privy Council did not appear to see the interim order as the kind of absolute barrier that the Court of Appeal had.

Conclusion

This paper presents a patchwork of judicial approaches to what are difficult issues. It is a cliché but an apt one, given the fact that four important judgments have been issued between the time of the conference and the publication of this volume, that we live in interesting times. Courts downunder have struggled with creating a coherent theory of government liability in general, and it is not surprising that there is an array of different approaches to complex issues like vicarious liability which one suspects are not necessarily the best doctrine to begin articulating why the Government ought to compensate or not compensate sexually abused children. While at times such incoherence is obviously frustrating, sometimes it has, as with *Prince*, the prospect of taking the law on new adventures. One can only hope that the cases in this area will continue to become more and more historic as our systems for protecting children get better and better. As much as the common law can adapt to new circumstances, let us hope that having so adapted it will no longer be needed.

Notes

1 In addition to the issues discussed here the cases often involve limitation problems. Limitation issues are not discussed in this paper.
2 *S v Attorney-General* CA 43/02 (15 July 2003) paras 71–72.
3 *Sullivan v Moody* [2001] HCA 59; 207 CLR 562.
4 *Enever v The King* (1906) 3 CLR 969.
5 *Cubillo v Commonwealth (No 2)* (2000) 103 FCR 1, as quoted by the Australian Law Reform Commission ALRC Report 92, *Liability of the Commonwealth at Common Law and in Equity* para 25.10. The doctrine has been repealed in New South Wales, and partially abolished in Queensland and The Northern Territory, and reform of the principle has been recommended by the Commission.
6 *Williams v Minister, Aboriginal Land Rights Act 1983* (No 2) (1999) 25 Fam LR 86.
7 *Cubillo v Commonwealth of Australia* [2001] FCA 1213 in which the Full Federal Court refused to allow the plaintiffs to allege on appeal that the Commonwealth had owed a duty to the plaintiffs to prevent them being physically abused in schools. The claims of abuse had been made at the earlier trial as a way of substantiating the damages that had been suffered as a result of the supposed wrongful removal.
8 *Murphy v Brentwood District Council* [1991] AC 398.
9 *X (Minors) v Bedfordshire County Council* [1995] 2 AC 633.
10 *Stovin v Wise* [1996] AC 923.
11 See the recent decision in *Attorney-General v Carter* [2003] 2 NZLR 160 in which the Court of Appeal seemed to discount the possibility in a negligent inspection case that once there had been a finding that there was no duty of care that it would be appropriate to essentially undo that finding by allowing an action to proceed by way of breach of statutory duty.
12 *Stovin v Wise* [1996] AC 923, 935–936, using the terminology of Mason J in *Sutherland Shire Council v. Heyman* (1985) 157 CLR 424.
13 *Invercargill City Council v Hamlin* [1994] 3 NZLR 513 (CA).
14 *Attorney-General v Carter* [2003] 2 NZLR 160 CA.
15 (1998) 192 CLR 330.
16 *Brodie v Singleton Shire Council* [2001] HCA 29.
17 *Crimmins v Stevedoring Industry Finance Committee* (1999) 2000 CLR 1.
18 *Graham Barclay Oysters Pty Ltd v Ryan* [2002] HCA 54.
19 *Attorney-General v Prince and Gardner* [1998] 1 NZLR 262 (CA).
20 *Attorney-General v Prince and Gardner* [1998] 1 NZLR 262, 285 (CA).
21 *G v Auckland Hospital Board* [1976] 1 NZLR 638 (SC).
22 Whether many of the claimants were in fact entitled to lump sum payments was a questionable matter.
23 *S v Attorney-General* CA 43/02 (15 July 2003) para. 29.
24 *S v Attorney-General* [2002] NZFLR 295.
25 Injury Prevention, Rehabilitation, and Compensation Act 2001, s.36.
26 Accident Rehabilitation, Compensation and Insurance Act 1992, s.63(3):
(3) For the purposes of this section, where a claim involves medical misadventure or conduct of a kind described in section 8(3) of this Act, the personal injury shall be deemed to have been suffered on the date on which the person first received treatment for that personal injury as that personal injury, being treatment of a kind for which the Corporation is required or permitted to make payments either directly or under an agreement or contract or arrangement under section 29A of

this Act, irrespective of whether or not it makes any payment in the particular case.

27 *S v Attorney-General* [2002] NZFLR 295 paras 175–176.

28 *W v Attorney-General* (3 October 2002) CP 42/97 Wellington para. 144.

29 Accident Compensation, Rehabilitation and Compensation Act 1992, s.63(3).

30 *S v Attorney-General* (15 July 2003) CA 42/03 para. 26.

31 See Geoff McLay 'Nervous Shock, Tort and Accident Compensation: Tort Regained' (1999) 30 VUWLR 197–220.

32 *Donselaar v Donselaar* [1982] 1 NZLR 97 (CA).

33 *Daniels v Thompson* [1998] 3 NZLR 22 (CA).

34 *W v Attorney-General* [1999] 2 NZLR 1 (CA).

35 Injury Prevention, Rehabilitation, and Compensation Act 2001, section 319 provides:

(1) Nothing in this Act, and no rule of law, prevents any person from bringing proceedings in any court in New Zealand for exemplary damages for conduct by the defendant that has resulted in:

(a) personal injury covered by this Act; or

(b) personal injury covered by the former Acts.

(2) The court may make an award of exemplary damages for conduct of the kind described in subsection (1) even though:

(a) the defendant has been charged with, and acquitted or convicted of, an offence involving the conduct concerned in the claim for exemplary damages; or

(b) the defendant has been charged with such an offence and, at the time at which the court is making its decision on the claim for exemplary damages, the charge has not been dealt with; or

(3) In determining whether to award exemplary damages and, if they are to be awarded, the amount of them, the court may have regard to:

(a) whether a penalty has been imposed on the defendant for an offence involving the conduct concerned in the claim for exemplary damages; and

(b) if so, the nature of the penalty.

36 See *M v L* [1998] 3 NZLR 104 , 112 citing *Carrington v Attorney-General* [1972] NZLR 1106; *Monroe v Attorney-General (Police)* [1985] 11 NZ Recent Law 342; *Pettersson v Royal Oak Hotel Ltd* [1948] NZLR 136.

37 *S v Attorney-General* (15 July 2003) CA 42/03 paras 88–89.

38 *S v Attorney-General* (15 July 2003) CA 42/03 para. 93.

39 *Monroe v Attorney-General* (27 March 1985) High Court, Auckland, A 617/82.

40 *McLaren v Somerville* [1996] 3 NZLR 424.

41 *A v Bottrill* [2001] 3 NZLR 622 (CA).

42 *A v Bottrill* [2001] 2 NZLR 622 para. 42.

43 *S v Attorney-General* [2002] NZFLR 295.

44 *S v Attorney-General* [2002] NZFLR 295, paras 277–279.

45 *A v Bottrill* [2002] UKPC 44 [2003] 1 AC 449 [2002] 3 WLR 1406 para. 26.

46 *W v Attorney-General* (3 October 2002) CP 42/97 Wellington paras 164–166.

47 *W v Attorney-General* (15 July 2003) CA 227/02 para. 61.

48 *W v Attorney-General* (15 July 2003) CA 227/02 para. 53.

49 *Attorney-General v Prince and Gardner* [1998] 1 NZLR 262.

50 Geoff McLay, 'Convicted Killer Can Use Social Welfare – *Prince* – the Strange Fate of *Bedfordshire* Down Under' (1999) 11 CFLQ 75 and with W.R. Atkin

'Suing Social Welfare Agencies – A Comparative View from New Zealand' (2001) 13 CFLQ 287–310.

51 *B v Attorney-General* [1999] 2 NZLR 296.

52 See the discussion in Geoff McLay and W.R. Atkin 'Suing Social Welfare Agencies – A Comparative View from New Zealand' (2001) 13 CFLQ 287–310.

53 *B v Attorney-General* (16 July 2003) PC1 of 2003 para. 30.

54 *B v Attorney-General* (16 July 2003) PC1 of 2003 para. 30.

55 *B v Attorney-General* (16 July 2003) PC1 of 2003 para. 27.

56 *TC v State of New South Wales* [1999] NSWSC 31 revised 12/02/99 and *TC (by his Tutor Sabintino) v The State of New South Wales* [2001] NSWCA 380 (31 October 2001).

57 Similar but not identical obligations are imposed by section 30–34 of the now Children and Young Persons (Care and Protection) Act 1998 (NSW). In particular section 34 provides:

(1) If the Director-General forms the opinion, on reasonable grounds, that a child or young person is in need of care and protection, the Director-General is to take whatever action is necessary to safeguard or promote the safety, welfare and well-being of the child or young person.

(2) Without limiting subsection (1), the action that the Director-General might take in response to a report includes the following:

(a) providing, or arranging for the provision of, support services for the child or young person and his or her family,

(b) development, in consultation with the parents (jointly or separately), of a care plan to meet the needs of the child or young person and his or her family that: (i) does not involve taking the matter before the Children's Court, or (ii) may be registered with the Children's Court, or (iii) is the basis for consent orders made by the Children's Court,

(c) ensuring the protection of the child or young person by exercising the Director-General's emergency protection powers as referred to in Part 1 of Chapter 5,

(d) seeking appropriate orders from the Children's Court.

58 *X (Minors) v Bedfordshire County Council* [1995] 2 AC 53.

59 *O'Rouke v London Borough of Camden* [1998] AC 188.

60 *W v Essex County Council* [1998] 3 WLR 534.

61 *Barrett v Enfield London Borough Council* [1997] 3 WLR 628.

62 *Attorney-General v Prince and Gardner* [1998] 1 NZLR 262, 285 (CA).

63 *TC v State of New South Wales* [1999] NSWSC 31 (revised 12 February 1999) para. 177.

64 *TC v State of New South Wales* [1999] NSWSC 31 (revised 12 February 1999) para. 184.

65 *TC (by his Tutor Sabintino) v The State of New South Wales* [2001] NSWCA 380 (31 October 2001) para. 124–125.

66 *TC (by his Tutor Sabintino) v The State of New South Wales* [2001] NSWCA 380 (31 October 2001) para. 148.

67 *TC (by his Tutor Sabintino) v The State of New South Wales* [2001] NSWCA 380 (31 October 2001) para. 142.

68 *TC (by his Tutor Sabintino) v The State of New South Wales* [2001] NSWCA 380 (31 October 2001) para. 142.

69 *TC v State of New South Wales* [2000] NSWSC 292 (12 April 2000).

70 See for the Australian approach to non-traditional fiduciary duties *Breen v Williams* (1996) 186 CLR 71. For its application in the child context involving the

question whether fiduciary law might be used to get around limitation periods, see *Paramasivam v Flynn* (1998) 160 ALR 203 but *Williams v Minister, Aboriginal Land Rights Act 1983 (No 1)* (1994) 35 NSWLR 497 (NSWCA).

71 *Deatons Pty Ltd v Flew* (1949) 79 CLR 370.

72 [2001] NSWCA 112.

73 *Bazley v Curry* [1999] 2 SCR 534.

74 *Jacobi v Griffiths* [1999] 2 SCR 570.

75 The leading case was *Commonwealth of Australia v Introvigne* (1982) 150 CLR 258.

76 *Lepore v State of New South Wales* [2001] NSWCA 112; (2001) 52 NSWLR 420, para. 40.

77 *Morris v CW Martin & Sons Ltd* [1966] QB 716 (CA).

78 *Lepore v State of New South Wales* [2001] NSWCA 112; (2001) 52 NSWLR 420 para. 55.

79 *Lepore v State of New South Wales* [2001] NSWCA 112; (2001) 52 NSWLR 420 para. 49.

80 *Lepore v State of New South Wales* [2001] NSWCA 112; (2001) 52 NSWLR 420 paras 98–112.

81 *Rich v State of New South Wales* [2001] QCA 295; [2001] Aust Torts Report 81–626.

82 *Rich v State of New South Wales* [2001] QCA 295; [2001] Aust Torts Report 81–626 para. 16.

83 *Rich v State of New South Wales* [2001] QCA 295; [2001] Aust Torts Report 81–626 para. 20.

84 *New South Wales v Lepore, Samin v Queensland; Rich v Queensland* [2003] HCA 4, (6 February 2002).

85 *Samin* 342. 'Negligent, even grossly negligent conduct is one thing, intentional criminal conduct is, and always has been altogether another. In my opinion, deliberate criminal misconduct lies outside, and indeed usually will lie far outside the scope or course of an employed teacher's duty.'

86 See the useful commentary on the decision by Steven White and Graeme Orr (2003) 11 Torts Law Journal 1.

87 *New South Wales v Lepore, Samin v Queensland; Rich v Queensland* [2003] HCA 4, (6 February 2002) para. 223 (citations omitted).

88 *New South Wales v Lepore, Samin v Queensland; Rich v Queensland* [2003] HCA 4, (6 February 2002) para. 233.

89 *Lloyd v Grace, Smith & Co* [1912] AC 716.

90 *Deatons Pty Ltd v Flew* (1949) 79 CLR 370.

91 *New South Wales v Lepore; Samin v Queensland; Rich v Queensland* [2003] HCA 4, (6 February 2002) para. 300.

92 Citations omitted.

93 *New South Wales v Lepore, Samin v Queensland; Rich v Queensland* [2003] HCA 4, (6 February 2002) para. 303.

94 *New South Wales v Lepore, Samin v Queensland; Rich v Queensland* [2003] HCA 4, (6 February 2002) para. 139.

95 Citing *Ramsay v Larsen* (1964) 111 CLR 16 at 25–26, 37.

96 *New South Wales v Lepore, Samin v Queensland; Rich v Queensland* [2003] HCA 4, (6 February 2002) para. 161.

97 *The Commonwealth v Introvigne* (1982) 150 CLR 258.

98 *M B v Her Majesty the Queen in Right of the Province of British Columbia* [2001] BCCA 227.

99 *S v Attorney-General* [2002] NZFLR 296.
100 *W v Attorney-General* (3 October 2002) CP 42/97 Wellington.
101 *W v Attorney-General* (3 October 2002) CP 42/97 Wellington.
102 *S v Attorney-General* [2002] NZFLR 295 para. 234.
103 *S v Attorney-General* [2002] NZFLR 295 para. 236.
104 *S v Attorney-General* (15 July 2003) CA 42/03 para. 68.
105 *S v Attorney-General* [2002] NZFLR 295 para. 187.
106 *S v Attorney-General* [2002] NZFLR 295 para. 190.
107 *W v Attorney-General* (3 October 2002) CP 42/97 Wellington para. 88.
108 *Sullivan v Moody* [2001] HCA 59; 207 CLR 562.
109 *Caparo Industries v Dickman* [1990] 2 AC 605.
110 *Sullivan v Moody* [2001] HCA 59; 207 CLR 562 para. 49.
111 *Sullivan v Moody* [2001] HCA 59; 207 CLR 562 para. 42.
112 *F v Wirral Metropolitan Borough Council* [1991] Fam 69; [1991] 2 All ER 648.
113 See the analysis of Jane Wright in her paper to this conference.
114 *Prince v Attorney-General* [1998] 1 NZLR 262, 291 (CA).
115 *B v Attorney-General* (16 July 2003) para. 30.
116 *Perre v Apand Pty Ltd* [1999] HCA 36.
117 *Tame v New South Wales; Annetts v Australian Stations Pty Ltd* [2002] HCA 35, 5 September 2002.
118 *Graham Barclay Oysters Pty Ltd v Ryan* [2002] HCA 54 para. 238.
119 The reverse point might be made in the United Kingdom where since *Spring v Guardian Assurance plc* [1995] 2 AC 296 it has been accepted that a duty of care might be laid over the top of qualified privilege in some circumstances, that the child welfare agencies might be sued in negligence for impugning the reputation of those under investigations, such investigations might be met by a pleading of witness immunity.
120 *Sullivan v Moody* [2001] HCA 59; 207 CLR 562 para. 15.
121 *Sullivan v Moody* [2001] HCA 59; 207 CLR 562 para. 62.
122 *Hill v Chief Constable of West Yorkshire* [1989] AC 53.
123 *X v Bedfordshire County Council* [1995] 2 AC 633.
124 *Evans v London Hospital Medical College (University of London)* [1981] 1 WLR 184.
125 *X v Bedfordshire County Council* [1995] 2 AC 633, 755.
126 *Darker v Chief Constable of West Midlands* [2001] 1 AC 435.
127 *B v Attorney-General* [1999] 2 NZLR 296 para. 32.
128 *B v Attorney-General* [1999] 2 NZLR 296 para. 51.
129 *B v Attorney-General* [1999] 2 NZLR 296, para. 26–27.
130 *B v Attorney-General* [1999] 2 NZLR 296 para. 32.
131 Citing *South Pacific Manufacturing Co Ltd v New Zealand Security Consultants & Investigations Ltd* [1992] 2 NZLR 282, 297, in which the Court of Appeal had held that private investigators employed by an insurance company to investigate fires did not owe a duty to those whose property had burnt down.
132 See the approach of the English Court of Appeal in *L & P v Reading Borough Council* (12 March 2001) EWCA 346; [2001] 1 WLR 1575.
133 *B v Attorney-General* (16 July 2003) PC 1 of 2003 para. 32.

Chapter 8

Child Abuse and the Failure to Protect: Liability of Public Authorities in Canada

*Margaret Hall**

Introduction

Canada has been in the vanguard in the development of the civil action for sexual abuse generally,[1] and in the doctrines pertaining to public authority liability for abuse. Canadian law continues to evolve, and the recent decisions of the Supreme Court of Canada in the British Columbia 'trio' of appeals (*KLB*, *MB* and *EDG*) will shape the law in this area to a considerable extent.

The potential liability costs for governments, in particular with regards to the residential schools for aboriginal children, are considerable, and as governments seek to control costs they may turn more often to Alternative Dispute Resolution and other alternative approaches. Several provincial jurisdictions in Canada have implemented alternative approaches to providing compensation for abuse ('redress programmes').[2] In December 2002 the Minister for Residential Schools Resolution announced a comprehensive 'resolution framework,' a 'unified and holistic' plan to facilitate the settlement of abuse claims out of court. An Alternative Dispute Resolution process will be available through the framework for applicants alleging physical and sexual abuse. Complainants who choose instead to pursue out of court settlement or proceed with litigation will, like ADR participants, have access to health and personal supports, in addition to commemorative activities such as healing conferences, monuments, and reconciliation feasts.

Development of non-traditional redress programmes has not replaced more traditional avenues of compensation, however; child abuse plaintiffs have continued to access the Courts, individually and through the mechanism of the class action.[3]

* Director of Legal Research and Writing, University of British Columbia.

Negligence: General View

The distinction between 'operational' matters and matters of 'policy' works to limit the potential negligence liability of public authorities in Canadian law. Public authorities may owe a duty of care not to be negligent only with regard to 'operational matters'; no duty of care can be owed regarding matters of policy unless the ostensible 'policy' decision is so unreasonable that it falls outside the ambit of judicially conferred discretion.[4] The line between matters of policy and matters of operation is not always a bright one, but the characterisation is a crucial, threshold step. Once that threshold has been crossed, and a duty of care established, that duty may be negated where considerations of policy exist which ought to limit or negative a duty of care in the circumstances.[5]

Within this limited purview a public authority, like any other defendant, may be negligent if it *acts* in a particular way so as to breach the duty of care or if it *omits* a particular action in circumstances where that omission constitutes a breach of the duty of care. Omissions will constitute a breach where they occur in a course of action undertaken by the defendant, or where a special relationship of proximity exists between the plaintiff and the defendant.[6] The common law does not impose liability for 'pure' omissions, or nonfeasance: 'There is no distinction more deeply rooted in the common law than that between misfeasance and nonfeasance, between active misconduct working positive injury to others and passive inaction.'[7]

Public authorities act negligently where oversight and management of the child's 'case' (where the child is in care) has been carried out in a negligent manner. The failure to intervene may constitute negligence where the omission is interpreted as occurring in the course of action or where a special relationship of proximity exists, giving rise to a duty of care requiring action. *X v Bedfordshire County Council* concerned the liability of a public authority for its failure to protect children at known risk on the basis of a special relationship requiring action. The House of Lords in *Bedfordshire* held that, although the facts established a sufficiently proximate relationship between the children and the authority, a duty of care was properly excluded for reasons of policy.[8]

In the subsequently decided case of *Barrett v Enfield Borough Council*[9] the House of Lords held that the duty of care owed by a local authority to a child already in care should not be excluded on the basis of policy. The relevant factors in the *Bedfordshire* case (the 'policy' reasons on the basis of which liability was excluded),[10] where the children were still in the care of their parents, did not apply once the decision had been made to take the child into care.

Barrett and *X* together created a strong incentive not to take children into care; a local authority could be found liable in negligence regarding discharge of their duty to a child in care but would be immune from liability regarding children who had not been taken into care, even where (as in *X*) the risks to the child in the community are high, clear and known. The decision of the European Court of Human Rights regarding the *Bedfordshire* case (*Z v UK*)[11] has diminished that incentive, perhaps significantly, but not absolutely. The European Court found that the decision of the House of Lords to exclude liability in this class of case – regarding the decision whether or not to take a child into care – was not the exercise of a 'blanket immunity' and did not therefore abrogate the plaintiffs' right to a fair trial as guaranteed by Article 6 of the European Convention of Human Rights. This kind of limited exclusion for reasons of policy was an acceptable interpretation of the English common law.

The Court did find, however, that the UK was in breach of Article 3 (the right not to be subjected to torture and inhuman or degrading treatment) by failing to protect the *Bedfordshire* children from serious and long term neglect and abuse. Under the Human Rights Act the UK judiciary is under a statutory obligation to take account of the European Court's interpretation of Convention rights. Nevertheless, the threshold for the human rights action (torture and inhuman or degrading treatment) would seem to be a high one, higher than the statutory threshold for intervention by a local authority (local authorities are not restricted to intervention in situations of torture or inhuman or degrading treatment). The ultimate scope of treatment prohibited by Article 3 has yet to be determined; 'whether the human rights remedy will be sufficient to balance the deficiencies of the common law remains to be seen'.[12]

No comparable analysis or distinction exists in Canada, although the issue has not been settled conclusively either way; the duty of care in the second class of case, where the child 'at risk' has not been taken into care, has seldom been considered. The liability of public authorities in the first class of negligence case (where the child is 'in care') is well established in Canadian law.[13]

Negligence: Oversight, Supervision and Case Management

Public authorities owe a duty of care to children and young people in their care; that duty will be breached where reasonable care is not taken to ensure that the child's environment is safe and healthy. The child's vulnerability, and the high degree of responsibility inherent in the decision to take a child into care, create a high standard of care or 'special diligence' to be exercised by the public authority in the discharge of its duty. That duty will be breached where an authority should have known that environment was unsafe and/or unhealthy, either because of single causative incidents of sexual or physical abuse or where the course of treatment resulted in a 'cumulative' harm. Actual knowledge is not required. 'Good faith' decision-making defence will not comprise a defence regarding non-discretionary operational matters, or where the decision taken is so unreasonable that it could not have followed a proper exercise of oversight.

The federal government was found directly liable[14] in negligence to a former child resident of an aboriginal residential school in the case of *FSM v Clarke*.[15] The government's duty of care in that case arose from its assumption of control and responsibility over the child, removing FSM from his home, placing him at the school, and delegating parental authority over the child to the school and its principal (who subsequently delegated that authority to the dorm supervisor who perpetrated the abuse). Canada's decision to discharge its duty of care in an 'institutional manner' for large numbers of children did not negate its relationship of proximity to the individual child plaintiff, nor the duty of care that relationship created.[16] Nor did reasons of policy justify limiting or excluding a duty of care in the circumstances;[17] on the contrary, reasons of policy made it crucial that the duty of care *not* be excluded in this context:

> The placement of children in the care of the Crown is not just theoretical where children are removed from their home, placed in institutions controlled by Crown personnel, and isolated from parental input and responsibility. Who is legally responsible for these children? Assumption of guardianship over Indian children by the Crown cannot be viewed as a hollow task devoid of responsibility when governmental objectives were being pursued through the policy of institutionalization of Indian youth.[18]

The government's duty of care required it to 'take reasonable care that [the plaintiff] was in a safe and healthy environment while at the institution', a requirement that the plaintiff be placed in a reasonable environment and that that placement be subject to ongoing and adequate supervision. It was not necessary that the government actually know about the abuse and fail to take action in the face of that knowledge, if the circumstances were such that the reasonable defendant *should have* known:

> The [government] administrator should have been aware of the behaviour of children on the schoolground and childhood gossip which was apparent to a relatively novice teacher at a local school who acted swiftly to deal with the matter. If he was not, then he was wilfully blinded by his own desires to avoid detection of lax moral conduct and sexually abusive behaviour at St. George's.[19]

In another residential school case (*WRB v Plint*),[20] however, the Court found that, given awareness about sexual abuse at the time the assaults were alleged to have taken place, the administrator could not have been expected to know about abuse in the school; nor was there sufficient evidence of actual knowledge. Students who had themselves suffered abuse at the hands of Plint were apparently unaware that others had had similar experiences, for example, even where those students had come into contact with each other. Nothing, apparently, was ever said, by anyone, either as gossip or otherwise.

The provincial Crown was found liable in negligence regarding its failure to adequately monitor and supervise a foster care placement in the case of *KLB v British Columbia*.[21] The Court of Appeal upheld the finding at trial that the duty of care owed by social workers to children in care required for its proper discharge a 'special diligence', a higher standard of care 'flowing from the responsibility of the Superintendent inherent in apprehension and the vulnerability of children taken into care'.[22] This special standard of care applied to both placement and ongoing supervision following placement.

Under the circumstances, the provincial authority had breached this standard of care. As described by the trial judge:

> The facts of this case are troublesome because there is no specific singular conduct or incident that stands out as so abusive as to be causative of obvious damage, with the exception of the beating and sexual assault of [K]. The other incidents, while abusive in nature and cumulatively leading to deleterious effect, do not stand alone as sufficient to cause the psychological and personal difficulties, which the plaintiff described. With the exception of the beating of [K], not one alone would have been sufficient at the time to end the foster relationship. It was the repeated hitting, misconduct, and humiliation that founds the cause of action here.
>
> The crown is liable for failure to adequately monitor and supervise the P/H homes and for failure to regularly and adequately assess the homes. The conduct of the social workers fell below the standards historically established for monitoring the P. home in a situation of overplacement. The same is true for the H. home. Discipline was not discussed. These breaches of the duty of care created the risk from which it could reasonably be seen that the children would be harmed.[23]

The Crown sought to rely on a common law defence of 'good faith', whereby decisions made in the exercise of discretion would never be negligent if made and carried out in good faith.[24] In this case,

> the fault was not in the exercise of discretion to place the children in the foster homes but in failing to discover the facts that would have engaged the proper exercise of that discretion. The course of action would have been clear if the facts had been discovered through reasonable supervision and investigation.[25]

If the social workers had exercised adequate oversight, a 'good faith' decision to leave the children in the home and take no action would not have been possible, given the conditions under which the children were living.[26]

The finding of direct negligence was upheld by the Supreme Court of Canada, subject to a limitations defence (that the limitations period for an action in negligence had expired). The Supreme Court held that it was

> reasonably foreseeable that some people, if left in charge of children in difficult or overcrowded circumstances, will use excessive physical and verbal discipline. It is also reasonably foreseeable that some people will take advantage of the complete dependence of children in their care, and will sexually abuse them. To lessen the likelihood that this form of abuse will occur, the government must set up adequate procedures to screen prospective foster parents. And it must monitor homes so that any abuse that does occur can be promptly detected.[27]

A definition of *systemic* negligence – an environment in which negligent management and oversight created conditions in which children were not protected from abuse – is developing with regards to the abuse and neglect of children in institutional settings. Certification of a class action brought on the basis of systemic negligence in a boarding school for the deaf (Jericho Hill) was upheld by the Supreme Court of Canada in 2001 (*Rumley v British Columbia*);[28] that case has yet to proceed, and the definition of 'systemic negligence' in this context will no doubt be more fully explained in the future. It is interesting to note that peer abuse was identified as a significant problem and source of damage at Jericho Hill; 'systemic negligence' connects abuse perpetrated by residents to an institutional responsibility for permitting or even facilitating environments in which peer abuse is allowed to occur (the so called 'culture of abuse' phenomenon).

Negligence: Failure to Protect

The decision not to act has been interpreted as an omission in the course of action where the risk to the child in the family setting was known. Inaction in this context was a breach of the standard of care. The outcome where a reasonable worker *should have* appreciated the risk to the child does not appear to have been considered in any Canadian case.

The liability of a social worker for failing to remove a child from an abusive situation – the failure to intervene – was considered by the Manitoba Court of Appeal in *AJ v Cairnie Estate*.[29] The social worker in that case had been called in to investigate the plaintiff's complaints of sexual abuse by her step-father, which she had disclosed to a school counsellor. Following the social worker's involvement with the family, the plaintiff suffered further abuse including rape. The social worker did not carry out a further investigation, nor did she apprehend the child or otherwise act to remedy her situation within the family home. A new social worker was eventually assigned to the case, whereupon the plaintiff was apprehended immediately and placed in foster care.

The social worker's evaluation of whether or not to apprehend the plaintiff was characterised in this case as an 'operational decision made in the usual course of the social worker's duties' (unlike the House of Lords characterisation of the decision not to intervene in *X* as a matter of policy, albeit the decision was potentially so unreasonable as to fall outside of the ambit of discretion and, therefore, immunity). The professional standard of care at the time should have required an investigation, especially in light of the existing evidence of previous abuse. By not acting, the social worker had breached that standard causing further damage to the plaintiff, for which the government as the social worker's employer was vicariously liable. There was no evidence of direct negligence on the part of the province; no evidence that the province had failed to supervise the social worker Mrs. Cairnie, or that her supervisors knew of her incompetence. The policy test or 'branch' (which had worked to exclude the duty of care in the *Bedfordshire* case) was not considered.

Vicarious Liability

Vicarious liability is a form of strict liability whereby an employer may be liable for the torts of an employee where they are committed in the course of employment. Traditionally, the doctrine has excluded most intentional torts, including sexual assaults, as purely independent acts committed for personal gratification and outside of the scope of employment.[30] With a set of landmark decisions in 1999, however (*Bazley v Curry*,[31] and its companion appeal, *Jacobi v Griffiths*[32]), the Supreme Court of Canada held that an employer would be vicariously liable for child abuse perpetrated by an employee where the risk of abuse was created by the terms and conditions of employment. In the *Bazley* case, the perpetrator's employment in an intimate and unsupervised parental role created a high risk that what did happen would happen; only the employer was situated so as to control or alleviate that risk:

> The opportunity for intimate private control and the parental relationship and power required by the terms of employment created the special environment that nurtured and brought to fruition Curry's sexual abuse. The employer's enterprise created and fostered the risk that led to the ultimate harm. The abuse was not a mere accident of time and place, but the product of the special relationship of intimacy and respect the employer fostered, as well as the special opportunities for exploitation of that relationship it furnished. Indeed, it is difficult to imagine a job with a greater risk for child sexual abuse.[33]

The perpetrator was employed as a house master at a home for emotionally troubled children, where he was given authority to play a parent-like role in the lives of the child residents in terms of both emotional and physical intimacy (including such acts as bathing and preparing for bed). These 'parental' duties were carried out unsupervised.

Following *Bazley*, the federal government has been found vicariously liable for sexual assaults committed in residential schools for aboriginal children in a number of cases (see, *FSM v Clarke*; *DW v Canada (AG)*;[34] and *VP v Canada (AG)*).[35]

Jacobi v Griffiths, by contrast, was a case in which abuse had been perpetrated by the director of a Boys' and Girls' Club. A majority of the Court concluded that there was an insufficient connection between the director's position and the creation of risk that abuse would occur; no intimate, private and parent-like control had been created, as the children remained living with their own parents. The perpetrator had used his position at the Club to foster a friendship with the children and it was this friendship, rather than the nature and terms of his position with the Club, which facilitated his abuse of the child plaintiffs. The 'mere opportunity' for abuse afforded by the Club was not enough. Note however that in *Bazley* the Supreme Court stated that the total control found in that case (institutional care) would not be an essential element in every case supporting vicarious liability for child abuse.

A provincial government was held to be vicariously liable for assaults on children in foster care in the cases of *KLB v British Columbia* and *MB v British Columbia*. Unlike *Bazley*, the foster care cases did not involve an underlying employment relationship, with the relationship of foster parents to the Crown characterised as one of 'independent contractor.' Following the decision of the BC Court of Appeal in *A(C) v C(JW)* ('*Critchley*'), decided prior to the Supreme Court of Canada's decision in *Bazley*, the Court found that the 'true nature of the relationship' rather than the mere 'label' attached to it was the determining factor, specifically, the measure and degree of *control* exercised by the Crown over its 'independent contractors'. Regarding foster parents, the Crown's control of contractual arrangements, approval of foster homes, supervision and funding of care, and authority to remove children at any time, comprised a degree of overall control sufficient to justify a finding of vicarious liability. On the basis of the policy principles discussed in *Bazley*, specifically fair compensation, deterrence and the ability to prevent or reduce harm, vicarious liability was also justified in this context. Mackenzie JA, giving concurring reasons in both *KLB* and *MB*, preferred the doctrine of non-delegable duty in cases involving an independent contractor (as opposed to employment) relationship.[36]

KLB[37] and *MB*[38] were appealed to the Supreme Court of Canada together with *EDG v Hammer*,[39] also a decision of the British Columbia Court of Appeal. The Supreme Court held that the relationship between foster parents and the state could *not* support a finding of vicarious liability on the basis of the underlying relationship between foster parents and the government. Foster parents did not act as government agents in their day-to-day activities, and operated, like other parents, free from close government control. Indeed, the independence of foster parents was inherent in their role and the purpose of fostering itself – to give children the experience of private family life. Justice Arbour dissented, noting that the government and no one else was ultimately responsible for the child in care as his or her legal guardian. The connection between the tasks assigned to the foster parents and the wrong committed was close enough to sustain vicarious liability despite the absence of day-to-day control:

> It is clear that the foster care arrangement reflects the highest possible degrees of power, trust and intimacy. The relationship does more than provide the opportunity for child abuse; it materially increases the risk that foster parents will abuse.
>
> Because foster homes generally operate free from day-to-day supervision, some foster parents may believe that they can take advantage of foster children without being detected. Unlike the situation in *Jacobi*, foster children are required to remain in the physical custody of their foster parents. They have nowhere to go to escape abuse in the short term. The power relationship between foster parents and foster children gives rise to its own set of concerns: foster children may submit to their foster parents even when their foster parents are abusive. Children may fear their foster parents more than they would other adults.... It is difficult to imagine a relationship requiring greater power or authority for its successful operation than the foster care relationship.[40]

A recent decision of the Saskatchewan Court of Appeal (*HL v Canada (AG)*)[41] involved what appears to be a further extension of the vicarious liability principles discussed in *Bazley* in a non-residential setting (note however that this case was decided before the decisions in the British Columbia 'trio', released in October 2003). The plaintiff attended at a boxing club run by William Starr, an employee of the school and the administrator of the residence, out of the premises of a residential school for aboriginal children. With the encouragement of the Department of Indian and Northern Affairs

(DIAND, the government department with responsibility for the residential schools) Starr organised and was involved in carrying out various extra-curricular activities for residents of the school and for residents of the surrounding Indian reserves. One of these was the boxing club, in which Starr was heavily involved as organiser and coach. Unfortunately, Starr (who subsequently received a criminal conviction) was a habitual abuser of young boys. The plaintiff lived on a local reserve and was not a resident at the school; nor did he attend at the school as a day student. He alleged that he was abused by Starr at the boxing club on three separate occasions.

The government argued that, as the terms of Starr's employment did not confer a total and parent-like authority *vis a vis* the plaintiff (unlike the position of the perpetrator in *Bazley*) there was an insufficient connection between Starr's employment and his abuse of the plaintiff. The plaintiff was not a resident of the school and was free to come and go as he wished. This argument was rejected, on the basis that DIAND's encouragement of his extra-curricular activities had conferred power, influence and authority on Starr not just in relation to the residents and students at the school, but in relation to the wider Indian community. Although Starr's position entailed no physical intimacy, his role involved a 'job related' *emotional* intimacy with vulnerable children such as the plaintiff; together with the power and authority of his position, going as it did far beyond his administrative duties at the school, a sufficient connection was established between the terms of Starr's employment and his abuse of the plaintiff to justify the imposition of vicarious liability.

Non-Delegable Duty of Care

Certain relationships have been found to give rise to a *non-delegable* duty of care, in which ultimate responsibility for performance of the duty cannot be delegated to a third person.[42] Where the duty of care has been breached by the delegee, therefore, the delegator remains legally responsible.

The British Columbia Court of Appeal found that the relationship between the Crown and children placed in foster care gave rise to a non-delegable duty of care in *KLB v British Columbia* and *MB v British Columbia*[43] by reason of the Superintendent of Child Welfare's assumption and exercise of parent-like control over the family and living situation of the child under the *Protection of Children Act*.[44] With this control the Superintendent assumed 'a particular responsibility for [the foster child plaintiff's] safety, in circumstances where the plaintiff might reasonably expect that due care (if not special diligence) would be exercised. In other words, the relationship between the Superintendent and the plaintiff in the circumstances fell within the class of relationships which, on a policy basis, supported a finding of non-delegable duty'[45] and responsibility for performance of the duty remained with the Superintendent despite his delegation of that duty to the child's foster parents.[46]

A non-delegable duty of care was also found in the residential school case of *WRB v Plint*.[47] The Court held in that case that the responsibility for residential schools conferred on the government by the *Indian Act*[48] created a duty of special diligence which was not discharged by delegation of responsibility for day-to-day running of the schools to the churches and, through them, their employees.

An argument of non-delegable duty was unsuccessful in the case of *EDG v Hammer et al*,[49] an action brought against a School Board regarding the abuse of a student by a school janitor. In that case the lower court had reached a finding of no vicarious liability of the basis on an insufficient connection between the terms of the perpetrator's employment and the risk of the abuse. Mackenzie J.A., giving the majority decision for the British Columbia Court of Appeal, concluded that the claim for breach of non-delegable duty must fail on the same basis:

> [t]he rationale for breach of non-delegable duty is to extend liability for torts of independent contractors in appropriate cases where there would be vicarious liability if the independent contractor were an employee. I do not think that vicarious liability and non-delegable duty should overlap to permit inconsistent results for the same tort by an employee. The duplication of vicarious liability and non-delegable duty would create doctrinal confusion for no valid policy purpose.[50]

As vicarious liability could not be supported in this factual context, nor could breach of non-delegable duty.

The Supreme Court of Canada concluded that the duties set out in the applicable legislation (the *Protection of Children Act* and the *School Act*, respectively) did not provide a basis for imposing a *general* non-delegable duty to ensure that no harm was caused to a child in care by his or her foster parents (in *KLB* and *MB*)[51] or to ensure that no harm was caused to a student by a school employee (*EDG v. Hammer*). Only duties imposed by statute are 'non-delegable'and no specific duty to ensure that no harm was caused through the abuse or negligence of foster parents or school employees could be inferred from the statute in either case. A general non-delegable duty could be inferred only where supported by the language of the statute.[52]

Breach of Fiduciary Duty

A fiduciary relationship is characterised by the following 'general characteristics':[53]

- the fiduciary has some scope for the exercise of power;
- the fiduciary can unilaterally exercise that power or discretion so as to affect the beneficiary's legal or practical interests; and
- the beneficiary is peculiarly vulnerable to or at the mercy of the fiduciary holding direction or power.

Where a fiduciary relationship exists, the fiduciary's duty is to exercise this power and discretion in the best interests of the beneficiary, a higher duty than the duty of care in negligence.[54]

The Supreme Court of Canada described the relationship between parent and child as 'intuitively fiduciary' in the case of *M(K) v M(H)*:

> Even a cursory examination of these indicia [from *Frame*, cited above] establishes that a parent must owe fiduciary obligations to his or her child. Parents exercise great power over their children's lives, and make daily decisions that affect their welfare. In this regard, the child is without doubt at the mercy of her parents.[55]

A fiduciary relationship also exists where a person who is not a biological parent is charged with responsibility for the care of children. The government owes a fiduciary duty to young people in its care, for example.[56] A fiduciary relationship may also come into being where an ongoing professional relationship exists between a social worker and a child, even where the child has not been taken into care.[57] Schools also owe a fiduciary duty to their pupils.[58] Public authorities, like other fiduciaries, will be liable where the fiduciary duty has been breached.

A 'strict' test for breach of fiduciary duty was set out in the case of *AC v CJW*[59] (*Critchley*), requiring that a defendant fiduciary personally take advantage of the relationship to his or her direct or indirect personal advantage. The '*Critchley* test' significantly restricted public authority liability for breach of fiduciary duty in child abuse cases. In the case of *EDG v Hammer* (the school board case involving a janitor perpetrator), for example, while a fiduciary relationship existed, there was no breach within the meaning of the *Critchley* 'test'. Also applying the *Critchley* test, the court found that the fiduciary relationship between the foster child plaintiffs and the provincial Crown was not breached by the failure to adequately supervise their foster placement in *KLB v British Columbia*; negligent supervision, while actionable as a tort, did not involve a conflict between duty and self-interest.[60]

The Anglican church in its role as administrator of a residential school for aboriginal children *was* found to have breached its fiduciary duty to a student resident at the school in the case of *FSM v Clarke*. In that case the Court found that the Anglican authorities knew of the abuse and undertook to assist the plaintiff (to the exclusion of the federal government), but did nothing – apparently – to protect the Church's interests and reputation. In this the Church preferred its own interests over those of the plaintiff, meeting the criteria for breach as set out in *Critchley*.

On appeal to the Supreme Court of Canada in the *KLB* and *EDG* cases, the Court held that there was no broad fiduciary duty owed by the government and school, respectively, to act in the best interests of the child. Breach of duty – and liability – arose from conduct, not results; it was impossible for any fiduciary to always know what acts would prove to be ultimately in the other person's best interests. The parental duty and, by analogy, the duty owed by the government to the child in care and by the school to the pupil, is a duty of loyalty; a duty to act selflessly in the interests of the child (not to achieve his or her best interests) and not to prefer one's own interests or the interests of another. This analysis widens the requirement of exploitation set out in *Critchley*; loyalty is also breached when the fiduciary prefers the interests of another (not his or her own interests) over the interests of the child.

The federal government in Canada owes a fiduciary duty to aboriginal people as 'Indians' in addition to the fiduciary duty owed to children in its care, and recent legal developments involving residential schools claims have addressed this aspect of fiduciary duty and its breach as claimants assert their right to damages for cultural losses. In *Bonaparte v Canada*[61] family members of former students argued that the policy of assimilation that was pursued through the residential schools (with the objective of eradicating the culture of aboriginal peoples) deprived them of their right to receive their culture and language from the older generations. Family members also claimed for loss of care, guidance and family life, arguing that the harmful impacts of institutionalisation continued to reverberate long after the period of instititutionalisation had come to an end. A lower court dismissed the claim on the grounds that the 'secondary' (family member) plaintiffs had not been born at the time of the events in issue.[62] This decision was reversed by the Court of Appeal, finding that the issue of whether the federal government's fiduciary duty to the secondary plaintiffs as 'Indians' had been breached was sustainable as a triable issue:

> Fiduciary law in Canada, particularly in respect of the Crown's relationship with aboriginal peoples, is a very dynamic area of Canadian law. The nature and extent of the particular obligations that may arise out of this relationship are matters that remain largely unsettled in the jurisprudence.[63]

Class Action

'Class actions' are lawsuits in which the claims of many people with common interests (a 'class') are decided in a single court proceeding. That proceeding is brought by a representative plaintiff on behalf of the class. A class action must be 'certified' before it can proceed, that is, the court must determine that there is an identifiable class of persons whose claims raise common issues, that the representative plaintiff fairly represents the interests of the class, that the pleadings show a cause of action, and that a class action is the preferred process through which the common issues involved in the case should be resolved.

A class action was commenced in 1998 on behalf of a class consisting of former students of the Jericho Hill School for the Deaf who were abused while attending the school and/or failed to receive an adequate education, secondary victims of abuse (individuals accused by former residents of the school as a result of abuse at Jericho Hill), and family members of students who were abused (where those family members suffered damage as a result of the abuse). Certification was granted on appeal to the British Columbia Court of Appeal,[64] although the class was restricted to include only former students suffering damages as a result of sexual abuse at the school (secondary victims and family members were excluded). Despite differences among class members, whose claims spanned a period of 42 years, the duty of the school to reasonably protect its students from sexual abuse was 'clear and immutable throughout the period the school was in operation'.[65]

The claims of the class members proceeded on the basis of 'systemic negligence', 'the failure to have in place management and operations procedures that would reasonably have prevented the abuse'.[66] Claimants would not be required to prove that abuse was perpetrated by any individual student or teacher at the school. 'Systemic negligence' would apply to the class members *as a class*, apart from any negligence that could be proven in individual cases.

The decision certifying the action on these terms was upheld in the Supreme Court of Canada, finding that the issue of 'systemic negligence' was common to all members of the class despite differences between the individual experience of class members.[67] The systemic negligence being argued was not specific to any one class member, but to all class members as a group. Finally, on the question of whether the class action was the preferred process through which the common issues should be resolved, the Court found that the Jericho Individual Compensation Programme (a 'redress programme' through which former students were compensated outside of the court process) was not an 'adequate alternative' to a class action in this case (and so the JICP did not obviate or diminish the utility of the class action); '[a]mongst other limitations' the JICP limited individual recovery to $60,000 and did not permit complainants to be represented by counsel before the panel. 'The JICP simply cannot be said to be an adequate alternative to a class proceeding.'[68]

The province of British Columbia alleged that the plaintiffs were attempting to use the class action to try individual cases of abuse and an action for de-certification was brought by the province in 2003.[69] The Court agreed, and the common issues were amended to emphasise the focus on systemic negligence as opposed to individual issues of alleged abuse.[70]

A class action brought on behalf of former residents of the 'Mohawk Residential School' was refused certification in *MCC v AG of Canada*,[71] a decision rendered prior to the Supreme Court of Canada's decision in the *Rumley* case. That decision was upheld by a split decision of the Ontario Divisional Court.[72] Dissenting in that case, Justice Cullity found that the allegations raised the common issues of systemic negligence and breach of the government's fiduciary duty to Indians in Canada where

> the very purpose of the Crown's assumption of control over the primary plaintiffs was to strip the Indian children of their culture and identity, thereby removing as and when they became adults, their ability to pass on to succeeding generations the spiritual, cultural and behavioural bases of their people.[73]

The dissent described the class action as 'preferable' in this case because of the special vulnerability of class members, which made it less likely that they would be able to access the court as individuals:

> Each of the representative plaintiffs referred to the poverty of many of the former students, their inability to afford the cost of individual actions and the effect such proceedings would have on the continuing emotional problems from which they suffer as a result of their experiences at the Mohawk Institute.[74]

The Decision of the Divisional Court is being Appealed to the Ontario Court of Appeal

A 'national' class action is currently being pursued on behalf of former residents of residential schools for aboriginal children and family members claiming 'intergenerational' harm(s) (*Baxter v AG of Canada* filed in 2000). The 'alumni class' would include aboriginal persons attending residential schools in Canada between January 1, 1920 and December 31, 1996.[75] The 'family class' would include a spouse (to include a common law or former spouse), child, grandchild, parent or sibling of an alumni class member, and any 'other persons' recognised by the Court. The family class has since been narrowed to include only children and parents.

The common issues asserted in the *Baxter* case include, but go far beyond the 'systematic negligence' at issue in *Rumley* (the Jericho Hill case). *Baxter* asserts that the residential schools and their policy of assimilation was designed to and in fact did interrupt the transmission of aboriginal culture and languages between the generations, in contravention of the Crown's fiduciary duty and in breach of the plaintiffs' aboriginal and treaty rights (the damage arising from systematic negligence is also stated as including loss of language, culture, and traditions). Unlawful confinement is also being alleged on the basis of the apprehension of many students and their enforced separation from family through compulsory school attendance. The plaintiffs will also argue that the residential schools were in contravention of Canada's commitments under international conventions to which it is a signatory.

Conclusion

The liability of public authorities for the abuse of children in their care has become a high profile issue with the proliferation of lawsuits filed by former residents of the 'Indian schools' run by the federal government and churches in this country between 1879 and 1986. According to the Office of Indian Residential Schools Resolution, 12,064 claims had been filed as of November 1, 2002.[76] Case law developing the common law causes of action in the area of public authority liability for child abuse – negligence, vicarious liability, breach of fiduciary duty, and a non-delegable duty of care – have exposed the federal government in particular (with responsibility for the residential schools) to enormous liability costs. Public authority liability in Canada is, accordingly, both a legal and a public policy issue. Initiatives to restrict liability through legislation,[77] together with the decision of the Supreme Court of Canada in the trio of British Columbia appeals, may curtail the future development of this area of the law.

The emergence of the class action and the theory of 'systemic negligence' being developed through the class action litigation is important, addressing in a particularly apposite way the common experiences of children suffering harm 'in the care of' the State (rather than focusing on isolated incidents of abuse) and the issue of responsibility for those harms.[78] If systemic negligence creates environments in which abuse is more likely to occur and be perpetuated, the legal responsibility of public authorities is both right and just.

Notes

1 See Feldthusen, Bruce, 'The Canadian Experiment with the Civil Action for Sexual Battery'. In Nicholas J. Mullany, ed., *Torts in the Nineties*. Sydney: LBC Information Services, 1997, 274.
2 See (2000) Report of the Law Commission of Canada, *Restoring Dignity: Responding to Child Abuse in Canadian Institutions*. The author is currently preparing a follow up report for the Law Commission.
3 See *Rumley v BC* (1999), 180 DLR (4th) 639 (BCCA); (2001), 205 DLR (4th) 39 (SCC).
4 See *Just v British Columbia*, [1989] 2 SCR 1228.
5 The second branch of the test from *Anns v Merton London Borough Council*, [1978] AC 728 (HL), broadly analogous to the 'policy test' as set out in *Caparo v Dickman*, [1990] 2 AC 605 (HL) and applied in *X v Bedfordshire County Council*, [1995] 3 All ER 353 (HL), that it would be 'fair, just and reasonable' to impose a duty of care in the siutation.
6 See discussion, Hall, 'Duty to Protect, Duty to Control and the Duty to Warn' (2003) *CBR* Vol. 82.
7 Bohlen, 'The Moral Duty to Aid Others as a Basis of Tort Liability' (1908) *U. Pa. L. Rev.* 217 at 219–221; see, *Smith v Littlewoods*, [1987] 1 All ER 710 (HL).
8 Following the analysis in *Caparo v Dickman*, [1990] 2 AC 605 (HL).
9 [1999] 3 WLR 79 (HL).
10 The fairness of a duty of care given the involvement of multiple agencies; the social worker's delicate task *vis a vis* parents; the need to avoid 'cautious and defensive' decision making.
11 [2001] BHRC 384 Eur. Ct. HR
12 Hall, 'Child neglect and the right to protection: *Z and Others v United Kingdom*' (2003) *Journal of Social Welfare and Family Law* Vol. 24 (4) at 454.
13 See *KLB v British Columbia*, [2003] SCC 51
14 As opposed to vicarious liability, which is discussed separately, *infra*.
15 [1999] BCJ 1973 (BCSC). The residential school system for aboriginal children in Canada was run jointly by the federal government and the Catholic and Protestant churches between 1879 and 1986. Thousands of lawsuits are currently pending regarding abuse which is alleged to have occurred in the residential schools.

16 The government had argued that because of the large numbers of children in the residential system, it could not be liable in negligence for a failure to supervise their care.
17 Applying the second branch of the test as set out in *Anns v Merton Borough Council* [1978] AC 728 (HL).
18 *Supra* note 9, at para. 162.
19 Ibid., at para. 180.
20 (2001), 93 BCLR (3d) 228 SC, appeal pending.
21 (2001), 87 BCLR (3d) 52 (BCCA).
22 Ibid., at para. 11.
23 *Supra* note 17 at para. 6–8.
24 Relying on the case of *G(A) v Superintendent of Child and Family Service* (1989), 38 BCLR (2d) 215 (BCCA), where the Court dismissed an action for an alleged negligent apprehension of children on the basis that the social worker in the case had been acting in good faith.
25 *Supra* note 12 at para. 13.
26 See also *A(C) v C(JW)* (1998), 60 BCLR (3d) 92 (BCCA); also, *MB v British Columbia* [2000] BCJ No. 909 (SC); [2001] BCJ No. 586 (CA). *KLB*, with its 'companion' appeals in the British Columbia Court of Appeal *MB v British Columbia* and *EDG v Hammer*, were appealed to the Supreme Court of Canada, where they were heard on December 5, 2002. As of writing, judgment has yet to be rendered.
27 *KLB v British Columbia* [2003] SCC 51 at para. 15, per McLachlin C.J.
28 [2001] 3 SCR 184.
29 [2001] M.J. No. 177 (CA); [1999] 11 WWR 82 (Man. QB).
30 Certain exceptions have long been made, e.g. the 'bouncer' and 'dishonest employee' cases (*Griggs v Southside Hotel Co.* [1947] 4 DLR 49 (Ont. CA); *Lloyd v Grace, Smith and Co.* [1912] AC 716).
31 [1999] 2 SCR 534.
32 [1999] 2 SCR 570.
33 At para. 58.
34 [1999] SJ 742 (Sask. QB).
35 [1999] SJ 723 (Sask. QB).
36 See also, *K(W) v Pornbacher* (1997), 34 CCLT (2d) 174 (BCSC) finding a Roman Catholic diocese vicariously liable for sexual abuse committed by a priest; but see *John Doe v Bennett* (2002), 218 DLR (4th) 276 (CA). A school board was found not vicariously liable regarding abuse committed by a teacher in *SGH v Gorsline* [2001] 6 WWR 132 (Alta. QB); see also *EDG v Hammer* (1998), 53 BCLR (3d) 89 (BCSC).
37 [2003] SCC 51.
38 [2003] SCC 53.
39 [2003] SCC 52.
40 *Ibid.*, at para. 94. See also *MB v British Columbia* [2003] SCC 53; *EDG v Hammer* [2003] SCC 52.
41 [2002] SJ No. 702.
42 *Lewis (Guardian ad litem of) v British Columbia* [1997] 3 SCR 1145.
43 *MB v British Columbia* [2002] 5 WWR 327 (BCCA); *KLB v British Columbia* (2001), 87 BCLR (3d) 52 (BCCA)
44 RSBC 1960, c. 30–33.
45 *MB* at para. 82
46 See also *E(JAK) v British Columbia* [2002] BCJ No. 597 (SC).
47 (2001), 93 BCLR (3d) 228 (BCSC).

48 SC 1951 c. 29.
49 [2001] BCJ No. 585 (CA).
50 Ibid. at para. 75. This distinction was recently applied in the case of *MR v British Columbia*, [2002] BCJ No. 2614 (SC).
51 [2003] SCC 51; [2003] SCC 53.
52 See, *Lewis (Guardian ad liem of) v British Columbia*, [1997] SCR 1145.
53 *Frame v Smith* (1987), 42 DLR (4th) 81 (SCC).
54 *Cairnie Estate*; see, M. Hall, (2003) 'Intuitive Fiduciaries: The Equitable Structure of Family Life' *Canadian Journal of Family Law* vol. 19.2.
55 [1992] 3 SCR 6 at para. 180.
56 *Critchley*; *KLB*; *MB*
57 See *Cairnie Estate, supra*. In the circumstances of that case no ongoing relationship existed sufficient to found a fiduciary relationship, although the contact between the social worker and the plaintiff was a relationship of sufficient proximity to give rise to a negligence duty of care.
58 *EDG v Hammer*.
59 (1998), 60 BCLR (3d) 92 (BCCA).
60 At para. 23. See also, *SGH v Gorsline*, [2001] 6 WWR 132 (Alta. QB); *WRB v Plint* (2001), 93 BCLR (3d) 228 (BCSC).
61 March 27, 2003 No. C37702 Ont. CA
62 *Lafrance Estate v Canada*, [2002] OJ No. 112 (Ont. SCJ).
63 Ibid. at para. 32.
64 *Rumley v BC* (1999), 72 BCLR (3d) 1; see also, decision of the BC Supreme Court, (1998) 65 BCLR (3d) 382.
65 Ibid, at 8.
66 Ibid., at 9.
67 [2001] 3 SCR 184. See also, *White v Canada*, [2002] BCJ No. 1821 (BCSC).
68 Ibid, at para. 38 per McLachlin CJC. See also *Rumley v BC* [2003] 12 BCLR (4th) 121 (SC).
69 *LR v British Columbia* [2003] BCJ No. 313 (SC).
70 Ibid., para. 90.
71 [2001] OJ No. 4163 (Ont. SCJ).
72 (2003) No. 1267.
73 Ibid. at para. 25.
74 Ibid. at para. 46.
75 (a) Aboriginal persons, resident in Ontario, who attended Residential Schools in Ontario during the Class Period; (b) Aboriginal persons, resident in Ontario, who attended Residential Schools elsewhere in Canada during the Class period; (c) Aboriginal persons, wherever resident in Canada, who attended Residential Schools in Ontario during the Class Period; (d) Aboriginal persons, wherever resident in Canada, who attended Residential Schools in Canada other than in the provinces of Ontario, British Columbia and Quebec during the Class Period; and (e) Such other persons as the Court recognizes or directs.
76 550 had been resolved in out-of-court settlements according to statements made by Minister Ralph Goodale, November 20, 2002.
77 The liability of public authorities through vicarious liability and non-delegable duty is currently the subject of a civil liability review being carried out by the province of British Columbia (and the potential subject of legislative reform).
78 See Hall (2000) 'After Waterhouse: Vicarious Liability and the Tort of Institutional Abuse', *The Journal of Social Welfare and Family Law* (Issue 2) 159–173.

Chapter 9

Child Welfare and State Liability in France

*Duncan Fairgrieve**

The French system of state liability is fêted as one of the most liberal in the world. Having shrugged off the notion of monarchical immunity at a very early stage, the law on governmental liability has been developed by the French administrative courts into a sophisticated remedy for administrative wrong-doing.

However, appearances can be deceptive. Despite the ostensibly liberal approach, French administrative law subsequently transpires to be in reality much less generous than first might appear. The sphere of child abuse claims is no exception to this trend. Rules which seem very generous actually result in surprisingly few concrete cases. There would appear to be few direct cases on the questions examined by the English courts in the cases of *X (Minors) v Bedfordshire County Council*[1] and *Barrett v Enfield LBC*.[2] This conundrum between apparent liberalism and resultant absence of cases will be explored in this chapter.

The chapter will be structured as follows. First, a thumbnail sketch of the French system of public authority liability will be made. This will be followed by an assessment of the way in which the French administrative courts have dealt with child abuse cases. Thirdly, the various control mechanisms in French law will be examined and an attempt made to explain why there is such a dearth of cases.

Governmental Liability in France

The French law of governmental liability is the product of the case law of the administrative courts over the last 130 years. The result is a complex set of rules. Limits on space prevent one from making a detailed analysis of this highly developed system.[3] An overview will nonetheless be given.

In French law, jurisdiction over public law cases, including claims for damages, falls to the administrative courts.[4] The inception of the modern regime of liability can be traced back to the seminal case of *Blanco* in which the

* Director, Tort Law Centre, British Institute of International and Comparative Law; Maître de Conférences, Sciences Po, Paris.

Tribunal des Conflits, with some audacity,[5] explicitly rejected the application of the rules stated in the Napoleonic *Code Civil*.[6] It was decided that the rules of administrative liability were of a *distinct* and *special* character. *Private rights* had to be balanced with *requirements of the general public interest*. Administrative liability could be neither 'general nor absolute'.

In the many years since the *Blanco* judgment, the principles of administrative liability have been developed by the courts, generally in a pro-claimant direction. Received opinion is that French administrative law constitutes one of the most liberal on offer anywhere. This is illustrated by three principles.

A fundamental tenet of French administrative liability is that *any* illegal administrative decision will *per se* constitute fault capable of giving rise to liability.[7] This results in an extremely broad conception of the notion of 'fault'. *Faute* in French administrative law covers areas which, in terms of categorisation, would fall within the ambit of strict liability in English law. The illegality-fault equation in French law leads to liability for breaches of legality which neither the defendant nor a reasonable person in the defendant's position could have foreseen. Clearly these types of situation would fall outside the scope of liability for fault in English law. In the common law, where courts have recognised a right of action for breach of statutory duty by virtue of the mere breach of the provision, this has been categorised as strict liability.[8]

Under this generous French rule, minor errors such as mere procedural unlawfulness or an error in the assessment of the facts of a case will suffice to constitute wrongful behaviour. In the famous case of *Driancourt*,[9] the administration was sued for financial loss caused by its licence-granting activities. A bar owner was awarded 50,000 Francs for the loss of profits caused by an unlawful prohibition on the use of neon lights, juke-boxes and pinball machines in his establishment,[10] even though the unlawfulness derived from a relatively minor error.

Of course, the causal creator of loss is not solely administrative decisions. Physical acts operate outside the rule that public law illegality entails fault.[11] In cases where a policeman strikes a prisoner, a doctor acts negligently during surgery, a teacher abuses a child, one cannot conceive of these as unlawful administrative decisions. This brings us onto the second point.

Over and above unlawful administrative decisions, the conception of *fault* in French administrative law is classically based upon the notion of a *faute de service*, or a public service-related fault. This notion is a quintessentially elastic conceptual device.[12] The stretching process has predominantly been in favour of claimants.

In determining whether a *faute de service* has occurred, reference is often made to a *malfunctioning* of the administrative machinery.[13] The reference to systemic failure has led the French courts to focus upon *results* rather than *reasonable behaviour*.[14] This illustrates a shift from conduct to consequences.

The standard of *faute de service* is not a homogenous one. In certain areas, the claimant must show a *faute lourde*, gross fault, in the exercise of public functions, rather than the basic element of *faute simple*. This requirement has been applied to disparate areas, including police work, regulatory activities, and the tax authorities. However, the courts have started to whittle away these areas,[15] and have considerably reduced the spheres protected by this pre-condition of liability. This is thus another manifestation of a pro-claimant stance.[16]

The third major factor establishing the French system's liberal credentials in this area is the existence of a sophisticated no-fault regime of liability.[17] The state can thus in some circumstances be held liable for harm it has caused whether or not it acted reasonably; whether or not it could have done any better in the circumstances. No-fault liability applies in diverse circumstances, for instance in the sphere of medical liability (backed up by a radical new statutory scheme),[18] as well as risk-based dangerous activities.[19]

In sum, there are various reasons why French governmental liability has been perceived as a very liberal system; and certainly as more generous than English law.[20] However, showing *faute de service* or the occurrence of a head of no-fault liability is not *per se* sufficient. The claimant must also show that the fault was accompanied by the infliction of loss and, importantly, that there was a causal link between the fault and that harm. We will examine these aspects at a later stage.

French Administrative Liability and Child Abuse Cases

It has already been noted that there are many elements of French governmental liability which appear extremely generous to claimants. The broad notion of administrative fault would be of assistance to claimants in child abuse cases. Presumptions of fault also potentially help claimants.[21] And yet, there are few decisions concerning child abuse cases against public bodies. One rare exception is the 1987 decision of *Ouaras*.[22] In the absence of other authority, this case must be considered to set down the basic principles. A three-year-old girl was sent by social services, with the agreement of her parents, to stay with a host family in the Netherlands for a period of three months. The foster family had been selected by a childcare association with whom the social services had already had dealings. Tragically the child died following serious ill-treatment by the foster family. The childcare association was not insured, and so the parents turned to the state for compensation.

The *Conseil d'Etat* found the state liable. The social services had failed to take sufficient precautions to ensure that the foster family was capable of looking after a child of such a young age. It was wrong to have placed such a young child in a family, the members of which did not speak French, especially when it was known that the foster mother had a history of emotional difficulties and had endured a disturbed upbringing.[23] The social services had actively encouraged the parents to place the child, thus playing an active and decisive factor in the parents' decision. Even though the actual placement had been organised by an intermediary organisation, the social services wrongfully failed to make proper checks on the foster family and protect the child from abuse.

The notion of fault was thus conceived broadly in this case. The reasoning applied by the court could theoretically be extended to many other scenarios, for instance where a child was *directly* placed with an inappropriate foster family by social services, or where there had been continuing failure to supervise a placement properly. However, such claims have not been brought before the courts.

Other parallel claims have appeared in greater numbers before the courts. In particular, there are many cases mirroring the facts of the English case of *Dorset Yacht*[24] in which the French courts apply a regime of no-fault liability for damage caused by escapees from liberal prison and borstal regimes. The reasoning underpinning this line of case law is that such liberal custodial schemes have beneficial effects for society as a whole, and it is thought inequitable that those harmed (if the risk of escape materialises) should go uncompensated. So, liability can arise without proof of fault for loss caused by those who have taken advantage of these liberal regimes to escape and engage in criminal activity. This case law has been applied to youths who have escaped from open borstals,[25] and it equally covers those detained in public and private institutions.[26] Admittedly however these cases are far removed from the scenarios envisaged in this paper as covered in the English cases of *X (Minors)* and *Barrett*.

Explaining the Differences

We have thus seen that exact parallels to the English cases are difficult to come by in French law. Evidently, the absence of cases may be explained by the lack of circumstances giving rise to the claims. This is a relatively difficult factor to corroborate, but it is an improbable explanation. France is unlikely to be one of the rare countries in which this societal phenomenon is absent. Alternatively, the circumstances may have arisen, but legal actions simply not pursued.[27] It is submitted however that the real explanation for the differences lies elsewhere. One may attempt to explain these by reference to substantive, procedural and institutional factors.

Substantive Control Mechanisms

Although there are many aspects of French administrative law which, from a common law viewpoint, seem extremely liberal, on a closer look one discovers that there are ways in which liability is circumscribed. Despite the ostensible liberalism of French law, the rules of *responsabilité administrative* have been moulded to provide for potent control mechanisms.

This can be seen in a variety of ways. First, looking closely at French administrative law cases, it is clear that an analysis of the case law reveals that the notion of causation plays an extremely important role in circumventing the liability of the administration.[28] The basic principle of causation in French administrative law is that the claimant's harm must be *direct* which entails, in effect, that there must be a direct causal relationship between the defendant's *faute* and the victim's loss.[29] Most commentators have asserted that the stipulation of causal directness is expressed by the courts through the test of *la théorie de la causalité adéquate*.[30]

The test of causal directness is very malleable, and academic commentators have remarked that the test of causation in French law is often applied stringently in order to reduce the burden of liability on public bodies.[31] There are examples of the use of causation to reject damages claims for malpractice in the educational sphere.[32] This would no doubt apply to potential child abuse claims, where causation is commonly contested.[33]

In French administrative law, account is taken of contributory fault, whereby a wrongdoer may reduce or even exclude his or her liability by showing fault of the victim.[34] It is clear that the French administrative courts have been particularly harsh to the injured victim when assessing contributory fault.[35] The French courts make an 'extensive interpretation of the notion of the victim's contributory actions'.[36] The sphere of child welfare is no exception to this trend.[37]

There is also another important point to emphasise. Unlike in English law, an obligation of joint and several liabilities does not arise for multiple wrongdoers in administrative law cases.[38] So, where a third party contributes to the occurrence of the claimant's injury, then the *administration* will be liable to pay solely the portion of loss for which they are responsible.

Similarly, control mechanisms would appear to apply at the level of quantum. It is clear that the measurement of damages for personal injury and dependency loss reflect unfavourably upon the French system.[39] The sums awarded are often rather low, compared with the standards of the common law. This is particularly striking in child law cases. One example is the decision in *Giraud*, concerning the failure of a school to teach a child the core subjects of the national curriculum, in which the Minister of Education was ordered to pay the equivalent of (approximately) £100 damages.[40] In such cases, the courts would be unlikely to entertain claims for lost earnings,[41] unlike the well-known English case of *Phelps v Hillingdon LBC*.[42] The parsimonious approach to quantum thus limits the effects of the wide conception of fault.

Procedural Control Mechanisms

There are also a variety of procedural barriers to bringing actions. One of these is the chronic delay in the French judicial system, with proceedings spanning decades.[43] This factor may well discourage the bringing of claims.

A more potent factor is the strict limitation period in French administrative law. A 1968 statute lays down that debts owed by the State are only payable for four years from 1 January following the date on which the debt arose.[44] This provision applies equally to debts arising in contract and delict. The reference period generally commences on occurrence of the loss. But the courts have also held in other cases that the limitation period does not start to run until the victim of the delictual act is aware of the origin of the loss and that the act could be attributable to the administration.[45] It is unclear how the courts would determine the starting-point for the limitation period in child abuse cases, but it is likely that the brevity of the period in French law, and the generally strict application made by the French courts,[46] would result in a reduction in the number of claims that can be brought in an area where there is likely to be a large gap between the occurrence of the harm and realisation of the potential action in damages on the part of the victim.

There is also a more nebulous factor which might be mentioned as having an influence on these claims, one which might be termed as a socio-legal or cultural factor. In France, it is only relatively recently that revelations have emerged regarding abuse of children in institutions or schools. In the wake of the criminal actions which have been brought, one might well witness an increasing number of damages actions.

Institutional Framework

There is another particularly potent reason explaining the lack of child abuse tort cases in French law. This is intricately linked to the institutional structure of child welfare in France.

The French system for child protection is organised in a very different way from its British equivalent.[47] It is impossible in this forum to detail the specific legal provisions governing child protection in France. There are various features of the French set-up which should, however, be mentioned.

The basis of the French system is an Order (*Ordonnance*) of 23 December 1958, which allows the judge to intervene with regard to any juvenile under 21 years old whose health, safety or morality is at risk or if the conditions of his or her upbringing are gravely compromised.[48]

The system for child protection is closely linked to that dealing with juvenile delinquency:

> The procedures, the states of mind of the professional workers and the facilities used are in many ways similar, whether the juvenile is an offender or in need of protection.[49]

Importantly, the role of the judiciary in child protection cases is primordial. It is the judge who plays an important role in determining the appropriate measures to ensure child protection. Generally, jurisdiction over such cases is conferred upon the *juge des enfants* (children's judge). Thus the *juge des enfants* directs the work of the social workers involved in their cases. Even after the decision of the court has been made, the judge is regularly consulted by social workers in respect of any important decisions concerning the child's welfare. The judge's input into the system of social work is facilitated through the writing of regular reports on the child's progress, the reviewing placements, visits of children's homes, meetings with stakeholders, and participation in key administrative committees.[50] The close relationship between social workers and the *juge des enfants* is described by Ely and Stanley:

> Children's Judges have at their disposal their own social work service (*Education Surveillée*) which assesses, supervises and, on occasion, receives juveniles into its residential facility, as the Judge directs. The municipal social services refer to the

> Children's Judge those clients with whom they have not been successful in working on a voluntary basis. Additionally, any organisation, citizen, or parent may make a referral to or ask an audience of the Children's Judge if they apprehend a risk to a child. Juveniles may also refer themselves to the Judge if they feel at risk.[51]

The provision of social services, particularly child welfare, is remarkably heterogeneous in France. In deciding appropriate provision, the *juge des enfants* can choose between a wide range of facilities from both the public and private sector. In particular, voluntary organisations often provide for supervision or residential care for children and young adults. The public sector social welfare organisations, known as the *Direction départementale des affaires sanitaires et socials* (DDASS), corresponds roughly to the English social services but if the family does not cooperate with a voluntary approach, or is in conflict with the DDASS, the decision must be made by a judge. A child can be referred to *juge des enfants* by a large number of people, but usually this will be the school, social services or the *Parquet* (Public Prosecutor). Parents or the child themselves can make an application to the judge.

This institutional set-up impacts on the law of liability in a variety of ways. Unlike in the United Kingdom, the crucial decisions concerning child welfare are not in the hands of social services, but are in effect taken by judges. Any challenge of the major decisions concerning the long-term welfare of children must be channelled through the judicial process.

Tort claims which are directed at the provision of child welfare are thus inevitably directed at this decision-making process. Establishing the liability of the judiciary is, in France as in many other countries, a difficult process.[52] It is rare for the claimant to be able to show that decisions concerning child welfare were unconnected with the judicial process,[53] particularly given the fact that most important decisions are required to be ratified by the judge.

Conclusion

The generosity of the French courts is in some respects more apparent than real. Child abuse cases before the French administrative courts are no exception. Whilst the notion of fault is broad and could potentially have been marshalled by claimants in their favour, the French courts have in fact shown a keen awareness of the need to keep state liability within reasonable limits. We have outlined the various factors, both substantive and procedural, which provide substantial obstacles for claimants to mount.

This fact also illustrates a wider point concerning the use of comparative law. It underlines the importance of placing the abstract application of substantive legal rules within a wider framework. It is impossible to determine the utility of legal rules for comparison unless one investigates the manner in which the wider procedural, and crucially, institutional, factors have impacted on them. This observation should not be seen as fatally undermining the value of comparative research.[54] However, it does emphasise the importance of the taking of account of broader influences, such as procedural differences and alternative means of redress.

Translations of French Administrative Law Cases

1 TC 8 February 1873, *Blanco*, D.1873.3.17
Fault liability – inception of modern state liability.
2 CE 26 January 1973, *Driancourt*, [1973] Rec 78
Illegality entails fault.
3 CE 27 January 1988, *Giraud*, [1988] Rec 39
Educational negligence – failure to teach subject on national curriculum.
4 CE 23 September 1987, Monsieur et Madame *Ouaras*, Req 64.037
Child abuse – damages claim.

TC 8 February 1873, Blanco, *D.1873.3.17*

Decision in French
Tribunal des Conflits
Blanco
8 février 1873
Vu les lois des 16–24 août 1790 et du 16 fruct. an 3;
Vu l'ordonnance du 1er juin 1828 et la loi du 24 mai 1872;
Considérant que l'action intentée par le sieur Blanco contre le préfet du département de la Gironds, représentant l'Etat, a pour objet de faire déclarer l'Etat civilement responsable, par application des articles 1382, 1383 et 1384 c. civ., du dommage résultant de la blessure que sa fille aurait éprouvée par le fait d'ouvriers employés par l'administration des tabacs;

Considérant que la responsabilité qui peut incomber à l'Etat pour les dommages causés aux particuliers par le fait des personnes qu'il emploie dans le service public, ne peut être régie par les principes qui sont établis dans le code civil pour les rapports de particulier à particulier;

Que cette responsabilité n'est ni générale, ni absolue; qu'elle a ses règles spéciales qui varient suivant les besoins du service et la nécessité de concilier les droits de l'Etat avec les droits privés;

Que, dès lors, aux termes des lois ci-dessus visées, l'autorité administrative est seule compétente pour en connaître:

Art.1. L'arrêté de conflit est confirmé.

Translation
Whereas the action brought by Monsieur Blanco against the Prefect of the Department of Gironde (representing the state) seeks to have the state declared liable in damages, under Articles 1382, 1383 and 1384 of the Civil Code, for the harm resulting from the injury sustained by his daughter due to the actions of workers employed by the Tobacco Administration;[1]

Whereas the liability which may be incurred by the state for loss caused to individuals by the actions of persons which it employs in the public service cannot be governed by the principles laid down in the Civil Code to regulate the legal relationships of individuals;[2]

That this liability is neither general nor absolute; it has its own special rules which vary depending upon the needs of the service[3] and the necessity of reconciling the rights of the state with private rights;

That, therefore, according to the terms of the aforementioned laws, the administrative body[4] has sole jurisdiction in this case.

Article 1. Confirmation of the decision finding a conflict of jurisdiction.

Translator's notes

1 At the time of the case, the state had a monopoly on the production, distribution and sale of tobacco. It exercised this function acting as the 'Tobacco Administration'.

2 When using the word 'individuals', the *Tribunal des Conflits* was referring solely to *private* persons.

3 The *Tribunal des Conflits* is referring here to the *public* service, as it explicitly recognised in the second paragraph of the judgment.

4 Although the original text states that the administrative *authority* would have jurisdiction to resolve the dispute, the *Tribunal des Conflits* clearly intended that the Administrative *Court* was to decide the case.

CE 26 January 1973, Driancourt, *[1973] Rec 78*

Decision in French
Conseil d'Etat
Ville de Paris c/ Sieur Driancourt
26 janvier 1973
Req 84.768
Vu la requête sommaire et le mémoire ampliatif présentés pour la ville de Paris représentée par le Préfet de police, ladite requête et ledit mémoire enregistrés au secrétariat du Contentieux du Conseil d'Etat les 10 septembre 1971 et 17 janvier 1972 et tendant à ce qu'il plaise au Conseil d'annuler un jugement en date du 22 juin 1971 par lequel le Tribunal administratif de Paris l'a condamnée à verser une indemnité de 85 745 F au sieur Driancourt en réparation du préjudice qui lui a été causé par une décision du 7 décembre 1962 du Préfet de police lui prescrivant de cesser l'exploitation de jeux installés dans son établissement sis Avenue Victor-Hugo a Paris (16eme);

Vu l'ordonnance du 31 juillet 1945 et le décret du 30 septembre 1953;

Vu le Code général des impôts: Considérant que, par décision du 7 décembre 1962 prise à la suite d'une plainte émanant du président de l'Association des amis de l'avenue Victor-Hugo, le Préfet de police a enjoint au sieur Driancourt de mettre fin à l'exploitation de différents appareils à jeux installés dans l'établissement dont l'intéressé était propriétaire, 85, avenue

Victor Hugo, à Paris (16eme); que cette décision a été annulée pour excès de pouvoir sur la demande du sieur Driancourt par un jugement du Tribunal administratif de Paris, en date du 27 octobre 1964, qui n'a pas été frappé d'appel; que par un second jugement en date du 22 juin 1971 le même tribunal a condamné la ville de Paris à payer au sieur Driancourt une indemnité de 85 745 F; que la ville de Paris fait appel de ce jugement; que, par voie de recours incident, les héritiers du sieur Driancourt demandent que l'indemnité allouée soit portée a 170 745 F avec les intérêts de droit à compter《de la requête》de leur auteur;

Sur le principe de la responsabilité: Considérant que l'illégalité de la décision du Préfet de police du 7 décembre 1962 a été constatée par un jugement passé en force de chose jugée; que cette illégalité, à supposer même qu'elle soit imputable à une simple erreur d'appréciation, a constitué une faute de nature à engager la responsabilité de la puissance publique; que le sieur Driancourt était en droit d'obtenir réparation du préjudice direct et certain qui a pu résulter de l'application de cette décision illégale;

Sur le montant du préjudice: Considérant qu'en allouant au sieur Driancourt la somme de 50 000 F au titre de la privation des bénéfices provenant de l'exploitation des appareils à jeux qui avaient fait l'objet de la décision d'interdiction, la somme de 25 745 F au titre de la perte résultant de la revente de ces appareils et celle de 10 000 F pour troubles dans les conditions d'existence de l'intéressé, le Tribunal administratif de Paris a fait une exacte appréciation de l'ensemble des circonstances de la cause; que la ville de Paris n'est, dès lors, pas fondée à demander la réformation du jugement attaqué;

Considérant, en revanche, qu'il y a lieu pour le Conseil d'Etat, faisant droit sur ce point aux conclusions du recours incident, de décider que l'indemnité globale allouée par le Tribunal administratif portera intérêt à compter《de la date de la requête initiale》, soit à partir du 18 juillet 1967.

Decide
Article 1: La requête susvisée de la ville de Paris est rejetée.
Article 2: La somme de 85 745 F que la ville de Paris a été condamnée à payer au sieur Driancourt par le jugement du Tribunal administratif de Paris, en date du 22 juin 1971, portera intérêt à compter du 18 juillet 1967.
Article 3: Le surplus des conclusions du recours incident des sieurs Driancourt est rejété.
Article 4: La ville de Paris supportera les dépens exposes devant le Conseil d'Etat.

Translation
Whereas following a complaint made by the President of the Association of the Friends of Avenue Victor Hugo, the Police Commissioner[1] ordered Monsieur Driancourt in a decision of 7 December 1962 to stop using various games machines which had been installed in the establishment he owned at 85,

Avenue Victor Hugo in the 16th Arrondissement in Paris; that on the application of Monsieur Driancourt, that same decision was found to be *ultra vires* and quashed by a decision of the Paris Administrative Tribunal on 27 October 1964, which has not been subject to appeal; that by a second judgment of 22 June 1971, the same Tribunal ordered the City of Paris to pay Monsieur Driancourt damages of 85,745 Francs; that the City of Paris appealed that decision; that by way of cross-appeal, Monsieur Driancourt's heirs claim that the damages awarded should be increased to 170,745 Francs with interest running from the date the claimant made his claim.

Concerning the issue of liability: Whereas the unlawfulness of the Police Commissioner's decision of 7 December 1962 was established by a judgment which is now subject to *res judicata*;[2] that this unlawfulness, even if it is attributable to a mere error of assessment, constitutes a fault which is capable of giving rise to liability of the public authorities; that Monsieur Driancourt may recover damages for any direct and certain loss which has been caused by this unlawful decision.

Concerning the issue of the amount of damages: Whereas the Paris Administrative Tribunal made an accurate assessment of the circumstances of the case in awarding Monsieur Driancourt the sum of 50,000 Francs, for the loss of profits from the machines which were the subject of the prohibition, and awarding the sum of 25,745 Francs for the loss sustained when these machines were resold, and 10,000 Francs for the troubles in the conditions of existence caused to Monsieur Driancourt; that the City of Paris is therefore not justified in requesting the reversal of the decision appealed.

Whereas, on the other hand, the Conseil d'Etat decides that interest on damages awarded by the Paris Administrative Tribunal should, in accordance with the arguments of the cross-appeal, run from 'the date of the initial claim', namely from 18 July 1967.

Held
Article 1. The appeal of the City of the Paris is dismissed.
Article 2. The sum of 85,745 Francs which the City of the Paris was ordered to pay Monsieur Driancourt by a decision of the Tribunal Administratif de Paris on the 27 October 1964, is subject to interest running from the 18 July 1967.
Article 3. The other grounds for the cross-appeal of Monsieur Driancourt are rejected.
Article 4. The City of the Paris is liable for the costs incurred during the *Conseil d'Etat* proceedings.

Translator's notes

1 The French phrase is 'Préfet de police'.
2 Force de *la chose jugée* (literally 'the quality of having been finally decided') is a complex notion with close similarities to the plea of *res judicata*.

CE 27 January 1988, Giraud, *[1988] Rec 39*

Decision in French
Conseil d'Etat
Ministre de l'Education Nationale c/Monsieur Giraud
27 janvier 1988
Req 64.076
Vu le recours du Ministre de l'éducation nationale enregistré le 22 novembre 1984 au secrétariat du Contentieux du Conseil d'Etat, et tendant à ce que le Conseil d'Etat:

1 annule le jugement en date du 4 septembre 1984 par lequel le Tribunal administratif de Lyon a condamné l'Etat à verser à M. Giraud la somme de 1 000 F, en réparation du préjudice subi par l'enfant de ce dernier du fait de la carence du service public de l'enseignement dans certaines matières;
2 rejette la demande présentée par M. Giraud devant le Tribunal administratif de Lyon; Vu l'ordonnance du 31 juillet 1945 et le décret du 30 septembre 1953;

Vu la loi du 30 décembre 1977.
Sur la régularité du jugement attaqué: Considérant qu'en invoquant à l'appui de sa demande au Tribunal administratif de Lyon tendant à ce que lui soit accordée réparation du préjudice subi par son enfant, élève de section d'enseignement spécialisé dans un collège public, du fait que, pendant l'année scolaire 1978–1979, une partie des enseignements prévus par les programmes de ces sections n'a pas été dispensée, la 'carence d'enseignement, due au fait que l'Etat n'a pas procédé à la nomination des enseignants nécessaires prévus par les textes en vigueur' M. Giraud entendait se prévaloir de la faute de l'administration; qu'ainsi, en retenant une telle faute, le Tribunal administratif n'a pas statué au-delà des conclusions dont il était saisi;

Au fond:
Sur la responsabilité: Considérant que la mission d'intérêt général d'enseignement qui lui est confiée impose au Ministre de l'éducation nationale l'obligation légale d'assurer l'enseignement de toutes les matières obligatoires inscrites aux programmes d'enseignement tels qu'ils sont définis par les dispositions législatives et réglementaires en vigueur selon les horaires réglementairement prescrits; que le manquement à cette obligation légale qui a pour effet de priver, en l'absence de toute justification tirée des nécessités de l'organisation du service, un élève de l'enseignement considéré pendant une période appréciable, est constitutif d'une faute de nature à engager la responsabilité de l'Etat;

Considérant qu'il résulte de l'instruction que l'enfant Giraud a été privé de sept heures d'enseignement hebdomadaire dont il devait bénéficier au cours de l'année scolaire 1978–1979; que l'Etat doit être déclaré responsable des conséquences dommageables pour l'enfant Giraud de la carence des services d'enseignement; que le manque de crédits budgétaires allégué par le Ministre de l'éducation nationale ne saurait, en tout état de cause, exonérer l'Etat de la responsabilité qui lui incombe;

Sur le préjudice: Considérant que le dommage subi par l'enfant Giraud est certain et direct; que le Tribunal administratif n'a pas fait, dans les circonstances de l'espèce, une excessive évaluation de la réparation due au requérant en raison des troubles dans l'éducation de son enfant en lui allouant une indemnité de 1 000 F;

Considérant qu'il résulte de ce qui précède que le Ministre de l'éducation nationale n'est pas fondé à soutenir que c'est à tort que, par le jugement attaqué, le Tribunal administratif de Lyon a condamné l'Etat à verser à M. Giraud la somme de 1 000 F.

DECIDE
Article 1er: Le recours du Ministre de l'éducation nationale est rejeté.

Translation
Concerning liability: Whereas the Minister for National Education's role of providing education in the general interest includes a legal obligation to guarantee the teaching of all the compulsory subjects on the syllabus, as defined by the statutes and regulations in force and in accordance with the timetables prescribed by regulation; that the breach of this legal obligation which, in the absence of any justification arising from organisational constraints, deprives a student from being taught over an appreciable period, constitutes a fault capable of incurring the liability of the state;

Considering that it transpires from the *instruction*[1] that, during the course of the 1978–1979 academic year, Giraud (a Minor) was wrongly deprived of seven hours of teaching per week; that the state should be held liable for the harmful consequences suffered by the child due to the shortcomings of the education services; that the lack of funds alleged by the Minister for National Education cannot in any way absolve the state from the liability which it has incurred;

Concerning the damages: Whereas the harm suffered by the child is certain and direct; that the Administrative Tribunal, in awarding the claimant[2] damages of 1000 Francs for troubles in his child's education, did not, on the facts, make an excessive assessment of the damages;

Whereas it follows from the above, that the Minister for National Education is not justified in claiming that the Lyon Administrative Tribunal wrongly ordered the state to pay Monsieur Giraud the sum of 1000F.

HELD
Article 1. The appeal brought by the Education Minister is dismissed.

Translator's notes

[1] The full elements of the case against the defendant as established by the inquisitorial procedure.
[2] The claimant was the child's father.

Conseil d'Etat 23 September 1987, Monsieur et Madame Ouaras, *Req 64.037*

Decision in French
Conseil d'Etat
Monsieur et Madame Ouaras
23 Septembre 1987
Req 64.037
Sur le rapport de la 1ere sous-section
Vu la requête sommaire et le mémoire complémentaire enregistres les 20 novembre 1984 et 8 février 1985 au secrétariat du Contentieux du Conseil d'Etat, présentés par M. et Mme Labcene OUARAS, demeurant 4, rue de Dijon a Epinay-sur-Seine (93800), et tendant a ce que le Conseil d'Etat:

1 annule le jugement en date du 30 mai 1984 par lequel le tribunal administratif de Paris a rejeté la requête des époux OUARAS tendant a ce que l'Etat soit condamne a leur verser a chacun la somme de 120 000 F, et a chacun de leurs enfants la somme de 15 000 F en réparation du préjudice subi du fait du décès de leur fille Nadia;
2 condamne l'Etat a leur verser la somme de 120 000 F, pour chacun d'entre eux, et de 15 000 F a chacun de leurs enfants ainsi que les intérêts et les intérêts des intérêts;

Vu le code des tribunaux administratifs;
Vu l'ordonnance du 31 juillet 1945 et le décret du 30 septembre 1953;

Vu la loi du 30 décembre 1977.

Sur la responsabilité de l'Etat:
Sans qu'il soit besoin d'examiner les autres moyens de la requête: Considérant qu'il ressort des pièces du dossier que, dans le cadre de son activité de service social, le service d'assistance technique, cependant de la direction départementale des polices urbaines de la Seine-Saint-Denis a propose en septembre 1977 a M. et Mme OUARAS de faire partir leur fille Nadia, âgée de trois ans, pour un séjour de trois mois auprès d'une famille néerlandaise d'accueil choisie par l'association belge 'Les Semeurs de joie'; que, partie le 21 décembre 1977 pour être hébergée par les époux H., la petite Nadia est décédée aux Pays-Bas le 16 janvier 1978 des suites des sévices que lui ont infliges lesdits époux H.;

Considérant que, dans les circonstances de l'espèce, et alors même que l'association 'Les Semeurs de joie' était favorablement connue du service d'assistance technique de la Seine-Saint-Denis depuis plusieurs années, ledit service, en ne prenant pas les précautions suffisantes pour s'assurer que la famille auprès de laquelle l'enfant allait séjourner présentait toutes les garanties nécessaires a l'accueil d'un enfant en bas age a commis une faute de nature a engager la responsabilité de l'Etat; que, des lors, M. et Mme sont fondes a demander l'annulation du jugement attaque, par lequel le tribunal administratif de Paris a rejeté leur demande d'indemnité;

Sur le préjudice moral: Considérant qu'il sera fait une juste appréciation du préjudice moral subi par M. et Mme OUARAS et par chacun de leurs enfants du fait du décès de Nadia OUARAS en condamnant l'Etat à verser une somme de 50 000 F a chacun des parents et de 10 000 F a chacun des enfants;

Sur les intérêts et les intérêts des intérêts: Considérant que les sommes susindiquées doivent porter intérêts au taux légal a compter du 15 juin 1982, date de la demande d'indemnité de M. et Mme OUARAS au ministre de l'intérieur et de la décentralisation;

Considérant que la capitalisation des intérêts a été demandée le 20 novembre 1984; qu'a cette date, il était du au moins une année d'intérêts; que, des lors, conformément aux dispositions de l'article 1154 du code civil, il y a lieu de faire droit a cette demande.

DECIDE

Article 1er: Le jugement du tribunal administratif de Paris en date du 30 mai 1984 est annule.

Article 2: L'Etat est condamne a verser a M. et Mme OUARAS la somme de 50 000F pour chacun d'eux, et a leurs enfants Taieb, Djida, Ourdia, Nasser et Souria la somme de 10 000 F pour chacun d'eux. Ces sommes porteront intérêts au taux légal a compter du 15 juin 1982. Les intérêts échus le 20 novembre 1984 seront capitalises à cette date pour porter eux-mêmes intérêts.

Apres avoir entendu: – le rapport de M. de Leusse, Auditeur, – les observations de Me Choucroy, avocat des Consorts OUARAS, – les conclusions de Mme de Clausade, Commissaire du gouvernement.

Translation

[...]

Whereas it transpires from the elements of the dossier that the technical assistance section of the Departmental Office of the Metropolitan Police of Seine-Saint-Denis, acting in its social service role, made a offer in September 1977 to Mr and Mrs Ouaras to send their three-year-old daughter, Nadia, for a three-month placement with a Dutch host family who had been selected by the Belgian Association, 'Les Semeurs de Joie'; that Nadia departed on 21 December 1977, was put up by Mr and Mrs H, and died on 16 January 1978 due to ill-treatment by Mr and Mrs H.

Whereas in the circumstances of the instant case, the technical assistance department of Seine-Saint-Denis failed to take sufficient precautions to ensure that the family with whom the child was going to stay had the necessary qualities to look after a child of a young age thus committed a fault capable of incurring the liability of the state, even though the department knew, and was favourably disposed towards, the 'Les Semeurs de Joie' Association; therefore Mr and Mrs Ouaras are justified in their appeal from the decision of the Paris Administrative Tribunal rejecting their claim for damages.

Concerning the moral harm:[1] Whereas it is a correct assessment of the moral harm suffered by Mr and Mrs Ouaras and by each of their children due to the death of Nadia Ouaras to order the state to pay 50,000 francs to each of the parents and 10,000 francs to each of the children.

Translator's note

1 'Non-pecuniary loss'.

Notes

1 [1995] 2 AC 633.
2 [2001] 2 AC 550, 572, 584–586.
3 There are a number of comparative law studies of governmental liability: D. Fairgrieve, *State Liability in Tort* (Oxford, OUP, 2003); B. Markesinis, J-B. Auby, D. Coester-Waltjen and S. Deakin, *Tortious Liability of Statutory Bodies: A Comparative and Economic Analysis of Five English Cases* (Oxford, 1999); J. Bell and A. Bradley, *Governmental Liability: A Comparative Study* (London, 1991); C. Harlow, *Administrative Liability: A Comparative Study of French and English Law* (Thesis, University of London, 1979); H. Street, *Governmental Liability: A Comparative Study* (Cambridge, 1953). See also W. Van Gerven, J. Lever and P. Larouche, *Tort Law* (Oxford, 2000) 358–394.
4 Although the majority of state liability claims fall within the purview of the administrative law courts, the French civil courts have gained jurisdiction in the following cases: accidents caused by vehicles belonging to the administration; claims concerning 'commercial' or 'industrial' public services; cases which entail a flagrant irregularity (*voie de fait*) by the administration infringing a fundamental freedom or a property right; activities of the judicial organ (*justice judiciaire*), including the *police judiciaire*.
5 G. Braibant, 'Le Rôle du Conseil d'Etat dans L'Elaboration du Droit' in *Mélanges René Chapus: Droit Administratif* (Paris, 1992) 91.
6 TC 8 February 1873, *Blanco*, D.1873.3.17. A translation of this case may be found at the end of this chapter.
7 See, for example, CE 26 January 1973, *Driancourt*, [1973] Rec 78. A translation of this case may be found at the end of this chapter. See discussion in R. Chapus, *Droit Administratif Général*, Volume 1, (15th edn, Paris, 2001) para 1454.
8 See discussion in D. Fairgrieve, *State Liability in Tort* (Oxford, OUP, 2003) 39–40.
9 CE 26 January 1973, *Driancourt*, [1973] Rec 78. A translation of this case may be found at the end of this chapter.
10 CE 26 January 1973, *Driancourt*, [1973] Rec 78.
11 In contrast with administrative decisions, the physical acts or *agissements* of public bodies cannot be quashed. Standards of legality may still sometimes have some

relevance. Occasionally, the *agissement* may constitute a *faute* due to the violation of rules laid down in statutes, regulations or secondary legislation. But in the majority of cases, no such breach will be apparent. In these cases, determining whether *agissements* give rise to fault cannot be made by reference to legality. Instead reference will be made by the courts to the whole circumstances of the incident in order to determine whether a *faute de service* has occurred.

12 See generally D. Fairgrieve, *State Liability in Tort* (Oxford, OUP, 2003) 102–105.

13 J. Moreau, 'Principes Généraux et Concepts Fondamentaux de la Responsabilité Administrative' Fascicule 700, Volume 8, *Juris-Classeur Administratif*, para 76; Rougevin-Baville, *La Responsabilité Administrative* (Paris, 1992) 58ff; Moreau, *La Responsabilité Administrative* (2nd edn, 1995, Paris) 66.

14 The mere fact that something has gone wrong can sometimes be considered to constitute administrative fault, even if the individuals were in fact doing their best, and could not reasonably have been expected to have done better. So, administrative fault was held to derive from the mere fact that a hospital ventilator (CE 9 May 1989, *Centre Hospitalier de Castelnaudry*, [1989] Rec 909) and firefighting equipment were defective (CE 28 June 1961, *André-des-Alpes*, [1961] Rec 440).

15 See Errera [1990] Public Law 571; Raynaud and Fombeur, AJDA 1998.418, 424. See case of CE 20 June 1997, *Theux*, Rec 253 concl. Stahl (emergency services); CE 29 April 1998, *Commune de Hannappes*, Rec 185, RDP 1998.1001 note X. Prétot, JCP 1999.II.10109 note Genovèse (fire-services).

16 Although, for the reassertion of *faute lourde* in the sphere of banking supervision, see M. Andenas and D. Fairgrieve, 'Misfeasance in public office, governmental liability and European influences' (2002) 51 ICLQ 757.

17 See generally R. Errera, 'The Scope and Meaning of No-Fault Liability in French Administrative Law' (1986) 39 CLP 157; D. Fairgrieve, *State Liability in Tort* (Oxford, OUP, 2003) chapter 5.

18 Law N° 2002–303 of 4 March 2002, *Gazette du Palais*, 4 April 2002, *Bulletin Législatif* 2002.113 (*Loi relative aux droits des malades et à la qualité du système de soins*). See generally C. Rade, 'La Réforme de la Responsabilité Médicale après la loi du 4 Mars 2002 rélative aux droits des maladies et à la qualité du système de santé' [2002] *Responsabilité Civile et Assurances* 4; Y. Lambert-Faivre, 'La loi N° 2002–303 du 4 mars 2002 relative aux droits des maladies et à la qualité du système de santé: L'indemnisation des accidents médicaux' D.2002 *Chroniques* 1367, 1371; M. Deguergue, 'Droits des Malades et Qualité du Système de Santé' AJDA 2002.508.

19 Where damages are granted to those that are adversely affected by public services which are dangerous or which run the risk of causing loss: for example, liability based on risk may arise when bystanders are injured by the police's use of firearms.

20 See D. Fairgrieve, *State Liability in Tort* (Oxford, OUP, 2003) chapter 9.

21 Presumptions of fault have been applied in the social welfare sphere: CAA Bordeaux 2 February 1998, *Fraticola*, JCP 1998.II.10041, but this case concerned loss caused by a child who had been placed in a foster family. See discussion in B. Markesinis, J-B. Auby, D. Coester-Waltjen and S. Deakin, *Tortious Liability of Statutory Bodies: A Comparative and Economic Analysis of Five English Cases* (Oxford, 1999) 34.

22 CE 23 September 1987, Monsieur et Madame *Ouaras*, Req 64.037. A translation of this case may be found at the end of this piece.

23 These factors are not explicitly spelt out in the judgment, but are detailed in *Commissaire du Gouvernement* Mme de Clausade's conclusions in the case (unreported).

24 *Dorset Yacht v Home Office* [1970] AC 1004.

25 CE 3 February 1956, *Thouzellier*, [1956] Rec 49; CE 14 June 1978, *Dodon*, [1978] Rec 258.

26 CE 19 December 1969, *Etablissements Delannoy*, [1969] Rec 596.

27 On a linked point, it should be noted that in France most cases which are litigated get to court – it is rather rare to settle claims with the French administrative authorities. There has been a marked reluctance on the part of the authorities to agree to settle claims, even where they are clearly liable on established principles. Moreover, the French Ombudsman, the *Médiateur de la République*, is unlikely to intervene in these cases. For alternative means of redress in French administrative law, see D. Fairgrieve, *State Liability in Tort* (Oxford, OUP, 2003) chapter 8.

28 See generally C. Guettier, *La Responsabilité Administrative* (Paris, 1996) 126–127; C. Harlow, 'Remedies in French Administrative Law' [1977] PL 227, 242.

29 M. Paillet, *La Responsabilité Administrative* (Paris, 1996) para 64; J-P. Dubois, *La Responsabilité Administrative* (Paris, 1996) 39; C. Gour, 'Faute de Service' in F. Gazier and R. Drago, (eds) *Dalloz Encyclopédie de Droit Public: Répertoire de la Responsabilité de la Puissance Publique*, para 255; Schaegis, *Progrès Scientifique et Responsabilité Administrative* (Paris, 1998) 209. See CAA Bordeaux 4 April 1991, *Francais*, [1991] Rec 1241; CE 6 July 1988, *Martin*, [1988] Rec 1061.

30 'Adequacy theory' or 'adequate cause theory'. See M. Deguergue, 'Responsabilité du Fait des Travaux et Ouvrages Publics' Fascicule 930 (1997), Volume 8, *Juris-Classeur Administratif* para 149; S. Rials, *Le Juge Administratif Francais et la Technique du Standard* (Paris, 1980) 166; J. Moreau, *Droit Public: Droit Administratif*, Volume 2, (3rd edn, Paris, 1995) 598. See also W. Van Gerven, J. Lever and P. Larouche, *Tort Law* (Oxford, 2000) 421.

31 C. Guettier, *La Responsabilité Administrative* (Paris, 1996) 17, 126–127; R. Chapelard, *Le Préjudice Indemnisable dans la Responsabilité Extra-Contractuelle de la Puissance Publique* (Thesis, L'Université de Grenoble, 1981) 177–178, 200; Deguergue, 'Responsabilité du Fait des Travaux et Ouvrages Publics' Fascicule 930 (1997), Volume 8, *Juris-Classeur Administratif* para. 149.

32 CAA Nancy 2 May 1996, *Ait Ahmad*, Req 95NC01869.

33 In English cases in the social welfare sphere, the courts have underlined the difficulties of showing that local authorities' negligent treatment of children in care actually *caused* compensatable damage (*Barrett v Enfield LBC* [2001] 2 AC 550, 574 and 590).

34 CE 23 February 1973, *Ville de Chamonix*, [1973] Rec 170. See further D. Fairgrieve, *State Liability in Tort* (Oxford, OUP, 2003) page 178.

35 B. Markesinis, J-B. Auby, D. Coester-Waltjen and S. Deakin, *Tortious Liability of Statutory Bodies: A Comparative and Economic Analysis of Five English Cases* (Oxford, 1999) 18; J. Moreau, *Droit Public: Droit Administratif*, Volume 2, (3rd edn, Paris, 1995) 599; J. Moreau, *La Responsabilité Administrative* (2nd edn, 1995, Paris) 80–81.

36 C. Guettier, *La Responsabilité Administrative* (Paris, 1996) 129.

37 See CE 23 July 2003, *Calon*, AJDA 2003.2329.

38 CE 11 May 1951, *Dme Veuve Pintal*, [1951] Rec 259; CE 28 October 1977, *Commune de Flumet*, [1977] Rec 412; CE 14 May 1986, *Commune de Cilaos*, [1986] Rec 716.

39 See generally D. Fairgrieve, *State Liability in Tort* (Oxford, OUP, 2003) chapter 7.

40 CE 27 January 1988, *Giraud*, [1988] Rec 39. A translation of this case may be found at the end of this chapter.
41 These would falter due to an insufficiently direct and certain causal link with the educational failure.
42 [2001] 2 AC 619. On this case, see B. Markesinis, 'Plaintiff's tort law or defendant's tort law? Is the House of Lords moving towards a synthesis?' (2001) 9 *Torts Law Journal* 168; D. Fairgrieve, 'Pushing back the Boundaries of Public Authority Liability: Tort Law Enters the Classroom' [2002] PL 288; J. Greenwold, 'Lawyers in the Classroom: the New Law of Educational Negligence' (2000) *Education and the Law* 245; M. Harris, 'Education and Local Authorities' (2001) 117 LQR 25.
43 CAA Nancy 18 March 1999, *Kurylak*, Req 94NC00324: concerning an accident in 1983, judgment at first instance given in 1988. France has been found in breach of Article 6 of the European Convention on Human Rights for the excessive slowness of its administrative justice system (eg *Cazenave de la Roche v France* [1998] Human Rights Case Digest 620). See also CE 28 June 2002, *Magiera*, Req 239575.
44 Article 1 of the Law of 31 December 1968.
45 CE 6 December 2002, *Commune d'Albestroff*, Req 230291.
46 M. Paillet, *La Responsabilité Administrative* (Paris, 1996) para. 544 et seq.
47 See generally J-F. Eschylle and M. Huyette, 'Autorité Parentale – Assistance Educative', Fascicule 20, *Juris-Classeur Civil* (Paris, 2001); P. Ely and C. Stanley, *The French Alternative: delinquency prevention and child protection in France with reference to the Dunkirk conurbation* (London, NACRO, 1990).
48 *Ordonnance N°* 58–1301 of 23 December 1958.
49 P. Ely and C. Stanley, *The French Alternative: delinquency prevention and child protection in France with reference to the Dunkirk conurbation* (London, NACRO, 1990), page 1.
50 Ibid. page 19.
51 P. Ely and C. Stanley, *The French Alternative: delinquency prevention and child protection in France with reference to the Dunkirk conurbation* (London, NACRO, 1990) 2.
52 The French administrative judiciary may be liable for acts of a judicial nature on the basis of a *faute lourde* as long as the claimant has not impugned the substantive content of a definitive decision (CE 29 December 1978, *Darmont*, [1978] Rec 542). However, the *Conseil d'Etat* has recently set aside this pre-condition of *faute lourde* regarding the violation of the right to a hearing within a reasonable time underpinned by Article 6(1) of the ECHR: CE 28 June 2002, *Magiera*, Req 239575. For further discussion of liability for judicial acts, see W. Van Gerven, J. Lever and P. Larouche, *Tort Law* (Oxford, 2000) 383. The French judicial judiciary, including the *juge des enfants*, is similarly protected by the law in respect of damages claims. The ordinary judiciary are liable only in the case of a *faute lourde* or a *déni de justice* (such as for excessive delay in giving judgment) and provided that the substantive content of the judicial decision is not concerned (article 11 of the Law of 5 July 1972). Also article 149 of the Law of 17 July 1970 provides for compensation where a person has been held in pre-trial custody and is subsequently released without charge or acquitted (no longer need to show abnormal loss: article 9 of the Law of 30 December 1996).
53 The *Ouaras* case is a notable exception: CE 23 September 1987, Monsieur et Madame *Ouaras*, Req 64.037.
54 A. Peters and H. Schwenke, 'Comparative Law beyond Post-Modernism' (2000) 49 ICLQ 800, 831.

Chapter 10

National Report on Germany

*Martina Künnecke**

Introduction

In Germany two spectacular child abuse cases in families, which due to omissions by local youth authorities ended tragically, have been reported.[1] These cases have put local youth authorities and the work of social workers into the spotlight. The subject has been widely discussed in the media and articles mainly written by legal practitioners: the dilemma of the social workers in fulfilling their difficult task between supporting the unity of the family and the protection of the individual child has become evident.[2] The work of local youth authorities has also been the subject of numerous petitions by individuals or initiatives to the Members of the *Länder* and the federal Parliament and the *Kinderkommission* of the *Bundestag*. Amongst other complaints the petitions are concerned with the supervision of children in care and the lack of co-operation with the biological family concerning the return of the child[3] similar to the factual circumstances in *Barrett v Enfield London Borough Council*.[4]

However, in Germany these particular cases have so far not led to claims in damages against local youth authorities for the negligent exercise of their public duties as can be witnessed in the English cases in *X v Bedfordshire County Council* and *Barrett*. The more serious cases have been subject to criminal prosecution, which have led to the sentencing of youth workers in 1999.[5]

Local youth authorities have so far not been sued for negligence. The recent decision by the European Court of Human Rights in *Z v UK*[6] did not receive much attention in Germany. However, some solicitors with a particular interest in childcare cases are familiar with the judgment and are currently preparing similar claims in negligence against local youth authorities. Whether these claims will be successful in German courts remains to be seen.

By describing the law of tortious liability of public bodies in Germany I will attempt to give reasons for the absence of such cases.

* Lecturer, University of Hull.

Brief Outline of the Tortious Liability of Public Bodies

This is tortious liability according to the Civil Code (BGB)[7] in connection with Article 34 Basic Law (GG).[8]

Similar to the position in English law the liability of public authorities in Germany is governed by the law of torts contained in section 839 Civil Code, which is concerned with damages for the breach of an official duty. However, the legal construction of this tort, which is a hybrid between public and private law, has been criticised for a long time. Liability for the wrongdoing of an official is a combined liability between the official and the state. However, the personal liability of the official is transferred to the state according to Art. 34 Basic Law (see below).[9]

This construction is due to its historical development from a purely private law liability in tort to a constellation in which the state accepts responsibility for the tortious acts of its civil servants. However, it is still not clear whether it can be regarded as a private or a public law remedy.[10] Due to its original private nature, the cause of action has to be filed in the civil courts and is outside the jurisdiction of the administrative courts. Similar to the position in English law, liability for breach of an official duty is governed by the law of torts, which is laid down in the *BGB*, the Civil Code that was drafted in 1900. Originally the liability of a civil servant for the breach of an official duty was dealt with purely as a private law matter contained in Art. 839 of the *BGB*. Accordingly the relationship between the state and its officials was considered as being of a private law nature. Therefore the official was liable personally for all unlawful acts. This reasoning is still clearly expressed in the *BGB*.

Accordingly, public bodies are liable in damages to individuals injured by their own (or their employees') culpable failure to perform properly any official duty owed to the individual. There has to be a causal link between the breach of the duty and the damage suffered. The provision contains three exceptions to liability. Liability is excluded where the breach of a duty is due to a negligent act only and the individual injured can obtain compensation from another source; secondly, where the victim did not make use of any legal remedy, which could have mitigated his damages; and thirdly where a statute expressly provides for such an eventuality.[11]

However, the aggrieved citizen was often unable to gain compensation from the civil servants. In order to protect the citizen claims were gradually allowed to be made against the state. Therefore the law changed around the second third of the 19th century and later the Weimar constitution from 1919 contained the provision, which is now contained in Art. 34 of the Basic Law:

> Should anybody, in exercising a public office, neglect their duty towards a third party liability shall rest in principle with the state or the public body employing them. In the event of wilful intent or gross negligence, a remedy may be sought against the person concerned.

Claims for tortious liability of the public authorities in Germany are dealt with by the ordinary courts. To make sure that the officials would not misuse the immunity granted to them from personal liability Art. 34 reserves a right of the state to recover damages from the official in question in case the breach of duty was wilful or grossly negligent.

The Requirements of the Tort in Child Abuse Cases

Duty of Care Owed to a Third Party

Both section 839 *BGB* and Art. 34 Basic Law require that the official duty must be owed to a *third party*. Whether a person is a third party in that sense depends on whether the object of the duty is directly to safeguard the interests of that person. If, for instance a policeman remains inactive while a theft is being committed, he is in breach of his official duty towards the owner, because his power to interfere is conferred on him not merely in the interest of the general public, but at the same time in the interest of each single individual. In each case it has to be seen whether according to the object and the legal provisions of the official task the affected interests should have been protected. Three conditions have to be met in order to establish a duty towards a third party. Firstly, the official duty must be capable of protecting individuals, secondly the plaintiff has to belong to the protected group of people and thirdly the damage must be included in the protective effect of the duty.[12] The establishment of such a duty owed to a third party is extremely difficult. The determination of which duties are capable of protecting third party effects is left to the courts. The decision on this issue is crucial for the success or failure of an action. The fact that section 839 *BGB* does not enumerate official duties, which confer rights on individuals, illustrates that the courts are given some leeway as to how to interpret the concept of duty. In the context of child care cases the establishment of such a duty is clearly to be found in the *KJHG* (*Kinder- und Jugendhilfegesetz* or *SGB VIII*). The duty to intervene in cases in which a child is at risk of injury by its parents is contained in section 2 *KJHG*. The official duties of the youth authorities are enumerated here and contain the provision of the educational assistance and other services and the taking of young children into care if necessary (see section 42 *KJHG*). Potential cases in negligence against public bodies would not fail at this early stage. There is little doubt that the local youth authority is under a duty to protect the welfare of children as soon as the authority obtains knowledge of the neglect. Such a duty of care was established in a case decided by the OLG Hamm, which was concerned with the claim of a mother whose daughter had been taken into care.[13]

However, some of the arguments put forward in the English decision in *X v Bedfordshire*, which are described as 'policy' arguments, appear alien to modern German reasoning. Amongst the policy arguments in *X v Bedforshire County Council* were those that imposing liability would make bad economic sense, that it would inhibit public authorities carrying out their duties, that the courts would be allowed to substitute the authorities' decisions by having a 'second guess' and that alternative remedies were available. However, a closer look into material stemming from the time when the German Civil Code was drafted early last century reveals that similar arguments were considered. However, a study has been carried out and revealed that the expenses for state liability cases amounted to only 0.015% of the total budget. It was discussed whether imposing liability would make civil servants too cautious. However, it was agreed that that would be better than allowing careless behaviour on the part of civil servants. Further, discretionary decisions may be reviewed and give rise to liability.[14]

Fault

Liability is only imposed on the official if he or she has wilfully or negligently breached the official duty. However, it has been shown that the element of fault does not constitute a particular problem in the establishment of a claim in negligence against public bodies.

Causality

The breach of the duty owed towards the plaintiff has to have caused the damage. This condition of liability may cause difficulties in cases where the authorities have a choice between different forms of action. In providing assistance to parents under the *KJHG* such as educational assistance, family therapy and other supplementary services or the taking of children into care, the authorities exercise a certain amount of discretion. A causal link between the breach of the duty of care and the damage can only be established if the lawful exercise of the duty of care would have avoided the damage with the highest probability.[15] In this context it is crucial to identify how the authority in acting lawfully would have decided the case. If the authority was exercising discretion it would be impossible to predict how the authority would have decided. The causal link can only be established in cases where there was only one correct form of the exercise of discretion (*Ermessensreduzierung auf Null*) or where it is absolutely clear how the discretion should have been exercised lawfully and that this exercise would have avoided the damage. In the case of *Barrett* it might have been difficult to establish what the only correct exercise of the authorities' discretion would have been.

Having outlined the difficulties in obtaining compensation under the provisions for official liability, an excursion into the constitutional framework of child care laws and the availability of primary legal protection in the form of judicial review of administrative decisions will follow.

The Constitutional Framework for the Law Governing Childcare

The law governing the relationship between the state, parents and their children is contained in different statutes such as the *BGB* (Civil Code), and the *KJHG* (a special law on the help for children and youths),[16] can only be understood in the context of the constitutional protection of the family as guaranteed in Article 6 of the Basic Law which reads:

Marriage and Family Shall Enjoy the Special Protection of the State

> The care and upbringing of children are a natural right of parents and a duty primarily incumbent on them. It is the responsibility of the community to ensure that they perform this duty.
> Children may not be separated from their families against the will of their parents or guardians save in accordance with a law in cases where they fail in their duty or there is a danger of the children being seriously neglected for other reasons.

When the Basic Law was drafted in 1949 in the light of Germany's history the main purpose of a written catalogue of rights was to protect the individual against infringements by the state (*Abwehrrechte gegen den Staat*). Accordingly, the constitution protects the unity of the family against state intervention. The child is considered to be part of the family. The care for and the bringing up of the children is considered to be the right and the duty of the parents. The state is under a duty to act as a guardian (*Wächterfunktion*), which can be enforced by local youth authorities or in extreme cases by the courts. Accordingly, the law on the help for children and youths states that the care and the education for children is the natural right and duty of the parents.[17]

Judicial Review of Administrative Decisions in Childcare Cases

The law provides for the power of the local youth authority to take children who are at a serious risk into care.[18] However, for the protection of the unity of the family the Law on the Help for children and youths provides for measures of help such as the counselling of the parents, and special living arrangements such as boarding. According to section 27 of this law it is the parents who hold the right to help in the caring for their children. The law was not intended to provide children with a right to receive help but contains the right of parents to receive help in the upbringing of their children if needed. The protection of the parents' rights to receive such help is enforceable in the German Administrative Courts. There is a wealth of cases concerned with judicial review of the decisions of youth authorities in granting or refusing such help.[19] Therefore the primary protection of these interests in Germany is very strong. This is due to the constitutional mandate in Article 19IV Basic Law, which provides for judicial control of administrative decisions. In other words, families who are not coping very well may request help in the upbringing of their children. If such help is refused by the youth authority, the decisions can be reviewed by the Administrative Courts.

To illustrate this point I have chosen a recent decision by the highest Administrative Court in Rheinland-Pfalz, in *Koblenz*.[20] The applicants were the parents of a boy aged 15 who suffered from serious behavioural problems, which were partly due to the mother's depression, and the lack of time of the father to look after his son. As the parents had difficulties in coping with the child and in order to prevent further social neglect of the child they applied for a placement of the child in a care institution. The local youth authority, however refused the request and offered help in the home in the form of a supervisor to aid and support the family *(Erziehungsbeistand)*. The parents applied for judicial review of the decision but were unsuccessful with their claim. The Administrative Court held that decisions concerning the review of pedagogic considerations were not fully reviewable as the decision-maker had a margin of evaluation *(Beurteilungsspielraum)*. Nevertheless the decision could be reviewed with regard to whether the decision-maker had taken irrelevant considerations into account and whether the decision was necessary and suitable. In applying these tests the court held that the decision had been lawful.

This decision illustrates that in the light of the constitutional protection of the family one of the main aims of child protection laws is the provision of help for parents in the upbringing of the children. The person entitled to these benefits is the parent and the decisions by the youth authorities are subject to review by the administrative courts. The intensity of review applied by the Administrative courts varies between different courts and is highly controversial.[21] Nevertheless, the case was aimed at illustrating that primary legal protection (often in speedy procedures) is of great importance in Germany. Negligence claims are secondary which is clearly stated in para. 839 III *BGB*. Accordingly, a negligence claim is excluded if the applicant has not exhausted other judicial remedies such as judicial review of the original decision. A hypothetical claim in negligence for damage caused by this decision would be bound to fail as the decision by the Administrative Court would be followed by the court dealing with the tortious claim.[22] The wealth of judicial review cases in childcare cases illustrates that the decisions of authorities concerning the provision of help in the upbringing of children are subject to judicial scrutiny. Many cases are concerned with the payment for services carried out by independent providers which parents have chosen and for which they request financial support from the youth authorities. Further, it has been suggested that individual citizens appear to know of their rights, even though they may not be aware of the statutory basis for their claims.[23]

Weak Legal Position of Children

Nevertheless, there are situations in which the help under the childcare laws has not been requested and the youth authorities failed to intervene in time to prevent tragic outcomes. In these cases there are no parents to sue local authorities. Here we need to look at the legal position of the child. The case of *Jenny*[24] illustrates that children may find themselves in a legal vacuum between the parental rights and the unity of the family structure and the reluctance of youth authorities and courts to separate them from the family for their own safety. Such care orders can only be made if the safety of a child is seriously at risk. According to section 1666a *BGB* the provision of help inside the family structure has to prevail over the separation of family and child. The youth worker in the case of Jenny should have informed his colleague in Southern Germany, where the mother and child had moved, of the special circumstances of the case. He was sentenced for being negligent in omitting this vital piece of information. The problem raised by this case was that children at risk often change their residence, which is intended by the parents to shake off the observation by the youth authorities. This has the effect that in the absence of a national register for abused children, children in these situations often fall through the net of childcare protection.[25]

Finally, due to the conservative mode of the family unit as protected in Article 6 of the Basic Law, children are not legally entitled to childcare measures themselves. The right to receive such help is primarily linked to the parental right. However, children from these deprived families are often not confident enough to sue youth authorities, the cases are not lucrative enough to be taken up by solicitors and the concept of the guardian *ad litem* is only just developing to improve the position of abused children in court proceedings. So far there are no guidelines for the legal representation of children.[26] Only three years ago the introduction of the concept of a guardian *ad litem* (*Verfahrenspfleger*), an independent representative of the child's rights was introduced into section 50 FGG (*Gesetz über die freiwillige Gerichtsbarkeit*). Despite comparative research into the function of the guardian *ad litem* before the provision was drafted, the role of the guardian *ad litem* has to be improved.[27] Often they are not independent enough to support a child's case in negligence against an authority.[28]

Conclusion

In conclusion, reasons for the absence of negligence claims in child abuse cases in Germany is due to the emphasis on the primary legal protection against decisions of youth authorities concerning the welfare of children. Due to the constitutional protection of the family unit in Article 6 Basic Law, child welfare provisions in the *BGB* and the SGB VIII are concerned primarily with the support of the parents in the upbringing of their children. They are entitled to measures of help as enumerated in the *KJHG* and these rights are enforceable in the Administrative Courts. Article 19 IV Basic Law guarantees the judicial review of such decisions. Accordingly, a wealth of case law concerned with child welfare matters can be found. Further, the law of tortious liability against public bodies is a secondary legal remedy, which is clearly excluded if legal remedies to prevent the damage have not been used.

In technical legal terms a claim in negligence would not fail at the early stage of the establishment of a duty of care. Such a duty towards children could be derived from the *KJHG* which puts youth authorities under an official duty to support the welfare of children. However, the requirement of causality could cause difficulties if the authority had discretion in exercising its powers. A claim could fail unless it can be shown that the authority was under a duty to perform its discretion in a particular way (*Ermessensreduzierung auf Null*).

The legal position of children however, is comparatively weak in this relationship between parental rights and the intervention of the state. For practical reasons they may fall through the net of social support and legal protection. This is due both to the fact that there is little control over children being moved from one jurisdiction to the next and to the emphasis in the law on the preservation of the family unit. A legal vacuum is further created by the lack of individual children's rights. The introduction of a *Verfahrenspfleger* in 1998, modelled on the British guardian *ad litem*, is a step in the right direction.

Since this paper was presented the Basic Right of children in care to a hearing by the relevant youth authority (Article 1, 2I and II1 Basic Law) and the tortious liability of the latter was addressed in a decision by the OLG Stuttgart in July 2003.[29] The decision came too late for inclusion in the main body of this article, its outcome is pending before the BGH[30] as of May 2004. The case concerned the abuse of two young children in foster care, one of whom died tragically of starvation. Both, the *Landgericht* and the *Oberlandesgericht* agreed that the youth authority had failed to comply with its statutory duties. According to the *SGB VIII* the youth authority was under a duty to acknowledge its own responsibility for the case, assess the foster family and observe the right of the children to be heard and to participate in their own fate. This constitutionally protected Basic Right of the child outweighed the right to the protection of the autonomy of the foster family (Article 6 Basic Law). Both courts agreed on the award of compensation amounting to €25,000. The decision by the *OLG* is to be welcomed[31] as it emphasises the right of the child to participate in its own fate. Nevertheless, in line with good German tradition, it has been criticised for simplifying complex questions of causation in the context of childcare and medical issues.[32] The decision of the *BGH* is eagerly awaited.

Notes

1 The case of 'Jenny', LG Stuttgart, 17.9.1999, 1 (15) KLs 114 Js 26273/96 and OLG Oldenburg, 2.09.1996, ZfJ 1997, 95.

2 Friedrichsen, Gisela, 'Musste Jenny sterben?', *Der Spiegel* 39/1999; Bringewat, Peter, 'Kommunale Jugendhilfe und strafrechtliche Garantenhaftung', *Neue Juristische Wochenschrift*, 1998, 944; Lehman, Karl-Heinz, 'Helfen ohne Risiko Justiz contra Sozialarbeit, Referat anlässlich der Fachtagung des DBSH Landesverbandes Niedersachsen am 1.6.2000 in der KFH'; Nolte, Susanne, 'Elternrecht, Rechte des Kindes und Kinderschutz bei Kindesmisshandlung Gegenpole im Spannungsfeld', *Kindesmisshandlung und Vernachlässigung*, December 2001, 77.

3 Wiesner, Reinhard, Problemaufriss zum Thema 'Kontrolle/Arbeit der Jugendämter', Tagesdokumentation 'Kindeswohl' – Dilemma und Praxis der Jugendämter – epd-Dokumentation Nr. 6/97 vom 3. Febr. 1997, p. 70 http://www.pappa.com/ja/wies_ja.htm.

4 [1999] 3 All ER 193.

5 LG Stuttgart, 17.9.1999, 1 (15) KLs 114 Js 26273/96.

6 *Z v United Kingdom* [2001] 2 FLR 612.

7 Abbreviation for *Bürgerliches Gesetzbuch*, in force since 1900.

8 Abbreviation for *Grundgesetz*, in force since 1949.

9 Fritz Ossenbühl, *Staatshaftungsrecht*, München, Beck-Verlag, 1998, 2.

10 Ibid., 6.

11 Section 839 Civil Code:

(1) If an official intentionally or negligently violates the official duty, which falls

upon him as against a third party, he must compensate the third party for the harm arising therefrom. If the official can only be charged with negligence, a claim can only be made against him if the person suffering harm cannot obtain compensation in another manner.

(2) If an official violates his official duty through a decision on a legal issue, he is only responsible for the harm arising therefrom if the violation of duty consists in a criminal act. This provision has no application to a refusal or delay in the exercise of the office, which is contrary to duty.

(3) The duty to compensate does not arise if the person suffering the harm has intentionally or negligently omitted to avert the harm by the use of legal remedy.

12 Ossenbühl, *supra* n.74, 58.

13 OLG Hamm, 20.11.1996 (11 U 61/96).

14 For an excellent discussion of these points see Markesinis, B.S., Auby, J.B., Coester-Waltjen, D. and Deakin, S.F., *Tortious Liability of Statutory Bodies, A Comparative and Economic Analysis of Five English Cases* (Oxford: Hart Publishing, 1999).

15 BGH VersR 1983, 1031.

16 Also referred to as *SGB VIII*.

17 Para. 1 (2) *KJHG*.

18 Para. 42 *KJHG*.

19 See Hinrichs, Knut, *Selbstbeschaffung im Jugendhilferecht – Zur Aktualität fürsorgerechtlicher Grundsätze in der Jugendhilfe*, forthcoming Peter Lang Verlag.

20 OVG Koblenz, 11.05.2000 – 12 A 12335/99.OVG.

21 See Hinrichs, Knut, *Selbstbeschaffung im Jugendhilferecht – Zur Aktualität fürsorgerechtlicher Grundsätze in der Jugendhilfe*, forthcoming Peter Lang Verlag.

22 BGHZ 9, 129, 132; BGH NVwZ 1984, 333; BGHZ 118, 235, 255 = NJW 1992, 2218

23 See Hinrichs, Knut, *Selbstbeschaffung im Jugendhilferecht – Zur Aktualität fürsorgerechtlicher Grundsätze in der Jugendhilfe*, forthcoming Peter Lang Verlag.

24 Jenny, 3, was found dead after having been abused and battered by the mother. The case was known to the local youth authorities. The case led to the criminal conviction of one social youth worker: LG Stuttgart, 17.9.1999, 1 (15) KLs 114 Js 26273/96.

25 Nolte, Susanne, 'Elternrecht, Rechte des Kindes und Kinderschutz bei Kindesmisshandlung: Gegenpole im Spannungsfeld', *Kindesmisshandlung und Vernachlässigung*, December 2001, 77.

26 Marquardt, Claudia, *Sexuell missbrauchte Kinder im Gerichtsverfahren*, Münster, 1999, 150.

27 Salgo, Ludwig, *Der Anwalt des Kindes*, Bundesanzeiger Verlagsgesellschaft, Köln, 1993.

28 Nolte, Susanne, 'Elternrecht, Rechte des Kindes und Kinderschutz bei Kindesmisshandlung Gegenpole im Spannungsfeld', *Kindesmisshandlung und Vernachlässigung*, December 2001, 77, 85.

29 4 U 42/03, *NJW*, 2003, 3419.

30 Az. III 254/03.

31 See Hinrichs, Knut, *Evangelische Jugendhilfe*, Kolumne Gesetze und Gerichte, 2004 forthcoming.

32 See Meysen, Thomas, *NJW*, 2003, 3369 [3372, 3373].

Chapter 11

Child Abuse Tort Claims in The Netherlands

*Cees van Dam**

Introduction

The legal framework of child protection in the Netherlands differs considerably from that in the United Kingdom. That is why it has been necessary to explain the Dutch legal framework of child protection when trying to answer the question about how claims like the ones in *Bedfordshire* (and *Z*) (the child not yet under protection), and *Barrett* (the child under protection) would have been decided by a Dutch court. In the following section, an analysis will be made of some possible explanations for the lack of cases on child abuse in the Netherlands; these problems, such as limitation, might also play a role in other jurisdictions. The last section will deal with the issues of damages and alternative remedies.

The Child Not Yet Under Protection: The *Bedfordshire* Case

In the *Bedfordshire* case five plaintiffs, born between 1982 and 1990, claimed damages for personal injury arising out of breach of statutory duty and negligence by the defendant council. The plaintiffs alleged that between 1987 and 1992 they had suffered parental abuse and neglect; that the council had received serious reports of such treatment but had failed to investigate the matter adequately or protect the plaintiffs from further harm; in particular, that it had failed to exercise their statutory duties to identify children in their area who were in need and to take measures to protect them from harm.[1]

In the case of *Z* the four applicants were siblings, born in 1982, 1984, 1986 and 1988. The family was first referred to social services in October 1987 by a health visitor as a result of concerns about the children, the parents' marital problems and allegations that the eldest one, Z, was stealing food. Over the next four years numerous referrals were made by neighbours, a family member and professionals, including the family's general practitioner, the children's

* Professorial Fellow in Comparative Law, British Institute of International and Comparative Law.

head teacher, a social worker and police officers. Between October 1987 and June 1992 no steps had been taken to remove the children from the care of the parents. Interim care orders were made on 7 December 1992 and full care orders on 14 April 1993. In June 1993 the Official Solicitor, as next friend for the children, commenced proceedings against the local authority claiming damages for negligence and/or breach of statutory duty.[2]

How would a Dutch court decide cases like *Bedfordshire*? In order to answer this question it has to be emphasised that the legal framework of child protection in the Netherlands differs substantially from that in the United Kingdom. The main Dutch institution in the field of child protection is the Council for the Protection of Children (Raad voor de Kinderbescherming, also referred to as CPC). The CPC is a public body and it is the only institution that is entitled to request the court to put a child under protection and to remove him or her from his parental home. The protection itself is carried out by child protection organisations. These child protection organisations are all private organisations and, contrary to the position in the United Kingdom, they do not have the possibility to put a child under protection or to change his protection regime.[3]

This framework implies that an important distinction has to be made between the care for children who are under supervision of a child protection organisation on the one hand and the care for children who are not yet under protection. With regard to this latter category only the CPC is entitled to request the court to take measures in order to protect the child; the child protection organisation is not entitled to do so. If it considers it necessary to protect a child or improve its protection, it has to ask the CPC to request the court to do so. If a child protection organisation prefers action and the CPC decides that action is not necessary, the CPC has the last word: there is no administrative action available to judge this decision.

This however does not exclude the possibility of filing an action in tort against the CPC for failing to request the court to put a child under protection. To put this issue in a broader perspective it has to be pointed out that, according to Dutch law, the main basis for liability is the breach of a statutory duty or the breach of an unwritten duty of care (art. 6:162 Burgerlijk Wetboek). The legislation regarding child protection mainly provides for statutory powers and not for statutory duties of the CPC. However, the lack of a statutory duty does not exclude the possibility that the CPC can be liable for breaching its unwritten duty of care. This can be the case if the CPC uses or omits to use its statutory powers in an unlawful way. According to Dutch tort law, liability of public bodies is not generally excluded: it is considered not to be just, fair and reasonable to give public bodies a general immunity to liability, because such an immunity leads to an undesirable avoidance of responsibility.[4]

An important justification for a duty of the CPC is its knowledge about the safety of children and its ability to interfere in family relations, whereas the potential victim does not have enough information about what an acceptable safety level is and is normally not capable of changing his situation without the help of others.[5]

In many cases the CPC and the child protection organisations receive information from doctors, schools or private citizens who report an abuse or report a dangerous situation. The Dutch Hoge Raad (Supreme Court) has decided that in such a case a public body has a duty to act.[6] This implies that it has to respond to the received information in a proper way by examining the extent of the risk and – if necessary – to take adequate measures to restrict or remove the risk. The receipt of the information does not in itself create liability for the public body but it deprives the public body of its defence that it did not know about the risk. Furthermore it has the burden of proving that it had reacted adequately to the complaint or the received information.

The extent of the duty of the CPC has to be established by weighing two elements: on the one hand the magnitude of the risk (that is, the probability of causing damage and the expected character and magnitude of the damage) and on the other hand the burden of taking precautionary measures and the character of the conduct and of the author of the damage.[7]

The foregoing amounts to the conclusion that in cases like *Bedfordshire* a Dutch claim has to be based on the fact that the CPC did not ask the court for protection for the child, although it knew that the child was in danger. At this stage, the CPC will put forward the policy defence. In this regard to that subject three general remarks have to be made. In the first place in the Netherlands public bodies, like the CPC, have to act at least in compliance with the so-called general principles of good governance, even if their acts have a pure policy character. This means that a public body is not allowed to act arbitrarily and that it has a duty to act fairly and a duty to treat equal cases equally. If it does not do so, it acts unlawfully and it might be liable for the damage caused. Secondly, the fact that the decision of a public body is a policy decision is no excuse for directly or indirectly infringing fundamental rights, such as art. 3 European Convention on Human Rights, which was the case in *Z*. It is therefore arguable that also in the Netherlands the CPC has to act if it knows about a child who is in a really dangerous or humiliating situtation. In such a case restricted financial means of the CPC are no justification not to interfere. Thirdly with regard to the policy issue, a public body must be able to make clear what its policy is and that it carries out that policy in a proper way. So, the CPC must make clear that it has, within its possibilities and means, a plan with regard to its main policies and goals, how it operates to achieve its goals and that it in fact carries out its plan.[8]

With regard to the policy issue it has also to be taken into account that there are many cases in which the CPC knows about a child or children in families with social, emotional and financial problems. They may also presume that in a number of these families child abuse may take place. However, there have to be sufficient legal grounds in order to successfully ask the court to provide protection measures. If the CPC obtains information about a case of child abuse, it will, on the one hand, have to act with all due speed. On the other hand, the CPC will have to investigate the accuracy of the alleged facts. So, generally speaking, a claim of a not-yet-protected abused child might only be successful, if it is clear that the CPC should have asked the court for guardianship for the child and that it did not do so or that it did not do so promptly. The facts in the case of *Z* are of course an example of such a clear case. However, the CPC would only have been liable if it could have been established that the court would have the order sought requested by the CPC. If that were not to be the case, there would not have been a causal connection between the omission of the CPC and the damage of the child. In practice the courts award about 95% of the requests of the CPC.

It is likely that the Dutch courts will apply a professional standard, which is related to the field of child protection. The courts are already applying this professional standard for instance in the field of liability of lawyers, auditors, physicians and psychiatrists. This standard is comparable to the one applied in English tort law.[9] This means that the child protection organisation has to act as a reasonably capable and reasonably acting professional. It has to be stressed that reasonable does not mean ordinary or passable but it means good. If the CPC obtains information about a specific case of child abuse, it is clear that the professional standard requires on the one hand that the CPC interferes promptly. On the other hand, the same professional standard demands that the CPC investigates the accuracy of the alleged facts; this might be quite difficult. So, the CPC has to make its way between Scylla and Charybdis: if it does not interfere promptly it can be sued by the child; if it interferes without reasonable grounds it can be sued both by the child and its parents. The criterion of reasonable grounds means that there were serious indications for child abuse, not there was proof of actual abuse.

The same goes if a child protection organisation observes that legal measures or additional legal measures should be taken in order to protect a not-yet-protected child. In such a case the child protection organisation can only ask the CPC to request the court for legal measures. This also means that an omission of a child protection organisation can only lead to a possibility of liability in clear-cut cases.

The foregoing can be illustrated by a Dutch case in the field of liability for child abuse. This is not a case in which the child protectors underacted but rather they overacted. This case also demonstrates that the CPC and child protection organisations have to steer clear of the rocks. A 14-year-old girl told her schoolteacher that she had been sexually abused by her brother. The schoolteacher called in the help of the regional organisation for mental health care. This organisation helped the girl to leave her parental home and to find her a new temporary home. A few weeks later it informed the CPC and then the CPC asked the court for protection and this request was awarded by the court. Later on it appeared that the girl had made up the story of sexual abuse. The parents of the girl and the girl herself filed a claim against the organisation for mental health care, which had helped the girl, alleging that it had acted unlawfully. The Hoge Raad held that in this case the organisation did not act unlawfully against the parents or the child by cooperating with the girl when she wished to leave the parental home. It was established that the organisation had at that time reasonable grounds to presume that the alleged facts were true. Furthermore, the Hoge Raad held that the organisation had acted with due speed when it asked the CPC within a few weeks to act in order to put the girl under protection.[10]

The Child Under Protection: The *Barrett* Case

In *Barrett* the plaintiff had been in the care of the local authority from a young age until his majority. He claimed damages for the psychiatric injury arising from the negligence of the authority and its employees during the time he was in their care. It was alleged that the authority was negligent in failing to arrange his adoption, organising inappropriate placements with foster parents and residential homes, not obtaining psychiatric treatment for him, and mismanaging both his re-introduction with his mother and his relationship with his half-sister. The House of Lords held that a duty of care should not be ruled out in this context.[11]

In the Netherlands the guardianship is carried out by child protection organisations. It is generally accepted that these (mainly private) bodies have a duty of care towards the child who is under its care and to carry out its task in a proper way. Whether this is the case will be tested by the courts with the help of a professional standard. This means that the child protection organisation has to act as a reasonably capable and reasonably acting professional (see section 2).

With regard to the alleged facts in the *Barrett* case it is likely that, according to Dutch law, the child protection organisation is liable if it did not provide the psychiatric treatment the boy needed or if it did not supervise the foster parents or the residential homes in a proper way. In such a case the organisation does not meet the professional standard. In principle the burden of proof lies with the boy but the organisation is obliged to disclose all its records about the treatment of the boy and about the way it supervised the foster parents and the residential homes. If the organisation does not provide this information, the court will generally decide that it has insufficiently disputed the statements of the claimant.[12] This will most likely lead to the conclusion that there was a breach of duty. If the organisation provides this information, whether a breach of duty can be established depends on the content of this information.

In this respect it is an interesting question whether the standard of care of a child protection organisation towards a child under protection is the same as the standard of care of parents towards their children. In most jurisdictions it is accepted that parents owe a duty of care toward their children, although this duty is generally not a high one and the distractions of everyday life must be taken into account.[13] This last aspect is less of a consideration for a child protection organisation. Moreover these organisations ought to know more about possible problems of children and how to handle them.

The Limitation Problem

There are few child abuse tort claims in the Netherlands. In the first place this might have to do with the fact that the Dutch were, at least until a few years ago, not very claim-conscious. Moreover, until recently even many lawyers were not aware of the possibility of suing supervisors such as governmental bodies. However the Dutch and their lawyers are waking up, and their claims consciousness is growing. This is partly due to the growing influence and help of legal aid insurers in order to claim compensation.

Another possible explanation for the lack of cases are the costs of litigation. The risks for the claimant are only limited if liability is established and the defendant has to pay the out-of-court costs of the claimant's lawyer (art. 6:96 Burgerlijk Wetboek). However, in most child abuse cases the answer to the liability question is uncertain and the victim may face a substantial financial problem if he loses the case. Of course this is not, or at least to a lesser extent, the case if the victim's lawyer is paid by the State. Although this latter possibility is restricted to the lowest income groups it may of course be especially relevant for young claimants. The financial risks for the victim may also be limited if the legal costs are covered by a legal aid insurance.

The most important hurdle to be overcome in Dutch tort law in cases like *Barrett* and *Bedfordshire* is the hurdle of limitation. According to article 310 section 1 of Book 3 of the Dutch Civil Code a claim for damages expires five years after the victim became aware of both the damage and the person responsible. In any case the claim expires twenty years after the event that gave rise to liability. The Dutch Civil Code does not have a special provision regarding claims of minors. This means that the beginning of the limitation term is not postponed until the day the victim reaches majority. The latter is the case in most other jurisdictions.

In cases of sexual crimes other limitation rules apply. In these cases the civil limitation term does not end before the end of the criminal term (art. 3:310 section 4 BW). This criminal term runs for twelve years from the day the victim reaches majority. This means that the victim of a sexual crime has the option to file a claim until her or his 30th birthday.[14] This special rule does not apply to cases of non-sexual crimes. In these cases the general rules of five and twenty years apply.

The practical consequence of these statutory limitation rules is that in most child abuse cases a young victim depends on his parents or legal representatives to file a claim before the limitation period expires. This is of course not a likely situation, especially not in cases where a parent or the legal representative is the person against whom a claim has to be filed.

This undesirable consequence of the statutory limitation system has been partially set right repaired by the Hoge Raad in two decisions in 1998 and 1999. In the first case a 35-year-old woman filed a claim against her brother-in-law, who was also her employer, for sexually abusing her from the age of 21 to the age of 30. It was held that the woman was not able to speak about the abuse, at least not before she reported the facts to the police at the age of 31.[15] In the 1999 case a 36-year-old man filed a claim against his father for maltreating him physically and mentally from the age of two until the age of 18 when he left the parental home. In this case it was also held that the man was not able to speak about the events until he was 35.[16]

In both cases, the Hoge Raad held that invoking the expiration of a claim by the defendant is unreasonable if the late filing of the claim was attributable to the conduct of the defendant. This is especially the case in cases of child abuse and of sexual abuse. In these cases the victim usually needs many years to deal with the events and will only be able to think of a possible claim after this process of coping. On the basis of the general principle of unreasonableness and the currently available psychological knowledge, the Dutch Hoge Raad has set right the evident shortcomings of the statutory system. This means that the short-term limitation period of five years starts at the moment when the victim is mentally able to talk about the abuse events. Since 1998 this short limitation period of five years is in most cases no longer a hurdle for a tort law claim.

The foregoing does not mean that limitation problems do not continue to play a role in cases of abuse. Dutch law limits a claim in any case to a period of 20 years after the event which caused the damage. This implies that a victim who was abused at a very young age might be confronted with an expiration of the claim before he or she is able to file it. Last year, the Dutch Minister of Justice has proposed to abolish the long limitation term for all cases of personal (physical and mental) injury. This new Act will not have retrospective effect, so it will not apply to old cases.[17]

Damages and Alternative Remedies

Cases of child abuse will mainly give rise to claims regarding psychological harm, which caused pecuniary as well as non-pecuniary damage. These heads of damage do not give rise to special problems, provided that the mental injury is diagnosed by a psychiatrist and that there is a sufficient causal connection between the conduct of the protection agency and the damage. Generally, compensation will be relatively modest: in serious cases it might range between €15,000 and €25,000 (= £9,000–£15,000).

If the abused child suffers from pure economic loss, he has a right to compensation, provided that there is a sufficient causal connection between the wrongful conduct of the CPC or the protection organisation and this head of damage. It would also be possible to claim for loss of potential revenue, if the abused child was not capable of holding down a steady job (or not able to obtain one) due to the psychological harm sustained during youth.

In the field of child abuse there are alternative remedies, although they can not replace a tort claim. There is a Fund for the Compensation for Victims of Crimes, but these payments are rather modest. The same goes for the financial remedies recommended by the National Ombudsman.

Concluding Remarks

Although in the Netherlands child abuse claims against public or private bodies are rare, there are nevertheless possibilities for a successful claim under Dutch law. However, the conclusion must be that there are better prospects for claims for children under guardianship than for children not yet under guardianship. Both the CPC (with regard to children not yet under protection) and the child protection organisations (with regard to children under protection) have to meet professional standards, but in practice the CPC is only liable if it did not interfere in a clear-cut situation, whereas a child protection organisation may also face liability if it did not take due care with regard to the child.

Notes

1 *X (Minors) v Bedfordshire County Council* [1995] 2 AC 633.
2 [2001] 2 FLR 612. Cf Jane Wright, 'The Retreat From *Osman: Z v United Kingdom* in the European Court of Human Rights and Beyond', in: Duncan Fairgrieve, Mads Andenas and John Bell (eds), *Tort Liability of Public Authorities in Comparative Perspective*, London 2002, pp. 55–80.
3 See about child protection in the Netherlands and its recent developments: M.R. Bruning, Rechtvaardiging van kinderbescherming, diss. VU-Amsterdam, 2001.
4 See C.C. van Dam, 'Liability of Public Authorities in the Netherlands', in: Duncan Fairgrieve, Mads Andenas and John Bell (eds), *Tort Liability of Public Authorities in Comparative Perspective*, London 2002, pp. 559–569.
5 Cp. C.C. van Dam, Aansprakelijkheidsrecht, 2000, nr. 1101.
6 HR 8 January 1999, NJ 1999, 319 (*Waterschap West-Friesland v Kaagman*); See also Van Dam, nr. 915.
7 HR 5 November 1965, NJ 1966, 136, note GJS (*Kelderluik*). This decision reflects to a great extent the famous Learned Hand Rule: see *United States v Carroll Towing Co.* (1947) 159 F. (2d) 169, 173. This formula has been more or less adopted in all the main European legal systems.
8 C.C. van Dam, Liability of Public Authorities in the Netherlands, in: Duncan Fairgrieve, Mads Andenas and John Bell (eds), *Tort Liability of Public Authorities in Comparative Perspective*, London 2002, pp. 564–566.
9 HR 9 November 1990, NJ 1991, 26; Van Dam, Aansprakelijkheidsrecht, 2000, nr. 913; see also *Winfield and Jolowicz on Tort*, 2002, paras. 5.55–5.56.
10 HR 25 September 1998, NJ 1999, 379, note S.F.M. Wortmann.
11 *Barrett v. Enfield LBC* [1999] 3 All ER 193.
12 This rule of evidence applies to professional liability cases: HR 20 November 1987, NJ 1988, 500, note WLH (*Timmer v Deutman*); see also 18 February 1994, NJ 1994, 368 (*Schepers v De Bruijn*).
13 *Winfield and Jolowicz on Tort* (2002), nr. 5.21. See also Münchener Kommentar-Hinz (1992), § 1664 N 1 ff.; *Prosser and Keeton on the Law of Torts* (1984), pp. 901 ff.; Broekhuijsen-Molenaar, Onrechtmatige daad in de relatie ouder-kind, in: *Als een goed huisvader*, Deventer 1992, pp. 133–148.
14 HR 8 September 2000, NJ 2001, 2, note CJHB.
15 HR 23 October 1998, NJ 2000, 15, note ARB.
16 HR 25 June 1999, NJ 2000, 16, note ARB.
17 Kamerstukken 26 824; this bill is still being discussed by the Dutch Senate (Eerste Kamer).

Index of Cases

Index

For Product Safety Concerns and Information please contact our EU representative GPSR@taylorandfrancis.com Taylor & Francis Verlag GmbH, Kaufingerstraße 24, 80331 München, Germany

Batch number: 10726013

Printed by Printforce, the Netherlands